2451

BOOBIES ON MY BOWSPRIT

BOOBIES ON MY BOWSPRIT

Richard and Maria Hauser

A Hearthstone Book

Carlton Press, Inc. New York, N.Y.

©1981 by Richard and Maria Hauser
ALL RIGHTS RESERVED
Manufactured in the United States of America
ISBN 0-8062-1598-4

To our children and grandchildren

CONTENTS

Chapter

1	Boobies on My Bowsprit	9
2	On the Way	13
3	Visiting Mexican Ports	30
4	Quiet Days on a Southeasterly Course (Wind? What Wind?)	50
5	The Panama Canal	75
6	Caribbean Adventure	87
7	Santo Domingo and the Dominican Republic	116
8	Puerto Rico and the Virgin Islands	146
9	Curaçao	159
10	A Narrow Escape	169
11	Costa Rica	180
12	Boobies on the Bowsprit	188
13	Homeward Bound	210

CHAPTER 1

BOOBIES ON MY BOWSPRIT

The farewell party was over; there had been a wonderful last gathering with all our children, friends and business acquaintances.

In a manner of speaking my wife and I were slowly casting off our lines. Our mobile home was sold, and we bent to the task of storing all our personal belongings in our daughters' homes. It would have been impossible to take everything along on our boat. *Antares* was bobbing gently at its moorings at the Shilshole Bay Marina. During the past year we had hardly been sailing: every minute which we could spare had been devoted to the task of getting the boat ready for the extended voyage we had planned.

Only six weeks now separated us from our departure date—February 19, 1976, a date which had arbitrarily been set a year before.

Although our funds were limited, we were able to make the last payments on the boat and turn to the selection of several pieces of equipment still needed aboard.

We had studied a book and several articles on windvanes, but found ourselves unable to make a selection because there were so many different ones on the market. I had to rely on the advice of the owner of my favorite marine supply store. I purchased a Hydro-Vane, manufactured in England, which I was assured had performed very efficiently on boats of several types.

For two days I labored in the ice-cold January weather to fasten the vane to the stern. On a trial run in Puget Sound, it seemed to perform very satisfactorily with a brisk 15-mph wind.

This was not to be our last major expense. We considered a good VHF radio to be an essential piece of equipment and purchased the best on the market that we could afford. To the price of the unit itself was added the cost of the antenna, wiring and installation by a professional.

Our dinghy had been thoroughly overhauled at our house, where it had rested peacefully in the living room. I had given it a new resin coating on the inside and to give it more flotation, I had filled the spaces between the bottom ribs with styrofoam. Over it I placed a new floorboard which received two layers of fiberglass. Since we intended to make the dinghy sailable, I built a well for a centerboard and a brace in the bow to hold the mast. After building and fastening a cradle to the cabin roof, we hoisted the dinghy into it and placed a snug-fitting canvas cover over the top.

There was an afterthought; keeping the dinghy upright on deck would give us the opportunity to collect rain water in it as our water tank holds only sixty gallons of water. In spite of the jaunty, sturdy look of the little boat, it is only eight feet long and not very reassuring as a lifesaving device to be used in the middle of the ocean.

Again I reached more deeply into my pockets for money and bought us a spanking new life raft which we fastened to the foredeck. This last acquisition put our minds very much at ease, because this type of life raft inflates in a few seconds and is ready to receive its occupants in the shortest time after a mishap at sea. By comparison, it requires at least fifteen minutes of valuable time to launch either the dinghy or the nine-foot Avon rubber boat.

Gradually our craft, *Antares*, was looking more and more seaworthy. To protect the helmsman in the cockpit. we added a spray dodger around the stern and sternquarter. We learned to appreciate this protection especially in following seas and winds. For the protection of sails and crew, we added a netting from bow to the main shrouds, which made *Antares* look positively salty.

Below, everything was shipshape, most of the provisions had been bought and stored. All canned goods had been marked with an indelible felt tip pen to avoid surprises should the labels get wet and come off.

Talking one day to a long-time friend, I jokingly asked him if he would like to come along. To my immense surprise he decided, there and then, to do just that. This unexpected development forced us to make a few changes in the bowels of *Antares*.

Maria and I rearranged the storing plan to make room for our new deckhand, Charlie. I gave him a list of essentials for the trip, such as woolen socks, warm underwear, mittens, caps and foul-weather gear, accompanied by suitable boots.

When Charlie arrived from Vancouver, Canada, his car looked like a moving van. He had brought along the proverbial kitchen sink! After one look at the two sea bags, the two bulging suitcases and assorted cartons, I told him that *Antares* was not a luxury liner, and that he would have to send two-thirds of the stuff back home. How well he followed my instructions I do not know, but I suspect that Charlie managed to sneak a lot more aboard than the alloted space would permit.

We were now rapidly approaching the departure date and a lot of last minute details needed my undivided attention. With one more crew member aboard, we added a considerable amount of stores to the already bulging storage compartments.

Six jerry cans of water brought our total up to ninety gallons. Three cans of diesel fuel complemented the one hundred gallons in the tank. Our cooking stove, heater and cabin lamps use kerosene as fuel, and after all had been filled, we stored twenty extra gallons aboard.

By then it became clear that the boat had reached the limits of its carrying capacity for it sat rather heavily on its red waterline.

There was just one more thing that bothered me; since the previous May there had not been an opportunity to take the boat out of the water for a thorough bottom-cleaning and painting. At this particular time of the year the weather and tides were most unfavorable, and since we were running out of time, we put it off. In our minds there was a beguiling picture of *Antares* careened on a palm-fringed beach where we could catch up on this work, and under much more agreeable circumstances.

Our passports and vaccinations had been taken care of, though we had to rush Charlie to the proper place to get his smallpox vaccine. The boat's documentation had been renewed and we thought we were all set to sail. For years we had been reading books and magazines about cruising yachts, but we had never found any particular or detailed information concerning the various legal papers a yacht is required to carry on a voyage to foreign ports. We had sailed so frequently and easily to and from Canadian waters with a minimum of requirements from the customs offices, that it never entered my mind how ignorant I was on this subject.

Our planned voyage would take us first to Brazil. Maria's parents live in Sao Paulo, and she desperately wanted to visit with her father who was very ill. She had put off the visit for the past sixteen years, and both of us were anxious to get there. We had worked out a somewhat vague schedule, but with possible dates and ports all the way to Santos.

We had based this timetable on the performance of our boat which had easily run up to ten and even twelve knots under favorable conditions. We had no reason to doubt that we could make daily runs of at least one-hundred miles. This would make it possible to reach Balboa in about six weeks without having to make port in between. We trusted ourselves and trusted our vessel.

We had been sailing it for five years; it had taken us, among other lengthy cruises, all around Vancouver Island, an 800-mile voyage.

We thought we knew *Antares* as well as our two preceding fiberglass boats—a twenty-one footer and a beautiful thirty-one foot ketch. The beauty of the latter, however, was not matched by her seaworthiness, for we soon discovered that her performance on the open sea could not be trusted.

Antares is a forty-five foot ketch-rigged wooden boat. The planking is plywood covered with fiberglass. Twin keels, attached to the rather flat bottom, give her the high speeds we had so far experienced in inland waters.

I was so confident that our first port-of-call would be Balboa, that I did not take any charts along for the Mexican or Central American coasts.

There were dozens of charts aboard covering Panama, the Canal Zone, the southern part of the Caribbean Sea and the area all around the South American continent, which we intended to circumnavigate. Our return home was to take us via Hawaii. To navigate on the open sea we would use plotting sheets from latitude to latitude.

We could now throw away the endless notes and lists made prior to the undertaking. Every item had been taken care of and one after the other scratched off. There was just one more item—not noted and not regarded in all our preparation—an old saying with which sailors have been familiar for as long as sailing vessels have crossed the oceans: A sailboat is not going to that and that port, but towards it, leaving always the possibility open that it might wind up in a quite different place.

CHAPTER 2

ON THE WAY

There were no crowds on the dock the day we left. We had said all our good-byes and only our friend across the slip was on hand to throw us our lines. Wistfully, he smiled through his handsome beard and wished us a good voyage. We had waited until well past noon, but it still was raining dismally with a slight wind from the south at three to five knots. As soon as we rounded the breakwater, we hoisted sails. Charlie, who was helping me, held, unaccountably, a burning cigarette between his lips. For any sailor, this is too much to bear, and I roared at him, "Once and for all, there will be no smoking while handling sails—understood?" Charlie was startled to speechlessness and quickly threw the offending item overboard. Maria, who was at the helm, raised her eyebrows and grinned. As a smoker herself, she knew the laws aboard ship and both of us knew that Charlie still had a long way to go until he learned all the do's and don't's.

We had not intended to set a record on this first day—as a matter of fact, we were on our way to Kingston, only seven miles across Puget Sound. But we had set a departure date and leave we did. Why, I don't know, because there were still several small jobs to be finished. I just had the feeling that if we stayed to finish up everything, we would never leave our mooring. Hardly a mile away, the first surprise of the trip started to appear. The jib fastening at the bowsprit came loose and I had to fasten it temporarily to the forestay. I went below after that and finished a bracket for our kerosene table lamp. Maria helped me put the finishing touches on the slats for the table. They acted as a railing to keep dishes in place at mealtime. It is not nice to lose one's soup bowl and have noodles or beans all over the carpet.

Looking out the hatch to see how Charlie was doing in the drizzly afternoon, I discovered that the wooden vane from the self-steering was gone. I had counted on such happenings, but not so soon. Good heavens, was that an omen?

We reached Kingston by nightfall, had a good night's rest and left early the next morning, about 0600. The weather was good. In bright sunshine, we were running before a southerly breeze at four knots. As long as we were in inland waters we did not follow any set routine of watches but relieved each other at the helm for short, loosely defined periods.

We were in good spirits and sailing along Whidbey Island, bays and a coastline which we knew very well. At Port Townsend and through Admiralty Inlet we were lucky to have the outgoing tide with us. Here we had frequently experienced very choppy seas with the south wind blowing over the incoming tide. The wind shifted as we sailed past Protection Island and we went on a broad reach. As we neared Dungeness Spit, the wind left us and we sat becalmed. It was clear that there was to be no more wind for the rest of the day, so we motored the remaining fifteen miles to Port Angeles.

We fastened to the guest pier and stayed for three days. We visited with many friends, some of whom had their boats berthed at the yacht harbor. All of them asked questions and gave advice and generally felt deeply envious that we had put our dreams into reality.

I am sure they would not have felt that way the day we left. For as long as we had been in port the weather had been perfect, for the Northwest. One could say, it had been outdoing itself! We pondered darkly about this state of affairs as we rounded into the Strait of Juan de Fuca. A miserable swell, cold rain and icy winds met us head on. Sailing was out of the question. Perhaps a more experienced sailor would have stayed in port. We 'greenhorns' had a schedule to follow and we plodded on, by motor, against all reason, to Pillar Point where we anchored for the night. We had just enough protection to spend a reasonably restful night.

I was the first to arise. After refilling the cabin heater I started shaving. Suddenly, a gust from the southeast blowing snow and hail before it, sent the boat reeling. Looking outside, I had the hair-raising impression that we were dragging the anchor. With my hand at the ignition key of the engine and with foam still around my mouth, I got my crew out to help. Charlie and Maria tumbled out of their bunks threw clothing on over their pajamas, and all three of us scrambled on deck.

I stormed forward and prodded the footswitch of the electric anchor winch. To my horror it remained mute. I turned and grabbed a line from the forward pinboard and managed to lash it to a link of the anchor chain. From there I ran it through the jib winch and all three of us heaved mightily.

Through mouthfuls of snow we chanted: "She is coming, she

is coming!" The chain, which was now accumulating on deck in muddy coils, refused to run through the howser below.

"Maria, go below and see what you can do from there," I shouted. "Charlie, secure the line to the cleat and stand by the helm; put her in gear when I give the sign." Miraculously, the motor of the anchor winch started purring. At my sign, Charlie slowly put the engine to forward and Maria somehow guided the chain to where it belonged. With a burst of speed we fled that ghastly place and made for open water.

Once in safety, I hoisted the mainsail and intended to let it go at that. But with main alone we had very poor steerage and decided to hoist the staysail also.

After that, we all took turns gulping hot cups of coffee and changing into more appropriate clothing.

The wind was steadily increasing, when a gust sent the genoa, which was still hanked to the stay, almost all the way up, the clew dragging through the water. Once more I rushed forward, fighting to get the sail down the stay and out of the water. Suddenly, the outhaul of the staysail parted. The boom, crashing on deck, proceeded to swing wildly from port to starboard.

Alarmed by the noise, Maria came on deck and helped me secure the genoa and fix the staysail. She then suggested putting a reef in the main. With the prevailing conditions, this was not going to be easy. I stationed Charlie at the main halyard winch and, taking the helm, brought *Antares* into the wind. Charlie started to get the sail down, but after only two feet of it was lowered, the winch promptly jammed.

Before Maria was able to guide the boom into the groove of the gallows, the mainsheet made a dash for independence by running off the cleat. Hastily, I exchanged places with Charlie, freed the winch and rehoisted the main. Maria secured the sheet and we both decided to forget about the reefing.

The wind was still increasing and had veered to almost due west. We had to remind ourselves that this was the end of February, early spring storms could be savage, even more so in the narrow confines of the strait. We were battling a full-fledged gale, the cross swells were banging and booming against the sides of the boat and I wondered how long all of us would hold together. We had barely reached Slip Point, and there was no adequate shelter between it and Neah Bay. I had no desire whatever to spend the night tacking back and forth, this was no light-hearted summer cruise. I brought the boat as close to shore as I dared, took all sail down and we continued under motor to Neah Bay. It was with a sigh of great relief that we let the anchor down and settled for the night. The bay was crowded with fishing boats: we were the only yacht among them.

The storm raged for another three days. Calling the Coast Guard station via VHF, we were informed that the winds were howling at fifty mph, gusting at times up to seventy.

We spent quiet evenings, sitting warm and cozy below, reading, writing letters or playing endless games of rummy. During the daylight hours though, there was enough work to be done to stave off any signs of boredom that might sneak up on us.

Checking out "Frieda," our 50-hp diesel engine, I discovered an oil leak and set about to trace its source. Soon enough I came upon the culprit, a crack in the oilpan. I cannot say that I was overjoyed at this discovery. It was just lucky I had done so while still in port. Searching further, I made more 'discoveries': the fillpipe for the oil had been lengthened with almost a foot of stainless steel pipe. This made the oil filling easier, but the addition was so heavy that, through the slight vibration of the engine, it had caused the crack.

I took off the whole contraption, sawed off the steel pipe and replaced it with a piece of rubber hose. I cleaned the area around the crack thoroughly and filled it with Marine Tex. It has done the job to this day. It all sounds so easy on paper, but in the narrow space of the engine room, with the boat swinging in the storm, I thought it quite an accomplishment.

Not liking to be idle, I occupied my hands fashioning two more pins for the boards which I had recently placed on the mizzen shrouds. In spite of all the work that had to be done, we were impatient to continue on our voyage. But the barometer was still hanging around at 29.4 mb and the weather report was not encouraging.

Maria was having some trouble with the amount of wet clothing piling up each time we went above decks. Stringing lines across the main cabin was not the happiest solution, with three people milling around, getting slapped in the face with wet socks. Since we have a completely enclosed head aboard, I fastened a rod there from wall to wall, fashioned from the handle of a derelict scrubber. Maria was happy and all of us dry. The head proved to be an excellent dryer when we placed the heater under the wet clothing and opened the porthole for ventilation.

Sunday morning was clear and brisk. We had confirmation from the Coast Guard that the weather was improving, so we made one more dash to shore: Charlie with letters to mail, I looking for the fuel dock and buying two more cans of kerosene, Maria in her constant search for fresh fruits and vegetables.

Once more we filled the diesel and water tanks to their capacity and motored out of Neah Bay. Before us was the Pacific, which, at the moment, was belying its name and there was no mistake about it: we were on our way.

The shelter of Neah Bay was behind us, with its mile-and-a-quarter of breakwater and little Waada Island at its entrance. Neah Bay is frequently shrouded in dense fog which rolls in from the sea and clings to its shores and surrounding hills. The noon sun, filtering through the fog, cast a silvery sheen over trees and drab buildings, wrapping in mystery the otherwise unattractive village.

To us it had been shelter and a springboard to the Pacific Ocean.

The fresh 30-mph wind whipped whitecaps from the fifteen foot waves left over from the previous storm. Using the power of the engine, we put a respectable distance between the boat and Tatoosh Island, the westernmost tip of the continental United States. With mizzen, staysail and reefed main, we pounded into heavy seas. Our course of 210 true did not agree too much with the southwesterly winds and we were making very little headway. Though baromeric pressure and temperature were rising, we were off to a difficult start. I attempted to engage the windvane but no matter how much I tried, it would not perform properly. After a few seconds on course, *Antares* would take over, gleefully making a mad dash to the southeast racing towards shore. Regretfully, I took the vane off and disengaged the auxiliary rudder.

It was cold and night was approaching. Maria and I were facing the prospect of having to steer the boat manually through our first night out. In an earlier attempt, Charlie had failed to hold the course, letting the boat run off in every which direction. He was extremely annoyed at this but we could not, for the time being, trust him at the helm during the night watches.

From the very beginning I had set up a schedule of three-hour night watches, starting at 1900 hrs, which we maintained for the rest of the trip. With three people on board, this timetable rotated by itself so that no one was favored or stuck with a watch he did not like. Every third night, one of us had two three-hour watches. It worked very well and agreed with all of us. But this first night proved to be a very lively one!

I had just gratefully stretched out in my bunk when Maria called for help at the helm. In the heavy seas the boat had swung off course, and she was unable to bring it back. She complained bitterly about the pressure she was experiencing on the rudder. She was mortified and almost in tears at having to call for assistance. I realized that we could, perhaps, loosen the sheets somewhat, but I was also determined, on this black and moonless night, not to give one inch towards the inhospitable Washington shore. Taking the easy way out, I jibed the boat and Maria helped me with the sheets. There was very little rest for any of us during the remainder of that night.

It was with more than relief that we greeted the new day. At last we could get at some of the problems which had crept up during the night hours. Maria winched me up the mizzen mast to retrieve the topping lift which had managed to slip off. With the boat hook, I freed the logline from the rudder; it had wrapped itself lovingly around it as we jibed and in consequence it had stopped recording our mileage. This meant that our dead reckoning would have to be estimated. This would cause us some anxiety in the following days which were heavily overcast, affording no chance to take any sun sights.

The wind would pick up in sudden gusts, whirling sleet, rain and snow about us in blinding gray sheets. On one occasion, poking my head out the hatch to see how my first mate was doing, I was just in time to see a big load of wet snow slide off the mizzen sail and bury Maria. Her expression could be summed up in the words: "Why me?"

I have often regretted not having taken a picture of her, she appeared to be a misplaced Santa Claus. But during those first trying days we seldom thought of our various cameras, loaded and ready to go into action though they were. We were too fatigued to think beyond the immediate needs of the boat and our bodies. None of us was seasick, but we experienced a numbness and slight headachy condition which made it difficult for us to remember the things which had happened the day before.

The remnants of the storm still trailed huge, mile-high cloud masses overhead, giving us now and then a brief glimpse of the sun. Winds were so varying in strength and direction that on some occasions we were forced to use the engine just to avoid being thrown about in the heavy swell. These unsettled conditions brought a lot of small mishaps which kept us busy night and day. At times it seemed that a mischievous gremlin was having the fun of his life making us scramble about setting things to rights again.

The head flowed over, soaking the carpets; we lost the top batten from the main while hoisting it; the flagpole at the stern was stuck in its socket and I had to take it all off—it was interfering with the windvane and the mizzen boom. Strange, grating noises came from the housing of the windvane and I had to take it apart and reassemble it. The log seemed sluggish in recording the mileage and I took it apart, too, greased it and put it back together again. We then timed it with the knotmeter and thought it fairly accurate.

A rattling noise from the stern sounded as if we were going to lose the aft section of the boat any minute. On close inspection, we saw that all the bolts from the self-steering assembly were ready to drop off into the ocean. Frantically we removed everything from the stern hold to gain acces to the bolts from the inside. I swung myself over the stern railing, armed with a wrench to hold the bolts, while Maria tightened the nuts, crouching inside the hold. I was glad to get my feet on deck again: with head down over the waves, lapping hungrily at my face and hands, I had had the feeling they were demanding a sacrifice in the form of my breakfast.

"Anything else to do?" Maria asked. "I only hope that the next emergency does not happen again when I'm sitting on the head. Have you ever tried to zip up your pants in a hurry?" Grumbling, she retreated to the galley where, tied with a safety harness to the handrail, she proceeded to fix us a delicious dinner. To her credit I must say that we always had good, hot and tasteful meals which lifted our spirits considerably.

Anxious to get an accurate position, we awaited the first signs of the sun finally approaching the noon zenith. Poised with sextant and stopwatch, we breathlessly waited for the right moment. ZIP! A dark little cloud brought itself neatly between the sun and the sextant sight and that was that. For days now we had been navigating on an assumed position and try as we might, all our sights and computations put us halfway to Japan. We were nonplussed. What would our celestial nagivation teacher think of us? Worse yet, would we ever know where we were? It seemed that the harder we worked at it, the worse the results became. We were, after four days at sea, still dependent on a very shaky DR position.

There seemed no end to the bad weather. Sitting at the helm during the nightwatch, I fingered and exchanged a handwarmer from glove to glove. I had another one tucked under my belt and felt reasonably comfortable.

Our speed had been anywhere from four to eight knots, and we had made innumerable sail changes with the changing conditions. I was already on the third boom vang from the main which kept snapping off in the violent cross seas and sending the boom up, coming to rest in the backstays of the main mast. This had an unnerving effect on Maria, whom I had relieved for the rest of the night. It was going to be a long haul for me. I hated to keep staring at the compass with no moon or stars to guide me or relieve my eyes.

Now and then I would nod off only to be startled by a sudden drenching rain squall. When the compass light started blinking, my first thought was that I was falling alseep, but looking closely I saw it blink once more and go out for good. All I could do was use the flashlight now and then to assure myself that I was keeping our course.

At dawn, Charlie came out to take over and I promised to refill the handwarmer and give it to him. As I took the one out from under my belt, I discovered that it had never burned properly and that I had kept it warm for half the night. The plesant warmth I had felt around my middle had all been in my head!

As I rummaged later among the many spare parts, I could not find a compass light bulb which would fit the socket of the burned-out one. While I set about finding a bulb of the appropriate size, thinking about how I would solder the connections back together again, I reflected on how many little things could sometimes create ridiculous problems I was hard put to solve. I found the solution for a missing soldering iron in the medicine cabinet. There was a small box containing a plastic material used to fix dental plates. It dries in seconds and is non-conductive. I was elated! After fiddling for hours in the rocking cabin, the compass light was working again.

Charlie called us on deck to come and admire a seal, the first sign of sealife after so many gloomy days. The little fellow swam around us, just as interested in us as we were in his antics. Perhaps it was wondering what we were doing out there at this time of year.

While on deck I had another look at the log and was not satisfied with the mileage it showed. I pulled in the spinner and found the blades almost straight. With a monkey wrench I bent the blades to give them a slight curve and let it run out again. Once more we checked it with the knotmeter as I did not know if all my 'doctoring' was going to be accurate enough, but it seemed again to come up reasonably accurate. In spite of our efforts, we still had only a vague and uneasy notion of our actual position. To Charlie's amusement, Maria had stashed away the almanac books and navigation tables with an air of utter frustration. I was worried, myself; the winds had shifted to the northwest and our course was now more easily maintained in a south southeasterly direction.

The fifth night was our lucky one—we met with a merchant ship which we contacted over the VHF radio and which gave us our position. No, we were not approaching Japan. We had sailed in a big arc and were actually fifty miles off the California coast at about the height of Eureka. Considering the conditions we had met, we had not done so badly after all.

The next day was the first warm and sunny one; all three of us felt good, for the first time above decks without the clumsy foul-weather gear hampering our movements. I was especially happy, knowing once and for all where we were and knowing that my crew had not the slightest desire to swim ashore at the first sight of land. I should have refrained from mentioning that Eureka was a scant two-hour flight from Seattle—I was almost thrown overboard.

We spent this beautiful day mostly basking in the sun and working with the windvane. The seas were smooth and the wind strong enough, we were skimming along at five knots and the self-steering should, at least under these conditions, work right. However, towards sundown we had to give up our efforts, except for very short periods; the self-steering mechanism was a failure.

During the night we passed Cape Mendocino and it lived up to its evil reputation—it gave us a send-off we would long remember. The wind had picked up after sundown and the seas started literally to boil. The cross swells gave us an incredible beating and it became almost impossible to keep the boat on course.

I reduced the watches to two hours each, as I had difficulty myself steering any longer than that. I was hesitant to have Maria out at the helm in all this raging, but I did need a short rest and reluctantly let her take over. All of us felt as if our arms would fall off any minute from the strain. On my last watch the boat was caught broadside by a mountainous wave and it swerved ninety degrees in a big lurch. The main boom was once again thrown high, the vane did hold this time, but the gooseneck slipped off its track, the outhaul of the sail broke and the boom crashed on top of the dinghy and across the lifeline. The sail, pushed by the wind, slid against the mast and flapped against the shrouds.

Any adjective to describe my feelings at that moment would be an understatement. I loosened the mainsheet and was able to place the boom in the outer groove of the gallows. After securing the sheet, I glanced at the knotmeter: we were still running at five knots, fouled up sail and all. At daybreak, all three of us joined forces and got boom and sail set right. Exhausted, I went below and fell on my bunk; all I wanted was a few hours of rest. The staysail runner overhead had been one of the last-minute additions. I began to wonder now about its usefulness. In the unsteady conditions the staysail swung back and forth, causing the most irritating noise. I decided it would have to go if I ever wanted to get a good rest again. This brought my thoughts around to the resolution we had made the day before: we would have to remove the rudder from the self-steering for it had interfered so strongly with the rudder of the boat that we felt it would not be safe to leave it trailing behind any longer.

We had given up on the idea of getting any help from the self-steering. Tossing around in my bunk, unable to sleep, I decided that NOW was as good a time as any to do the job. I got up, donned rubber pants and boots and, armed with a pair of pliers, went on deck. With the engine going, I ordered Maria to hold the boat into the wind. Charlie, giving me a hand as I climbed over the stern railing, remained on standby. With the pliers, I worked at the pin which holds the vane rudder to its shaft. Now and then I was dipped to my armpits into the icy waves but I was determined to get the job done. One more yank and the pin was out. With a mighty kick, the rudder dropped off, and I could retrieve it by a security line we had attached to it. I was rewarded by a happy shout from Maria: "I can steer again as easy as ever!" All the time it had been like steering a car in the wrong gear and with the brakes on. I returned to my bunk and slept like a log for a whole three hours.

After ten days out at sea, our position was eighty miles west of San Francisco. It was warm and sunny and completely calm. We motored for a few hours to recharge the batteries. At noon we had our lunch, sitting all three together at mealtime for the first time since leaving Neah Bay. It was an occasion to celebrate, and Maria made an especially nice lunch.

Because the wind refused to appear by evening, we took all sails down, put the anchor light up just in case, and the whole crew had a full night's rest.

Life was becoming increasingly easy with the rise of the temperature. Slowly, we had achieved a close-knit small community of three. Charlie had become a relatively good helmsman as long as the winds did not change, and he was always a cheerful companion, full of laughter, jokes and nonsense. We enjoyed his company immensely and were glad that he had joined us.

As we reached the height of Santa Barbara, we celebrated our first 1,000 miles. A special chocolate cake, made by a daughter in Seattle and kept for such an occasion, was a fitting reward. After dinner, Maria produced a fresh fruit salad of mouth-watering quality. With the passing of time we had come to enjoy the small pleasures of day-to-day living to their fullest. We came to realize once more how little is needed to be completely happy. Each day brought us closer together as we divided the chores and shared the sights. In our hectic lives on land the sight of a seagull would go unnoticed. Like children we daily discovered new pleasures. On my favorite watch from 0400 to 0700, I reveled in the sight of the sunrise, the start of a new day at sea. It brought a frigate bird which gravely circled the boat twice before flying off to unknown fishing grounds. It was followed by two seagulls which I could have sworn were the same ones which had greeted us the previous day.

Occasionally we would observe seals in their sinuous water ballet. We did our best to encourage their performance by clapping hands and shouting "bravo"; and our efforts were acknowledged with graceful turns and flips.

Through our RDF we kept a check on the shore stations we were passing; we had not seen land since Eureka and always kept well offshore. On March 17, we crossed paths with the first passenger liner, the *Royal Viking Star*. We called on it and had a nice long chat with the radio operator who gave us our position, for which we were very grateful.

By now we had crossed the border into Mexican waters and were nearing the Baja coastline. Not wishing to run into shore during the night, we tacked to a southwesterly course. I sat contented, watching the moon set, which was particularly interesting this night. On an otherwise cloudless sky, two layers at the horizon appeared to await the moon's descent. Slowly, their borders turned silvery and the moon slipped behind them, a tired being lying down to rest.

Soon a comet appeared, tail first. We had observed it for several nights now and we assumed it to be Kohoutec, too low on the horizon to be seen from land. Stars glittered above, and in one direction I witnessed an amazing phenomenon. Large, bright stars shone and disappeared in a flash. Sailing on, I realized that the stars were a lighthouse whose light rotated and flashed off the surrounding hills. Land? To starboard? This could only mean that we had Cedros Island on that side. This was an uneasy sensation.

We were poorly equipped with charts of this region, which we never had intended to approach. To be truthful, our only chart was a very small-scale one of the northeastern Pacific area and not well suited for navigation. It reached from Prince Rupert, Canada, on the north to Mazatlan in Mexico. To have a vague idea of our position relative to the coast, I had laboriously drawn in the squares in one-degree distances. The chart itself was divided every ten degrees.

When Maria came to take over I did not dare to go below. We had come closer to land and could clearly see the outline of hills, bays and shore. Soon Charlie joined us and we took turns at the wheel and as lookouts at the bow for the rest of the night.

In the early dawn we discovered the entrance to a bay and found a nook which looked like a promising anchorage. We inched our way in, passed beds of seaweeds, and let the anchor go in thirty feet of water. It had been a long and exhausting night and everybody slipped quietly into the bunks, grateful to be at rest after eighteen days at sea.

We slept well but not long. We had grown so used to the rocking motion of the boat that I think the stillness bothered us. On awakening, we turned to look at our surroundings. An impressive landscape of mountains and hills in all shades of brown, rust and yellow ringed the bay, all utterly devoid of vegetation, with the exception of a few scant dry bushes along the shore line. To our eyes, so accustomed to the green forests of the north, it was as desolate as a moonscape.

Maria, who had lived in Argentina, remarked that it looked very much like the coast of Patagonia.

Throughout the bay small fishing craft dotted the waters, and soon some of the boats passed us, the fishermen waving friendly hellos. One of the boats came alongside and a man motioned to ask if we wanted fish. Did we ever! Soon Maria was engaged in a lively conversation with the three men in the boat. She was happy to be able to try out her knowledge of Spanish, and to all appearances she was doing splendidly.

We exchanged three fish for a few packs of cigarettes: the fishermen were not too interested in money. As a bonus we received two abalone, and the Mexicans gave Maria a recipe for their preparation. Charlie exchanged two more packs of cigarettes for the two largest and most beautiful abalone shells.

This had been a very nice experience indeed. After the excitement had died down a bit, we turned to more important matters. Our cooking stove had been giving Maria some trouble and she had threatened to quit cooking altogether. I took advantage of the quiet afternoon and replaced one burner and fixed the second. At the same time I refueled the tank; then I turned to our running light, which had given us a few anxious moments by refusing to come on when needed.

We had a busy afternoon, each doing his best to make the boat shipshape. The pleasant aroma of fresh-baked bread followed us around, and in the evening we sat down to a well-earned feast. We had never eaten abalone before and were surprised at the truly delicate taste of it. The fish was superb and nobody could blame us for eating prodigious amounts of it That night not only the cat's tummy was bulging!

Oh, pardon me, in the excitment I totally forgot to introduce you to our fourth crew member. Meet Prince Igor, a regal white and orange tabby, who, with feline singlemindedness, has trained us to his catty ways. Until the weather turned to more amenable temperatures, he spent his days buried in Maria's sleeping bag.

Igor spent the whole of that afternoon basking in the sun. He inhaled deeply the many intriguing smells the breeze wafted over from shore. His tail twitched excitedly as flights of birds crossed overhead, among them a long row of about twenty pelicans. They always look to us like heavily laden air transports on their way to an important mission. That night Igor did not join us as we turned in early for a much needed rest, but chose to remain above deck.

We lifted anchor at 0700 and set our sails to a lively wind from the northwest; we headed towards the passage between Punta Eugenia and Natividad Island. Our speed was six to eight knots with the current adding another knot or two. The island proved to be as arid as the mainland appeared, with only a few houses scattered along the hillsides. Its coast was steep with rocks and reefs extending seaward, and the surf foamed and boiled skyward in thundering cascades. Even with the proximity of the mainland, it seemed very lonely to us.

On crossing the Bay of San Cristobal, which is ringed with tier after tier of mountain ranges in hues of gray-blue and reddish brown to ochre, we met another sailing boat. After several attempts we managed to make radio contact. Its crew was looking for an anchorage, but we could not give them any information as we did not have charts of the region. The voice of the skipper sounded strained. It must not have been very pleasant to battle against the wind and waves which were favoring us so well.

The favorable wind was to be the last one for many days to come. It slowly died away and we experienced days in which the total distance sailed varied from forty to seventy miles. This caused anxiety aboard, as I grew more tense after each day's run was computed. Instead of enjoying the slower pace and relaxing, I fretted about our slow progress and found that my patience was wearing thin. A lifetime of hard and continuous work, during which vacations had been few and far between, had conditioned me to be on the move constantly. Work as such was an ingrained habit I would not be able to shed for a long time yet. For now, I was compelled to keep busy, more so during my off-watches than at the helm.

While steering, I had noticed that the helm had developed too much play and I seized the first opportunity to crawl past the engine to the rudder assembly behind it. I tightened and then greased all the moving parts. Then I turned to our compass.

which, we had discovered, was mounted at an unfavorable angle. I set about to raise it by two-and-a-half inches from the binnacle. From the wood supply aboard, I selected two suitable pieces of mahagony and worked happily for two days on this project.

Maria took advantage of the sunny, warm days to hang out bedding and sodden carpets. She scrubbed and washed and rummaged for hours, infected by my own activity; then, with a sigh, sank down at the helm for her watch. "So help me God," she groaned, "I will never go cruising again on a boat with shag carpeting; the pieces weigh a ton when damp. Whatever happens to fall disappears into it, dissolving into a disgusting paste, matting it down into malodorous clumps."

Times at the helm were more like rest periods now, especially during the day when we could sit in the sunshine which grew warmer at each mile we made to the south. Frequently we read while on watch. We had a great and varied selection of books aboard, ranging from sailing manuals and adventures to nature books and science fiction.

I preferred history or biographical accounts and was engrossed at the moment with *The Birdman of Alcatraz*. Maria, who is a bookworm anyway, had enough to choose from. Any subject could interest her as long as there was something to be learned. Charlie enjoyed a lighter fare of criminal mysteries which he consumed at the rate of about one a day.

Remembering how good the fish we had eaten at our first anchorage had tasted, I decided that we should trail a line. Fish of any kind would be a welcome change from corned beef. Happy to have found another reason to keep busy, I hauled a big trawling reel with a five-pound weight from the hold. It had been a going-away present from my former business partner.

For want of a better location, I mounted the base of the reel to the underside of the hatch of the sternhold. While trawling, the hatch would have to remain open, secured to the stern-railing with a choke cord. The rod protruded vertically, which was no handicap to its performance.

We baited the hook after I had tied a blinker to the leader and watched the weight disappear below the surface. We settled down to wait; our expectations could not have been more suspenseful had we been holding a ticket on the Irish Sweepstakes. Again and again we lifted the line in the hopes of a catch. On this first try we not only lost the lure and the blinker the five-pound sinker was gone, too. So much for deep water fishing.

After this venture, anybody could have told that we were not exactly adept at the art of fishing. From this day on, we trailed 150 to 200 feet of line with a three-ounce sinker and a hook baited with artifical or fresh lure when available. In this manner, we caught a reasonable amount of fish for our table and for Igor, whose supply of catfood was rather on the skimpy side.

March 21 marked the start of spring very suitably with a warm and sunny day. We were twenty-two days under way, and to my disgust still off the Baja coast. Donning my diving mask and flippers for the first time, I went overboard. Not to my surprise, I found that *Antares'* bottom was covered end to end with a growth thicker than the shag carpet in the cabin above it. No wonder we were slowing down so much. To my disappointment, the water was still too cold to remain in it for any length of time. Bottom cleaning would have to be postponed until we reached warmer waters.

In this vicinity we met with our first whale, a huge animal, easily as long as our boat; we passed each other at a distance of half a mile, we on our way south, the whale north, probably on its way to the Bay of Vizcaino which harbors the entrance to the Scammon Lagoon. This lagoon can be entered only with the special permission of the Mexican government. It is under a wildlife protection act, for large numbers of whales gather there to give birth and parts of the lagoon are considered a whale nursery.

On one late afternoon, out of the mist surrounding it, we sighted a high bluff and I asked Maria if she could identify it. In the absence of charts, she had been studying the *US Sailing Directions* assiduously and told us that we had reached Cabo San Lucas, the southermost tip of Baja.

That evening, over dinner, I talked the situation over with Maria and we agreed that it would be a good idea to put into the next major port, Manzanillo. We set course for Cabo Corrientes on the western coast of the Mexican mainland. Our food and water supplies were still adequate and would have lasted easily another month. But the constant calms had forced us to use the engine with increasing frequency and our fuel supply had diminished rapidly.

Somehow, I had lived under the illusion that we could make Balboa, in the Canal Zone, in six weeks. This and many other of our misconceptions became apparent with the passing of time. We knew now that we would never reach Balboa in the next two weeks. We had to notify our families back home of this new development to spare them unnecessary worry.

Before a dazzling sunrise, Cabo Corrientes loomed ahead, 500 feet high with the mountains behind it rising to a height of 2,000 feet. With the dwindling wind we sailed along the coast, Maria reciting the landmarks from the *Sailing Directions*. Soon she grew confused with the seemingly endless repetitions of Piedra Blanca and Piedra Negra. "There are just too many white and black rocks around here—which is which?" We told her that it really did not matter, with the wind as it was, we would never be able to make it to Manzanillo on that same day.

That night, though, a good blow sent us scurrying along at an appreciable speed through a veritable soup of marine life. Not only in our wake, but in the following waves, long streaks and large patches of phosphorescence were stirred further into higher luminescence by the lightning-fast motion of the dolphins swimming along in the boat's shadow.

Besides the rushing of the waves and the sound of the wind, there were squeaks, snufflings and mighty splashings all around us. This region must be a fantastic fishing ground. We sailed through a dense population of squid which extended for miles along the coast.

At about 0600 the next morning, the wind died abruptly and left us to wallow painfully in the swell. We had kept well offshore during the night and motored the rest of the day until we reached Manzanillo at 1700. During our approach, we kept in radio contact with the yacht *Diana Lee*, stationed in the harbor. Her skipper guided us into the anchorage. Once inside the breakwater, we rafted up to his boat and shook hands with Bob and Jerry from San Diego.

We gladly accepted a dinner invitation and spent a very pleasant evening together.

During the course of our conversation, Bob assured us that as we wished to stay only two or three days, it would not be necessary for us to report to the harbor master. According to him, no boarding officials would come to the yacht. The following day, Bob and Jerry offered to guide us into town and show us the best places to shop for fresh staples.

CHAPTER 3

VISITING MEXICAN PORTS

Next morning early, we lowered our dinghy and rowed ashore. Bob and Jerry, who had been here for four weeks already, showed us the best spots to land. We had to scramble over slippery rocks up the embankment to the street into town.
Along the narrow sidewalk streamed a lively traffic of trucks, cars and buses. Bob led the way with Jerry, the three of us strung out behind them. Soon we came upon the town square, cool and shady under flowering trees rustling in the sea breeze. We contemplated the water fountain in its center with the rotating sculpture of a leaping marlin, the famous game fish so sought after by the sports fisherman visting Mexico.
It was just 10:00 a.m., already hot, and most of the benches around the square were occupied. Women in gaily colored dresses watched over little girls who, for all the world, walked about like living dolls. Older men were almost invariably clad in white shirts and dark pants, but the younger ones had long since adopted blue jeans and multicolored, clingy shirts. Most of the young working women wore smart pantsuits. We felt like most tourists on their first day in a strange country, slightly ebullient and a bit selfconscious.
Our short walk had made us thirsty and we eyed the refreshment stand with awe. Long rows of glass jars were filled to the brim with big hunks of fruit such as papaya, mango, orange and pineapple. Maria explained to us that they would be put into a liquifier with ice and sugar, beaten and served in tall glasses, much like a milkshake. How we came to love those delicious *jugos*!
For now, we each purchased a large coconut. The top was neatly chopped off and a straw inserted in a tiny hold. For the first time in my life I savored the cool, delicate and immensely refreshing water from a green coconut.
A few steps from the stand we found a store from which we could place our calls to home. For a small fee, a very serious looking gentleman put our collect calls through, and we all bunched around the phone in the booth he had assigned to us. The connection was made surprisingly quickly, and we had a nice chat with our family.
At the bank we exchanged our travelers' checks for wads of

Mexican currency and, led by our self-appointed guides, proceeded happily towards the market.

As we strolled through the narrow streets, favoring the shadowed side, I thought to myself: what do we really know about Mexico? Not very much, except from some vague concept about its colorful past. The only information we had on it was from friends who had spent a week in Acapulco or Mexico City and had complained about the water and the prices. Maria, the bookworm, had read extensively about the Aztec and Mayan cultures, but how could that be tied into today's world?

We found that there were no difficulties for Maria as far as communication was concerned. She chattered happily in a language she had grown up with in Argentina. Clearly, she was a step ahead of me and Charlie, whose whole vocabulary was limited to *si, no, buenos dias* and *muchas gracias!* We learned how much more one could enjoy the stay in a country when familiar with its language.

We marched into small stores whose wares spilled onto the sidewalk in wooden and plastic bins. Owners or clerks never pressed us into buying but gave courteous answers and advice to our questions.

Passing a watch-repair shop, Charlie dragged us in with him. His watch had stopped marking the hours quite some time ago. We crowded around the tiny counter as the watchmaker opened it for inspection. He turned mournful eyes on Charlie and sadly shook his head from side to side. There was no need to know a word in Spanish. We perfectly understood. Walking on, Charlie trailed behind, still stunned, and muttering over the rusty remains of his timepiece.

The big hall of the market was crammed with stand after stand, overflowing with produce, fish, poultry and meat. Smells, strange odors and aromas from spices hung in the air, pungent and unfamiliar to our nostrils. Maria grinned at us, as Charlie and I instinctively wrinkled our noses. "It takes some getting used to, doesn't it?" she said. Our appetites guided us more towards the fruits and vegetables. We started to select with happy abandon, unmindful of the mounds accumulating at our feet. The owner of the stand, a young woman, told us "I have sister in San Diego. I visit every year." She was obviously proud to speak in her halting English, while Maria kept up the conversation in Spanish. We listened, amused, to their bilingual exchange, while the vendor ceremoniously spooned four pounds of soft yellow butter from a large plastic bag into a smaller one.

At the end of this wild shopping spree, we found we had gone through all our Mexican pesos. We asked the owner of the stand if she would accept a travelers' check, to which she graciously agreed. We were thankful, for in smaller towns we did fare better with dollars or local currency. Travelers' checks were eyed with suspicion, and we usually had to show our passport, visa, and give our life history to the store owner before he would accept them.

It seems that some time previously, Mexico had been flooded with forged travelers' checks, and we could not blame the merchants for their cautious attitude.

At 1:00 p.m., the market, as well as all the other stores, are closed, only to be reopened between 2:00 or 4:00 in the afternoon. Business then continues until late in the evening. No Mexican worth his salt will wander the streets in the heat of these early afternoon hours. The house walls reflect the sunlight in fierce waves and turn the streets into veritable ovens.

We could not have carried all our purchased goods to the anchorage and so hailed a taxi which dropped us off opposite our bobbing dinghy. It had been worthwhile, as the price for the fare was negligible.

With barely three inches of freeboard, I carefully maneuvered our overflowing dinghy alongside the boat. Gratefully, we scrambled aboard, the fresh sea breeze drying the perspiration from our faces.

Enthusiastically, we fell over huge bowls of a delicious fresh tossed salad that Maria had whipped up in a jiffy. And then we did as the Mexicans do, we had a well-earned siesta.

Only reluctantly did we move from our reclining positions to slowly pick up from where we had left off. Maria remained aboard, up to her knees in produce to be stored away and rising bread dough overflowing the sides of a bowl. Yeast sure came to life quickly in this warm climate.

Charlie and I toted two seabags along with all the accumulated dirty clothing and went in search of a laundromat We found one, but it was not a self-service one. We left it all in the hands of a capable laundress, and sauntered off, happy to be rid of our heavy and smelly burden.

Manzanillo has all the charteristics of a prospering town; it bustles with activity and there is a definite air of progress about it. True, it might not be as clean or as charming as an old European town, but it was not dirty either. We could see everywhere efforts to clean, paint, build and rebuild. It was evident that Manzanillo was looking forward to a bright future. The harbor, not very large, but well protected by a long breakwater, is deep enough to accommodate ocean-going vessels. Freighters and tankers came and went daily. Two Japanese fishing vessels seemed to be stationed there and besides *Antares* and the *Diane-Lee*, countless Mexican fishing boats in all sizes dotted the quiet anchorage.

For the next two days we rowed back and forth innumerable times. To refuel at the commercial pier meant having to get permission from the harbor master, an encounter we wished to avoid at this time. With our jerry cans, we wandered over to the service station across from the anchorage. The owner regretted very much that he sold no diesel; but a few streets farther, he told us, there was one who did. In a fit of generosity, he loaded our cans and us into his car and drove us there. Not only that, he helped us in getting them filled and in reloading them into the car and drove us back to the anchorage, refusing any pay.

His kindness put me in an awkward position. I could not possibly tell him that I would have to repeat the trip four more times to fill our tank. He might have thought I was trying to take advantage of him. Besides, what else could I tell him but *muchas gracias?* I regretted being up against the language barrier in view of this man's generous gesture towards a stranger.

Another trip into town took us through winding streets. Here, we got lost and had to ask several times for directions. Finally, we found the only place in town which sold kerosene.

In a dark and murky recess, the store owner kept a few vats of what looked to me more like black diesel, but he assured me that it was the real thing. Once more we clattered through town with our cans and loaded them into a taxi to get back to the harbor. All this hauling and carrying was getting Charlie and me thoroughly tuckered out.

That evening, as I sat aboard *Diana Lee*, busily tracing from their charts of the Mexican and Central American coasts, Bob told me that we could get fuel and potable water across the bay, at Las Hadas. It would cost us ten dollars for a one-day stay, which, I thought, was not too much to pay to fill our water tank with clean, filtered water.

Maria had been hoping for a relaxed picture-taking tour of

Manzanillo, and both of us set out one morning with our cameras. I took along the gooseneck from the main boom, which had a crack and had to be welded, and the cable from the RPM meter, which had broken off. We found the welding shop close by and the gooseneck was promised for the next day. For the RPM cable, however, I could not find a replacement, nor could it be repaired. We wandered from one auto parts shop to another; there must have been dozens in Manzanillo.

In our search we had come to a part of town where houses were built on stilts over a shallow lagoon. Naked and half-naked children waded in the shallows, catching tiny crabs to be sold later to passersby on the street.

My mind did a quick flash-back to the North Sea, where we had spent so many vacations. There, my sister and I had done the very same thing, catching and collecting small crabs, not larger than our own small hands. My mother had cooked them for us, and we would savor every edible morsel out of them. I had never imagined that there were crabs in existence six and eight inches across, until I came to live in the Pacific northwest.

I had taken a few pictures here and there, but Maria had still not used her Rollei. By now our feet ached, it was hot and we felt tired and thirsty. The hunt for the cable had taken up too much of our time.

The next morning we picked up our laundry and went to the welding shop on the way. To our immense surprise, the gooseneck was ready also. The welder had done an excellent job on it and it cost me just three dollars. Who says you can't get anything done in Mexico?

In the afternoon, we said goodbye to Bob and Jerry and set out across Manzanillo Bay to the resort Las Hadas. We motored around the breakwater into a very modern and attractive marina. Atop a concrete pier stood a few fuel drums, and we gathered that that was the fuel dock. There were no bollards or cleats to make fast the boat; we had to tie our lines to odd pieces of wood and pipes sticking out of the ground on shore.

The surge was very strong and we slammed continuously into the concrete wall. I did not want to spend too much time at this pier and went in search of somebody, anybody, in charge of the fuel operation. After some time we managed to scare up an attendant, who ambled over and asked how much fuel we needed. "About fifty gallons," I informed him. He attached a handpump to one of the drums and gave us the end of a plastic hose to insert into the tank. We sat down and watched the liquid gurgle through it. This was most certainly much better than carrying the jerry cans through the streets of Manzanillo. Of course, for this service and convenience the price per gallon went up to thirty-two cents; in Manzanillo it had cost us seventeen cents.

From the pier, we now had to move over to the yacht dock, and I could see that we would have some fancy work to do, to moor stern-on with a bow anchor out. It all would not have been so difficult but for the strong surge inside the breakwater. By now we had declared this an engineering failure!

While I positioned the boat so that we could slip into the slot between two other yachts, Charlie was at the bow, preparing the anchor. Maria was busy meanwhile tying the sternlines. Charlie dropped the anchor but misunderstood my signal and let out too much chain. In consequence, with the help of the surge, we sped towards the dock and slammed into it with a sickening thud. We bounced off and away, too late for Maria to jump onto the dock and secure a line.

I rushed forward and took in some chain to avoid another encounter with the dock. This was not so good either, as now the gap separating us from it was too large to jump over. I lowered the dinghy over the side and sent Charlie to row over to the dock and take our sternlines. There, he promptly missed the line Maria had thrown to him.

I am not given to shouting, but by now I was so furious and frustrated that it took all my willpower not to bellow at my crew. We had thoroughly muffed this operation, and the boat moved like a yo-yo, not only away and towards the dock, but, alas, sideways into the other boats alongside. Finally, Charlie managed to get hold of one of the lines and by then, an attendant had come by. He took the second line, helped to tie both sternlines crosswise on the cleats of the dock and then he languidly slinked away.

We were all breathing hard by now. They decided that the best thing we could do to cool off would be to go for a swim.

What I would do with the shaft of the steering vane, which had acquired a nice S shape, I did not know yet. I still harbored the hope that some day I might be able to unlock the secrets of its function which had so far eluded me.

We walked along carefully-kept paths, under whispering palm trees and along dazzling white walls over which bougainvillaea and hibiscus spilled multicolored blooms. We stood, dazzled by a swimming pool much like a Hollywood set, complete with bathing beauties and officious waiters with cocktail trays.

While Charlie and I appreciatively eyed the beauties, Maria swam to an artificial island in the pool to get a look at the parrots we could hear but not see. Soon she was talking to them through the greenery; I swam to her, leaving Charlie to get his fill of shapely tanned legs and backs.

From the pool we moved to the beach, well protected from the strong surf by a breakwater and a small island. After having a good swim here, we moved again to the pool and finally to the showers. Maria came out, shivering a bit, and we had a hot cup of coffee aboard ship.

Fuel and water tanks were filled, we had a nice swim, and I saw no reason to linger anymore. We cast off our lines and brought up the anchor and set sails to a good breeze from the northwest.

I thought I could get a bit more speed if I added the mizzen to the main and working jib. I was about to do so when Maria, who was at the helm, looked up and asked, "How much faster do you want to go? We are doing six knots already. Do you want to fly to Balboa?" I was taken aback and just stood there, winch handle in hand, unable to say anything. Was this my first mate? Always in accordance with my decisions? What had brought on this outburst? "What do you mean?" I asked, finally able to speak. Maria's face was set in hard lines as she replied, "I mean that you are pushing a bit hard lately. It's all work, work and push, push. This was supposed to be a vacation, a fun trip and not a marathon. Oh, I think I am just tired," she trailed off.

I tried to remind her that it was really due to the malfunction of the vane that we had been pressed into working more than anticipated. As to my pushing, yes, I had the strong urge to go on, to get us to Brazil as fast as the lousy winds and the fouled bottom could carry us. It was, after all, her father who was sick and waiting for her.

I knew, also, that it was useless to continue; Maria could outargue me in nothing flat, and I was not eager to keep up this futile exchange. I was puzzled and hurt, I glanced back to where Las Hadas glimmered in the shadow of the hills, the first lights twinkling through the palms. For a moment, in my confusion, I thought of sailing back; but no, we were already rounding the Manzanillo Cape and out of the bay.

For the next few days, a strained atmosphere pervaded the boat and I felt miserable. I silently prayed that this would not be one of those instances where the first mate walks off the boat in the next port.

Perhaps I should have been a bit more perceptive; a few days later, when Charlie had been a short while at the helm, he complained that he was not feeling well and thought he would not last much longer out there. The regularly late afternoon wind was picking up and promised a good blow. I relieved Charlie and Maria administered aspirin to him and put him to bed.

Later, when she took over from me, I asked her what was the matter with Charlie. "Probably the same thing I had in Manzanillo," she said. "It's really bad; one feels sick, cold and generally miserable. I don't know why he is fussing so; he is whimpering and shivering like a puppy." I forgot about Charlie and asked her, "Why did you not tell me you were feeling sick?" "What for?" she replied. "It would have worried you and, anyhow, I did not know myself what was happening at the time." Oh! Women's logic! I could have slapped and hugged her at the same time. It explained to a certain extent the rotten mood she had been in as we left Las Hadas.

Once below, I looked in on Charlie. He was still whimpering and sighing in his beard. I felt amused and annoyed at the same time. Charlie was a dreamer with many romantic notions about the sea. He had let his whiskers grow into a shaggy beard, had brought along a pipe and pounds of tobacco in hope of complying with the boyhood image he had of a salty seaman. Little did he realize that all these outer frills would never transform him into an able sailor.

But who could have the heart to destroy this image he had of himself?

I thought about the dreams I had harbored myself about this voyage. It was developing so differently from what I had imagined it would be. In my mind's eye I had seen us rushing along, maybe even beating a little record or two. . . instead of ghosting miserably in the variable and fickle winds along the Mexican coast.

Lying in my bunk, I reflected about the three of us, people so different from one another, yet united in the effort to go from here to there in a nutshell of a boat. My love, my interest was concentrated in just sailing that nutshell, to prove to myself that I could do it; to compare myself with the others who had dared before my time and had succeeded; to realize a lifelong dream which I had nurtured since the time I could hold a book and read about the sea and the men who had conquered her or succumbed in the attempt.

I turned and tossed and my thoughts wound around Maria, doing her turn at the wheel. We still had a long way to go to truly know each other. We had met so late in life; could we really and truly become one? Could we become so close that nothing would tear the fine threads of the affection we feel for each other?

I am singleminded. Maria is the shades of gray in my black and white world. I decided that time would take care of our developing relationship. After all, older people cannot be as flexible, emotionally, as the young who are more susceptible and adaptable to each other's influences.

I must have slept finally, for the next thing I heard was Maria calling from the hatchway. It was my turn again. As I prepared a cup of hot chocolate, I saw Charlie had quieted down also and was fast asleep. It would do him good.

Luckily, he recuperated rather quickly from his sickness and could join us for the first meal from the Pacific mackerel I caught the next morning. Health, peace and contentment returned to *Antares* as she slowly made way, east southeast.

Hot, sunny days followed one another, the winds blew intermittently, and our daily runs grew shorter. In the calms, the swell remained strong, and we rocked mercilessly from side to side. Now and then a cross swell hit us broadside, booming against the hull; it made our teeth chatter as the sails flapped and slatted; and below, the cacophony of rattling pots, pans, dishes and cans drove Maria mad.

She named the cross swells "Mexican sideswipers" and desperately stuffed towels between the dishes to muffle the sound.

On such occasions, the only thing left to do was to reach for the ignition key and start motoring. We did a lot of it during those days. But not all of it was misery: we learned to compensate.

One of our daily delights was a swim over the side. Since Mexican waters are notoriously shark-infested, we did not take chances. We lowered all sails, trailed a life-ring attached to a line aft of the boat, and never, never dove in with a splash.

I was always the first to climb down the boarding ladder. Slipping quietly into the water, I first had a good look around the immediate vicinity of the boat. With my diving mask on I could see, it seemed, for miles in the utterly clear, deep blue of the ocean. Only when I gave the all clear sign would Maria or Charlie join me. One of us always remained aboard, closely watching the surrounding waters for telltale fins or ripples. We found that shampoo could be substituted for soap because it could be worked into a nice lather in the salt water. By all means, we were a very clean crew.

Should we find that one or more sharks were trailing behind us, we made use of a bucket to freshen up. Only once did I meet with one of these denizens of the sea and though I was not frightened, I cannot say that I was particularly anxious to make its acquaintance.

I saw it only after I had swum away from the boarding ladder and was halfway between it and the bow. We eyed each other for a moment, just long enough for me to notice a pilot fish, or remora, with its beautiful black and blue stripes, attached to the underside of the shark. Slowly, I turned around, quitely swam back to the ladder and hoisted myself up. It had taken a lot of self-control not to thrash about wildly in my retreat to safety. This, however, would only have aroused the shark's curiosity, and the possible implications sent ripples up and down my spine as I toweled myself dry.

On one particular day, we declared a Sunday aboard, even though the calendar showed it to be Wednesday. It had been a particularly rocky and miserable night and in this we found reason enough to gratify ourselves and indulge in some rest and culinary extravagance.

At breakfast, we had divided our last grapefruit, followed by cereal with fresh canned milk, a soft-boiled egg and toast with butter and marmalade. Freshly brewed and filtered coffee, with its incomparable aroma, spread a satisfying feeling around our middles.

We lolled in the cockpit, reading or sunbathing, and Maria and I fell over a game of Chinese checkers.

Lunch was equally a delight, as the butter melted over the slices of the freshly-baked bread accompanied by sardines, cheese and a salad.

Maria always managed somehow to complement our diet with fresh vegetables. Shredded cabbage and grated carrots were the base to which she added canned vegetables tossed with a variety of dressings enriched with the many spices and dried herbs she had insisted on taking along.

Late afternoon found us with our usual cup of coffee, today accompanied by a chocolate cake. We hoisted sail to the late breeze and at sundown we had dinner before we resumed our night watches. On the menu was fried, marinated tuna with fried potatoes. Maria had placed the leftover fish from the day before in a marinade with onion rings, thus conserving the fish which otherwise we would have been forced to throw overboard.

All this may sound as if our main preoccupation was with food. But we did not often feast like this, and food does become, to a certain extent, a main source of enjoyment, a means to celebrate and to unite us in the mutual pleasure of it. Nobody can eat a good meal and remain grumpy!

The next morning we found ourselves well past the Point of Papanoa. From this headland, a sandy beach curves for seventy miles to the Heads of Acapulco. In the absolute absence of wind, we motored all day along the coastline. The beach is fringed with palm trees and through the binoculars we could observe the traffic on the road which must run parallel to it for many miles.

By nightfall, we could see the glow of Acapulco's lights and since we had no detailed chart of the port, we decided to anchor offshore until morning. We had seen several fishing vessels anchored along the beach in this manner and it seemed to be safe.

It would be rocky, as the line of breakers testified to a rather heavy swell in this area. We could see that to attempt to land in a dinghy rowing through the heavy surf would be a wet experience and a very dangerous one too.

To our surprise, we did have a good rest. The weather remained calm and as we lifted anchor the next morning we knew that it would be no use to hoist sails, the sea was a mirror. With the roar of the breaking surf as companion, we motored along the shore as close as we dared and enjoyed the view of the land.

About noon we were closing in to the hills surrounding Acapulco Harbor and did not feel exactly edified by its desolate appearance. On barren red soil, hundreds of small shacks huddled in the dust. Here, evidently, lived the poor Mexicans their tattered houses exposed to the northwest and westerly winds. There was no sign of vegetation to relieve the drabness and all we could say in favor of that location was that the inhabitants surely had well-ventilated housing.

Rounding the head of the hill and entering the harbor through the Boca Chica passage, human habitation changed abruptly to hotels and villas surrounded by lush gardens and velvety lawns. How close we thought, lived the poor to the more fortunate ones in our society.

Coming further into the harbor we had a sweeping view of the bay and the city of Acapulco. Highrise buildings hugged the shore and marked the downtown section. Residential areas spread behind it and up the hillsides and the mountains which dominates the harbor to the east northeast.

At this time of year, the dry season, that mountain looked bare and strewn with large black boulders. We cruised around for some time looking for the yacht harbor. We found it, crowded to its capacity, and turned looking for anchorage. Among dozens of other yachts, we finally were able to drop the anchor without bumping into one. We pumped up our Avon and meant to get information from one of the nearby yachts as to the possibilities of finding a store or market close by. We rowed to an especially neat and bright little ketch which had drawn my attention instantly.

Maybe we did interrupt their siesta, for its occupants were singularly reluctant to part with any information, nor were they eager for a chat. They did tell us though that we would have to take a bus or taxi to get to any of the places we had mentioned. Gathering all our courage, we asked them if they could possibly take our letters and mail them on their next shore visit. To this they agreed and we handed them our letters and the money to cover the postage. We wished them a good voyage; they were on their way from San Diego and intended to sail around the world. The crew seemed to be a husband-and-wife team, about the same age as Maria and I. We returned to our boat, feeling a bit deflated, and I don't know how much this strange encounter influenced us, but we decided, unanimously to lift anchor and leave.

There was no immediate need to replenish our stores. We set sails to a nice brisk breeze. We were joined by other yachts which had come out of Acapulco for an afternoon cruise. We passed Bruja Point and had a glimpse of Puerto Marques with its many high, white hotel buildings.

Rounding Punta Diamante, we were in the open again where the wind had whipped up to whitecaps, rolling across the prevailing swell. Close to shore the waves were short and steep and as the boat heaved up the bow it slammed into a crosswave with a big whack. This broke the fastening of the headstay at the bowsprit and the sail started to flap violently, carrying its boom across the deck and making it almost impossible to pass it. I hastily doused and secured the staysail and inspected the damage. There was an extra eyepiece on the bowsprit but, I remembered, the screws I had used were short ones. I replaced them with longer ones and attached the stay temporarily to it, crossing my fingers that it would hold. To my surprise and relief it did hold until I could replace the original fastening, months later.

The wind, unfortunately, lasted only until sundown and we were back to engine power, which we honestly hated, but it was the only means of going on and avoiding some of the sickening motion we experienced when becalmed.

That evening we heard strange clanking noises from the engine room and, fearing the worst, I had an inspection tour. The air filter of the engine was vibrating frightfully and, taking a closer look with the flashlight, I discovered that all the screws holding it to the engine body had broken off. I had no replacement for it; therefore I took the whole filter off. Measuring the intake, I found a piece of pipe among my spare parts and inserted it there with a piece of very fine copper mesh. I robbed Maria's cleaning supplies of one plastic potscrubber and stuffed it into the protruding pipe. Presto, let's see how it works. I could pat my back again. It functioned so well that I never replaced the bulky airfilter.

At noon the next day, Maria announced that we had reached the height of Maldonado Point. She scanned the shore with the binoculars and checked and rechecked with the Sailing Directions. I could not quite believe it; if so, we had then made almost sixty miles. "Don't forget that we have the current in our favour," she said.

A bit later we sighted a Mexican tanker and after a few tries, our radio call was acknowledged by its communications officer. Since he had some difficulties with the English language, Charlie relinquished the mike to Maria and she had a nice long chat with the officer in Spanish.

He confirmed our position and proceeded to ask Maria our destination. As she reeled off the ports and places we intended to sail to, a clamor rose in the background and the officer told Maria that he had to hold his man back from swimming over and joining us! He also had a weather forecast for us: it would remain much as it had been, hot and windless and we would not have to fear anything in the Gulf of Tehuantepec.

This encounter reminded us that we were in the shipping lanes and that we would have to keep our eyes open during the night. Maria's watches, no matter at what time they fell, were particularly likely to bring a ship over the horizon. On sighting a light, both she and Charlie would yell for me to come. It took them a long time to be able to judge the distance or direction of another vessel at night.

Before coming on deck, I turned the running lights on and, if under sail, had the engine going. In very light winds, this was a necessary safety precaution, even if the rules of the road gave the sailboat the right-of-way. I have never indulged in the assumption that this would be so and did want to be able to dash out of the way if the need arose. Once on deck, I could take over at any moment or give my instructions to the helmsman. I have never regretted or resented being awakened during my rest time, but much preferred to assist and assure my crew in any task they felt required my presence. Once the danger of a close encounter was passed, I could return to my bunk and sleep.

As the forecast had predicted, it was very hot, but to us not uncomfortably so. By now, we had grown accustomed to the heat and to the sun. Our bodies were brown and, I suspected, as crisp as a strip of bacon in the frying pan. There was one danger Maria always warned us about—dehydration. She urged us to drink as much as possible, which for me was not so easy. I have never been much for drinking water except in the form of coffee or tea. But Maria got us accustomed to luke-warm water, made more appetizing by adding powdered orange juice; and in time, we came to appreciate and even ask for the welcome treat. Since there was no refrigeration aboard, we used our ingenuity now and then to get a cooler drink than one directly from the watertank. We wrapped wet towels around a container which we kept in any shadow available, but exposed to windward. It was amazing how much cooler our drinks were after using the age-old method of cooling by evaporation.

Our greatest pastime now was to behold the sweep of the coast, and the binoculars passed from hand to hand as we discovered one or more features on shore which aroused our interest. On one such occasion Maria discovered a lighthouse and we wondered what it was doing there in the middle of a stretch of coast with high bluffs and no port or point visible. We were too far out to tell and motored closer to have a look. No mistake about it, this was a tiny little bay, a cut, a veritable hole in the wall. Nestled around the shore, a small town spread and spilled over the hills blinking in the noon sun. We had come to Puerto Escondido (Hidden Port), a suitable name for this very pleasant small port.

We anchored abreast a golden, sandy beach and were surrounded immediately by a horde of brown, smiling boys, paddling on surfboards. The bolder ones asked permission to come aboard and climbed excitedly up the boarding ladder. They banded around Maria as soon as they found out that she spoke Spanish and had a million questions for her. She tried to answer as quickly as they were asked. I suspect she enjoyed this tremendously, while Charlie and I once more pumped up the Avon. The boys asked Maria if we had any luck fishing, all the while shyly caressing our fishing gear with knowing fingers.

When the Avon was put into the water and we had climbed in, they all fanned out around it and escorted us to shore with gales of laughter. We landed with a thud on the sand and one moment later dozens of little hands dragged the Avon over the sand and free of the surf.

We found the people of Puerto Escondido as friendly and as happy as their children. Our first dash was to an open veranda bar and we soon sat before frosty, tall glasses filled with iced orange juice. With the sea breeze rustling in the dry palm leaves of the roof, we savored our drinks, letting our eyes rove over the beach. On its southeast side the breakers rolled in, stronger and higher than to the northwest side which is protected by the bluff where the lighthouse stands sleeping in the sun.

Tents and campers had congregated in a wooded, fenced-in area and a holiday atmosphere pervaded all. We felt extremely relaxed and happy to have landed here at this time. We could visualize and foresee the time when hotels would line the shore and all its natural and primitive beauty would be lost in a maze of concrete buildings.

We walked a dusty road through the little town, passing

stands which sold everything from fruits to clothing and plastic household wares. The colors ranged from sunny yellows to lurid pinks and purples, and unbelievable shades of green. At the most prosperous-looking store, we stopped and gathered around the owner, a formidable looking lady, her jet-black hair held in a heavy coil at the neck. Her dark eyes swept over us, alert and searching, but not unfriendly. Maria convinced her that we could be trusted with our travelers' checks. She exchanged one for Mexican currency, but not before she had carefully noted down our passport and ID numbers. We were affluent again and could storm the stands where the fruits sent their sweet aromas aloft to mingle with the smell of frying fish, garlic and spices coming from the many open cooking fires of the small roadside restaurants.

But the beach was beckoning strongly, so we returned aboard to change into bathing suits and join the throng of swimmers. Soon, Charlie and Maria left me, to go and compete with the more daring swimmers at the southeast side of the beach where, with a great deal of shouting and laughter, they joined the body surfers in the breakers.

Meanwhile, I had swum once around the boat and was appalled at the green scum which had accumulated along the waterline. Climbing into the Avon and armed with a scrubber, I went all around and did a fair cleaning job. Maria and Charlie returned, breathless and laughing, and I was happy to see them enjoy themselves so much.

Hardly had we been aboard, when a runabout stopped alongside. Five young men in it asked politely if they could come aboard and see the boat. Over coffee and cookies, Maria kept a lively conversation going with the Mexican youths, while Charlie and I talked to the only one in the group with a smattering of English, a student from France on a tour of Mexico.

After they had left, we once more went into the water. It was irresitible. Maria met Chuck, from Seattle, and an acquaintance of his, a girl from Chicago who also knew Seattle well. We invited the two aboard and over a glass of fruit juice we told them of our voyage.

Slowly, as the evening dusk spread over the bay, the beach became deserted. I rowed our guests back to shore. Lights glimmered and soft music floated over to us. The lighthouse had awakened and flashed its warning ray across the darkening ocean as I climbed back aboard, tired and happy, leaving wet tracks on deck as I went along. Coming to the companionway, I lost my footing on the upper step and landed with a thud below. This would not have been so bad, had I not slammed my back as I tried to regain my balance. A sharp and agonizing pain spread over my back. I barely managed to take off my wet trunks and crawl into my bunk. To everybody's relief, after an hour's rest I felt fine and we forgot the incident.

The next day we swarmed into town and made several trips back to our Avon on the beach, depositing bags with fruits and vegetables. Walking up a dusty hill road, we found a 'supermarket' where Charlie and Maria pounced gleefully upon the cartons of Mexican cigarettes, which cost considerably less here than at home. Moreover, we found a package of dry yeast, an item Maria had not been able to find in Manzanillo.

By 1400 we had rowed everything aboard and we lifted anchor, regretfully, I am sure on Charlie's and Maria's part. But by now they knew better than to protest the skipper's decisions. As we sailed by the lighthouse, Maria turned and, throwing a kiss, murmured, "Good-by, Puerto Escondido, I love you!"

That evening we caught a small barracuda which went from the hook to the frying pan in a flash. Prince Igor always seemed to sense the excitement which comes over us when we have a strike. He rubs against Maria's legs and mews expectantly up to his mistress without stopping, until the head of the fish is cooked, cooled and served to him. I had entertained the vague hope that during the trip he would perhaps change his eating habits when the catfood we had along would give out. I had not reckoned on his feline stubborness. He refused any tasty leftovers from the table, even sardines, corned beef or any other morsel we thought he could not possibly resist. The only exceptions were boiled fish and condensed milk.

What had I expected from a 'prince?' Even if we had not cared for fish, it would have been mandatory for us to hang out a hook just to feed him. There were many occasions when we feared for his health and life as the days passed without even a nibble on our lines. During these times he would listlessly lap a few drops of condensed milk, his only sustenance for many days.

The heat made him suffer to a certain extent. His favorite place was on the cabin sole between our bunks, where he lay stretched out on his back with fore and hindlegs as far away from his body as possible.

His trust in us must have been limitless; he lay directly in our path when we had to go to the forward section of the bow. I have lost count of the times we reminded each other, "Watch it—don't step on the cat, there is a yard of him lying on the floor." We felt sorry for him; what would we have done if we would have had to wear a fur coat in 90-degree weather?

While we spent all day in the sun, he ventured on deck only at night. Then he scampered about, jumped over the dinghy or even sat atop the mainboom when the sail was down. Many a nightwatch he spent purring on my lap, lovingly digging his claws into my thighs. I had never before been especially fond of cats, but this one had somewhere found a soft spot in my heart. Perhaps because he is such a beautiful orange and white, long-haired tabby. We called him our "furry nuisance." but bestowed a lot of love and attention on him.

Windlessness was still with us the next morning. Disgruntled, I put away the fishing line. During the short breeze blowing offshore in the early morning, we had lost several hooks and lures. No fish today. All that remained to enjoy was a nice swim. I followed Charlie who had ventured first into the water today. Hardly had I made a few strokes when the sharp pain in my back returned, taking my breath away. It was sheer agony to climb the ladder back aboard and make my way below. Once in my bunk, I found I could not even move a finger. Each time I did, I had the impression of knives slicing my back to pieces. After a brief consultation with my crew, we decided to motor into the next port. The possibility that I had a broken rib was not ruled out; therefore, it would be better to seek a doctor's advice.

On our way to Puerto Angel, we met with another yacht. Charlie made radio contact with the *Sanssouci* from Portland, Oregon. Her skipper told us that they intended to put into Puerto Angel, that it was an easy landing. We remained in radio contact, in case Maria and Charlie needed assistance with anchoring the boat. But my crew came through with flying colors. I was proud of them as the boat swung at anchor and lay at a safe distance from the *Sanssouci*.

The more difficult task lay ahead: to get me to shore, maneuver the Avon through the surf and walk to the doctor's office which, incidentally, was just a few steps from the beach.

In a dizzy fog of pain, I found myself sitting in the doctor's office. He was very young but examined me competently and at length. Maria, beside me, translated that he could find no broken bone. To ease the pain, he wrapped my whole chest with stretch bandages and gave Maria two kinds of pills which I had to take alternately.

When it came time to pay for his services, we were dismayed since he told us that he could not accept our travelers' checks. We could exchange those in the next town, Pochutla. He said that he trusted us—we could pay him the next day. This fact began a chain reation of events I would rather forget. If anything should happen to any of us on the way to that blasted town, it could develop into a sticky situation as we had no visas to enter the country. It was one thing to seek anchorage or portage and another to venture inland.

We resolved that the best thing to do under the circumstances would be to put ourselves in the hands of the harbormaster and straighten out our confused notions about what permits or papers we really needed. This was perhaps the best opportunity, for we had entered the port under emergency conditions. Maria and Charlie rowed me back on board and returned to shore with our passports and ship's papers. It was too late in the day to go to Pochutla anyway; the bank closed at one.

When they returned, Maria reported that the harbormaster was not in, but that he would be the following morning.

My crew took off again the next morning, having to hire a taxi, as we did not even have the necessary change for the bus. They paid the doctor and the driver on their return and went back to the office of the harbormaster. There they were told that we all had to come to the captain's office.

It was still very painful for me to move about, and I grumbled all the way up a steep hill to the office of the harbormaster. He was not there but, we were told, we should go to his residence. One of his officers came with us to show us the way. Down the hill we went and up another, steeper yet, and my mood went from gray to black. In the blazing sun, the tight bandage around my chest felt hot and itchy.

Climbing up a winding row of stone steps we came to a house atop the hill where, under a thatched veranda, a man in a khaki uniform awaited us. One of his pudgy hands stroked lazily over a well-fed tummy while he motioned us with the other condescendingly, to a few chairs. He was soft spoken and told

Maria, in grave tones, that we were in the country illegally and that we were subject to a fine of 10,000 pesos and the possible seizure of the boat. He waited for the effect of these words to sink in as Maria, thunderstruck, translated them for me.

I was fuming. It was obvious that the official in front of us had pegged us as 'greenhorns.' Since he was in possession of all our papers, there was nothing we could do but try to minimize the high amount of money he was asking of us. The 'fine' was finally settled at $100, 1,200 Mexican pesos. As he, of course, could not accept this payment in anything other than in local currency, we had to pile into the next bus and once more make the trip to Pochutla.

Perhaps I should have taken a chance and put a call in to the nearest American embassy. I don't know what help or advice, if any, I would have received. At that moment all I wished for was to be off again, as quickly as possible after having satisfied the port captain's demands. I only hoped that these demands would stop there, with no further strings attached.

Hot and thirsty, we returned to our 'benefactor' who proceeded to count the pesos carefully. He stuffed them, satisfied, in his pocket and handed us our papers. We checked them but could not find the dispatch he had promised we would get when we paid the fine. He said he could not provide us with one, that we should leave soon for this was a military port and that "they" surely would deal much stronger with us if we stayed. We knew that all these veiled threats were meant to scare us and make us leave before we recovered our senses. To spite him, we stayed another night at anchor. Besides, I needed the rest, and I wanted to see Maria and Charlie on speaking terms again.

Apparently, on their comings and goings to and from shore, Charlie had not been too skillful at landing the dinghy and Maria twice had been dunked in the surf with the Avon riding over her and rolling her with the waves in the sand.

"Can you imagine," she fumed, "there I stood, dripping all over the doctor's nice clean veranda, puddles all around me, sand in my hair, water in my shoes!"

We got all our feelings sorted out nicely, though. Nobody can remain mad at Charlie for long and soon their friendship was restored. Puerto Angel, we won't forget you so soon and we hope that someday we may get even with your harbormaster.

The next day we set sails to a good wind. Here we come, Tehuantepec!

CHAPTER 4

QUIET DAYS ON A SOUTHEASTERLY COURSE
(WIND? WHAT WIND?)

While the *Sailing Directions* recommend an offshore course for merchant vessels in the Gulf of Tehuantepec during a norther, we had been advised to keep close to shore by yachting friends who had lived through one of them. I had not much choice; without detailed charts I would not sail too close to an unknown shore. The season for the northers had passed anyhow, and we set a course which roughly led from the Mexican western tip of the Gulf of Tehuantepec to Punta Guionos in Costa Rica.

The first day, Tehuantepec claimed several hooks and lures and try as we might we never got a single skipjack tuna, which abounded in this particular area. From noon to noon we had made twenty-five miles, mostly due to a favorable current, and I began to feel frustration mounting again inside me. Unable to keep idle, I had Charlie inflate the Avon and both of us went over to scrub the sides of the hull and as much of the bottom as we could reach with a longhandled scrubber.

I had attached long lines all around the boat and tried to dive to the keels to loosen some of the barnacles which had grown to an incredible size on them. I had to give up the idea because by the time I had worked myself far enough down to the keels and taken a single whack at them, I was out of air and had to surface. Maria told me I sounded like an asthmatic whale and that I should take better care of my back.

As another day passed, it became clear that no fierce norther was going to hit us. The sea became more and more like a glassy, undulating surface, as if a lake of molasses was holding us in place. It was as if we had come to the doldrums and would stay here for weeks at the mercy of elusive little breezes.

We hoisted sails, we got them down again only to raise them for another elusive puff. We repeated this so often in the course of a day that we grew weary of it. During the night, we observed spectacular lightning flashes far to the east in the direction of shore. They revealed mountains of clouds, which never came our way across the water. These were the first cloud formations we had seen in four weeks.

Easter Sunday rolled around and we still sat in the middle of

Tehuantepec Gulf without a breath to stir our restless sails. We were below when a strange sound of rushing waves reached us. We looked at each other in surprise. "Somebody coming?" asked Maria. The sound faded and came again, closer this time. We climbed up to the blistering hot cockpit and searched the water. "There, and there," we exclaimed in unison, pointing in different directions. We now saw it all, countless schools of fish, swarming, skimming, surfacing and rushing in well-coordinated patterns.

The water seemed to boil in patches, sometimes a quarter mile in width. The sight made us frantic. Grabbing the catcher, we tried to scoop up a few of the fish. But they never came quite close enough. It was maddening to sit here among millions of fish and not to be able to catch a single one.

The schooling fish had attracted a great variety of birds which wheeled overhead and, with shrill cries, plunged amid the fish feeding unashamedly on them. If only we knew how to fish as the Mexicans do, in small open pirogas, just with handlines which they throw far out and away and bring in with small, jerky motions of the wrist. We had seen them come home with boatloads of tuna mackerel and barracuda.

I had entertained the idea of going for a swim when, looking astern, I spotted almost a dozen sharks trailing lazily behind the boat. It would have to be the bucket again today. All three of us were watching the sharks and wondering why they did not join the birds and feed on the bountiful fish available. After a while, we could spot below the sharks the silvery flashes of tuna and other middlesized fish. Slowly it dawned on us; the tuna, as did the birds, fed on the smaller schooling fish. Yet, each trip to the surface would be the last one for many of them. The sharks, patiently patrolling the area, moved in and fed on the tuna. This had been a free lesson in the way of sealife in all its beauty and cruelty. The old adage "big fish eats little fish" could not have been demonstrated more clearly.

In a futile attempt to disperse the sharks from our proximity, I poked at them with the boathook. Lazily, they fanned out in a circle and returned, rubbing now and then against the bottom of the boat. I struck out once more and poked a hole in the skin of one of them; it did not seem to bother him at all. Marked as he was, we could follow his movements as he returned to his place astern. I knew it had been a foolish gesture on my part, caused by the age-old fear and revulsion man has for sharks.

The display we had witnessed continued all afternoon as we watched, fascinated, unable to take our eyes off the surface of the sea around us.

Since our sunsights worked out sometimes in strange and erractic ways, I hauled out the taffrail log again, took it apart and cleaned and oiled it once more in the hope of getting a more accurate mileage reading.

I felt that the sensor from the knotmeter must not be showing our correct speed because of the growth covering the tiny padded wheel but there was nothing I could do at this time to correct it.

Only many months later did I find that the index mirror on the sextant was out of alignment and that the sights we took and which now and then matched our actual position were pure coincidence.

Poor Maria, how hard she was working on those useless sights and how often had they caused needless arguments between us.

We had heard about husband and wife not seeing eye-to-eye on the subject of navigation but we had never believed it would happen to us. This fact alone could have turned my hair white had it not been that color already.

However bad our navigation was, after five days of very little sailing and much work on the part of our faithful Frieda, we found ourselves across from Chaperico, Guatamala's major port on the Pacific side.

A very fine mist obscured the low shore and only with the binoculars could we make out two freighters at anchor as well as a few palm trees.

Here, too, we met with the *Seaquest*, a beautiful ketch-rigged boat, built in traditional lines. She was out of San Francisco and on the way to Denmark. The Crew members had followed the advice of keeping close to shore and regretted having done so. They were trying to dry out now, for they had been drenched continuously by the heavy rainfall along the shore.

Engine problems had plagued them along the way but, as they had no clearance for Guatamala the *Seaquest's* skipper was considering the possibility of entering port in Acajutla, El Salvador.

The boat was better rigged for light winds than ours. It slowly pulled ahead and away from us and we knew we could never catch up with them. At noon, as the wind left us, we started our engine. To our surprise, we met with the *Seaquest* again two hours later; becalmed, her skipper was busy working on the engine.

We rafted up to them and we drifted together in the swell, visiting. Those were nice relaxing hours; we shared experiences, cups of coffee and all but devoured Maria's banana cake.

The skipper and I discussed engines and navigation while the girls exchanged recipes. Charlie was involved in a serious conversation with the skipper's brother and a friend of his about our fishing problems.

We found that the *Seaquest* was not doing much in the field of navigation either. I don't believe they had ever taken a sunsight. The only method they used was DR and depthsoundings off the coast It seemed interesting, but, I thought, would not be more accurate than our floundering efforts with the sextant.

Wind came up and we had to separate, but not before making a date to meet at Punta Arenas in Costa Rica. They hoped their chances would be better of making repairs on the engine there.

Since the wind was fair and we were making good speed, Charlie put the line out to see if his newly gained knowledge would help us to a good catch. We had seen schools of dorado swimming alongside, their bright rainbow colors flashing enticingly in the sun.

We did not catch a dorado that day; instead, a marlin took our lure and made off with it, jumping high out of the water twice, trying to shake off the hook and sinker. Of all the fish in the ocean, a marlin weighing at least 200 pounds had to get our 40-pound line! Part of our problem was the line, for we would have needed at least a 100-pound line, enough to hold a big fish fighting the hook.

The wind, a strong northwesterly, sent us skimming along at six to seven knots and nothing could have been better suited to lift our spirits. We already thought ourselves in Punta Arenas if only it kept blowing. A sound downpour drenched us thoroughly during the night. After it had passed, the wind slowly died again. We had been wishful dreamers to think that it would last.

By now the frustration was turning into desperation as we once more sat in the swell without wind. According to our pilot charts, regular northwest winds are supposed to blow at this time of year. But they had been all but absent on our entire trip down the Mexican and Central American coasts.

In view of the low level of our fuel supply, I had to put into the next port, clearance or no clearance.

That day we entered the port of Acajutla, guided into the anchorage by a very helpful radio operator. We sat nervously in the cockpit after hoisting our yellow flag, waiting for pratique. At the piers, not less than seven freighters were loading and discharging cargo. We had seen two more at anchor outside, awaiting their turn. A small rowboat detached itself from the pier and came toward us. Soon the boarding officer shook our hands and we sat down to parley. We indulge little in alcoholic beverages, but for this occasion I got out a bottle of a very fine brandy, another going-away present which came in handy now.

The conversation was one-sided as the official spoke no English and Maria had to deal with the details. We could go ashore, he told us, but should come the next day to the port captain's office.

Before he left, taking along our passports and ship's papers, he must not have been able to resist the temptation and sat down at the wheel.

A dreamy expression crossed his soft features as his hands caressed the varnished wood. He asked Maria if she too steered the boat. She assured him that our watches were always split three ways. Reluctantly, we thought, he left us then, a wistful smile still on his face.

We immediately followed him in our Avon and climbed the thirty-foot iron ladder up to the pier. Absolutely everybody we met had a friendly hello for us.

From his tower, the radio operator motioned us to come up to his perch. We climbed endless stairs. This was hard for our legs, no longer accustomed to this kind of exercise. Here we were shown around and additionally given much help in negotiating for the water and fuel supply.

The radio operator also told us where we could cash travelers' checks and advised us to take one of the taxis parked outside the gate of the port facilities. The drivers would help us to get wherever we needed to go.

True enough, we made the acquaintance of José, a young man who was delighted to have Maria at his side speaking his language. He drove us to a small restaurant a few miles inland. Here we not only reveled in delicious food and cool drinks, but the owner also changed several of our travelers' checks.

It was amazing how much easier relations became, how many obstacles were overcome, by the absence of the language barrier. This proved itself once more the next day when we paid our respects to the harbormaster sitting on the porch of the office building. He questioned Maria closely and at length about our home port, our destination, why we had no dispatch, or *zarpe*, as it is called in the southern ports.

Maria told him of all our problems and of our ignorance about such a document, and of how we had been treated in Puerto Angel. The port captain never smiled, nor did his sharp eyes leave her face.

After what seemed an eternity, he must have been satisfied; he motioned to one of the clerks and we went into the office with him where we finally, finally received a *zarpe*.

We were curious to know what it looked like. It is simply a piece of paper stating that such and such a vessel had been in such and such a port for a determined time, how many people were aboard and that it was sailing on a certain date to a certain port. Tonnage, length and width were recorded as well as the registration number. This is the most important document a yacht needs to enter and leave foreign ports.

Besides the *zarpe*, one must have a crew list in which is noted the names, passport numbers and function of each person aboard. I was the master, Charlie the deckhand and Maria was the *cozinera* (cook) of the yacht *Antares*. Few countries demand visas for yacht crews, a valid passport is sufficient.

It is not a waste of time to inform oneself at the respective embassies before taking off. We had known about the visas, but had not bothered to seek any, as we had never intended to put into any of the ports we had been forced to enter. However we had not been too well informed about the windless condition along these coasts. We were gaining our experiences the hard way. The price we paid for our *zarpe* in Acajutla was the regular fee of twelve dollars. In some ports it is less, in some more; it all depends on the port captain's orders.

We had found a helpful official in Acajutla and felt indebted to him for the fair treatment he gave us and for this final settlement of the red tape. It is, of course, a must to carry Coast Guard documentation aboard. Besides that, I had my title and insurance policy among my papers as well as the vaccination cards against smallpox which is still mandatory.

When we had presented ourselves to the Health Department in Seattle for this vaccine, we had been urged by the nurse to take one against typhoid. Malaria and yellow fever are still endemic in some parts of the South American countries, but the vaccines, as we had informed ourselves, are not effective for long periods of time. We, therefore, dispensed with those.

We felt so good coming out of the port captain's office that we could have hugged our taxi driver, José, ambling towards us. We had not found him at the gate of the port that morning. He explained that it was his birthday today and that he had taken the day off to celebrate.

But since we needed his services, he galloped off to get a car from his boss. He came with us as we made our purchases and even haggled with the vendors when he thought they were asking too much for their wares.

Once on the pier, he helped us heave the bundles down into the dinghy. I wanted to pay him, but he shyly refused the money; instead, he asked us if we would let him come aboard. He had never been aboard a yacht before and would much appreciate it if we would grant him this wish.

We took José along and had a drink with him in the cockpit. He had a long conversation with Maria, telling her of his desire to go to the United States in the hope of making a better living.

Maria explained to him gently that unskilled labor in the U.S. was not much in demand. To start a new life there, a certain knowledge of the English language would be mandatory.

On our voyage, we met many more young people asking the same question: "How can I go to the United States?"

We may have shattered a few dreams with the honest answers we gave those young aspirants to a bright future in a land they greatly admired and where they thought it was easy to make mounds of money, if one just got there.

Maria told him, "Look at us. We are by any standard old people. We have worked hard for a lifetime to come where we are now; it took that long. We, too, were strangers in paradise. Educate yourself, work hard and you will be able to make it in your own country, among your own people."

For this twenty-two-year-old, the answers did not seem to be satisfactory. Youth is impatient with life, it wants to take flight and achieve great things in the shortest time possible.

We understood him, but I doubt that he understood or believed us. We rowed him ashore and he promised to meet us at the grand ball which was given at the port facilities in celebration of its fifteenth anniversary.

We had been especially invited to these festivities and looked forward to the event. We spruced up for the occasion but, as we came to the ladder at the pier, we saw a large, black oilslick lapping at the lower rungs. It would not be easy to go to the ball without oily stains on our pants. We did not think it would be wise to leave the Avon unattended on shore and took our chances at the latter. We went to the ball, oil stains and all!

Drinks could be bought with the tokens one purchased at several stands where men sat behind wiremesh cages. For tables and chairs one had to pay in the same manner. We went from surprise to surprise, but the greatest was to come as the band struck a chord and rock-and-roll blasted out and, electrified, the dancers gyrated in the same manner as our kids do at home.

Several sailors from the merchant ships had come also and we saw them dance the bump with the señoritas in their long evening dresses.

A group of about ten girls, all dressed alike in pink evening dresses, circulated among the throngs of dancers. We approached the prettiest one and asked her the purpose of their attire. All of them were daughters of port employees competing that evening to be named Port Queen for the coming year.

The young lady we were talking to charmed us with her poise and the graceful movements of her hands. She was very slim and very, very young. Her finely chiseled features, large dark eyes, olive skin and jet-black hair contrasted pleasingly with the pink pastel of the gown.

She thanked us gravely as we told her we would applaud for her the most and the loudest. For this was the way in which the winner would be chosen.

We did not leave the party until long after midnight when our candidate had been elected and seated on the throne, roses in her arms, crown on her head, smiling shyly at the surrounding crowd.

On the next and last day of our happy stay in Acajutla, we remained aboard waiting for the call of the radio operator. He was to inform us of the exact time when we would have to move to the pier to take on water and fuel. Leaving Charlie and Maria to catch the call, I rowed to another motor-yacht whose owner had invited me aboard.

Jim Kelly showed me the boat he had bought in Miami to sell in San Francisco. He hoped to make a handsome profit with it. He had only one crew member aboard; the yacht steered itself by an autopilot. All there was to do during watches was to make sure the autopilot remained on course.

Jim had designed windvanes in the past and when I told him of the failure I had experienced with mine, he drew for me the details of one I could build myself.

A call came for the yachts to move to the pier and I shook Jim's hand in parting, thanking him for the drawing and the ice-cold beer from his ample store.

As we tied up at the pier, the tide was out and the pier was thirty feet above us. Dozens of hands grabbed our lines and tied us securely to the bollards above.

In Acajutla harbor, even in calm weather, there is such a strong surge that frequently the lines holding the freighters part and all hands have to rush to make them fast again.

We hoped our lines would hold, but we were not so sure that we would not eventually have our sides staved in against the concrete pilings. The freighter tied at the other side of the pier evidently had empty holds; it made a deep booming sound as it solemnly slammed into the pier. We could hear as its lines stretched to the breaking point and creaked and chaffed until the big ship swung back and boomed once more.

All this made us more nervous as Jim received the fuel hose ahead of us, for it took much longer to fill the huge tanks of the motor yacht. Jim was taken aback when he received his bill—a gallon of diesel cost seventy-cents in Acajutla! We fueled with seventy-five gallons and paid an additional two dollars for the water. This fee was to pay the fire department, which provides this service for the yachts, hauling the potable water to the pier in fire trucks.

Fervently, I hoped that there would be no major conflagration on shore while they were servicing us. We thankfully moved away from the pier with no damage other than a bent axis from the taffrail log.

We motored off away from the coast and by 1600 we had lost sight of it.

We were alone again, this time filled with many happy memories of that nice and hospitable port.

Day after day we drifted and motored more than sailed, now in a more southerly direction. The coast of El Salvador runs almost east-west, while Nicaragua's coast dips from the Gulf of Fonseca in a southeasterly direction towards Costa Rica. Between Cabo Sta. Elena and Punta Guionos is the Gulf of

Papagayos where we could hope for some wind. The coast here runs practically north to south and then sweeps sharply east southeast towards Cabo Blanco, which marks the western point of the Gulf of Nicoya. From that point we would have to sail northeast and north to Punta Arenas. I did not know if I really wanted to make such a large detour; it all would depend upon our fuel supply.

For now we had enough and, optimists that we always were, we were very convinced that there would be no further reason to put into another port before Balboa.

Sealife abounded in astonishing quantities. Closer to the coast, we had daily encounters with water snakes which, in Mexico, were caught for their skins and manufactured into belts. How barbarous, we thought. They are harmless and pretty creatures, brown on top with bright yellow and tan colors on the underside. Turtles abounded, too, looking like pieces of flotsam from afar, often with a bird perched on their shells.

We felt privileged one day to watch a huge manta ray jump high out of the water and fall back with a mighty splash. We had often heard the splash but had always been too late to see what had caused it. Sometimes I worried that one of these unique animals would get on our hook and suffer injury. In our book collection was a richly illustrated edition on sealife which we often consulted. I assured myself that manta rays were plankton eaters. What surprised me, though, was the fact that they belonged to the shark family. Even if we did not do much sailing these days, we certainly were learning a lot.

The temperature remained mostly around ninety degrees. Our daily runs were discouraging, averaging just fifty miles. This slow speed was what enabled us to observe and study much of the sealife around us. In a way, it contributed to taking our minds off the poor sailing conditions.

Dolphins had been almost daily companions from the coast of Baja on. We never tired of their presence and often stopped our activities to watch them frolic off the bow. Nights we knew they were present when we heard the funny snuffling sound they make when surfacing for air. Their sleek bodies left luminous trails in the water as they incessantly circled the boat.

Dolphins swim in the shadow of a boat to make their feeding easier. Their prey cannot detect them fast enough. One other thing was pleasant to know—if there were dolphins, there were no sharks around which, in turn, meant we could swim safely.

In our northern latitudes we had often seen killer whales, but no more than maybe five at a time. We, therefore, particularly enjoyed seeing a pod of about fifty swimming past us at a distance of about twenty feet. The waters foamed and boiled as they made their way northwest, seemingly in a great hurry to get wherever they were going. The next day we met another smaller pod of about twenty making their way in the same direction.

All this abundant sealife eventually yielded a bountiful catch for us. I had hauled a four-pound tuna aboard and, after cleaning it, more out of curiosity then anything else, I took the liver and put in the hook. Almost instantly I pulled an eight pound dorado out of the water. Maria clapped her hands happily.

"Cat," she said, "your hungry days are over." As some of the fish was still boiling, Maria cut a few strips of dorado and served them raw to Igor. He devoured them hungrily, but lost the whole lot on the carpet again. It had been too strong a fare for his empty tummy. He now lay at Maria's feet, patiently waiting until she had cooled the cooked fish enough and made sure there was enough broth with it in his dish.

This unexpected amount of fish kept Maria busy for the rest of the day. I had cleaned and filleted it all in the cockpit, but she had to prepare several dishes of it and marinate some so that it would keep.

But she could take her time with it. Since we had left Acajutla, I had relieved her at the watches during the daytime. Charlie and I split the day in two-hour turns and though Charlie did not especially enjoy this, he, too, saw that Maria was more than busy. Not only were the cooking and bread-baking her daily chores, but also the constant wrestling with our sights. After all this, she often took her notes and my logbook and sat down to write our reports to *Castoff* magazine in Seattle. She frequently had to write this report in longhand because the motion of the boat sent the carriage of the typewriter sliding this way and that and it was impossible to use it at those times.

Off Cabo Blanco, we again experienced the most windless days and it became apparent that our fuel would give out before we reached Balboa. Maria had suggested the ports of Quepos of Golfito in Costa Rica. Both involved detours from our course.

"It will take us days and days to get back on course again," I protested. "Especially Golfito, stuck up there in the Golfo Dulce."

We checked our chart of Panama and found that fifteen miles north of Punta Burica was Puerto Armuelles From Cabo Blanco, where we were at this moment, to Punta Burica, in a straight line, it is about 200 miles. If we went into Golfito it would lengthen our course by a good 150 miles more. We did not know what difference there was between Golfito and Puerto Armuelles.

If we had known, we would gladly have made the detour and been much happier with our next landing. But I decided to put into the Panamanian port to save time. Little did I know that it would cost us not only time but money.

Punta Burica lies off a long narrow isthmus with an island at the end of it. A reef connects the island to the isthmus, and there is no passage between them.

We sailed up to the island and rounded its southern shore in calm weather, catching a fish along the way. From then on we had to motor, almost straight north, to Armuelles. It is only a fifteen-mile stretch which, when one is anxious to get there, seems to lengthen to 150 miles.

At a distance, landmarks are very difficult to make out in this region for they are mostly obscured by haze. I could not see any evidence of a port in the vincinity and began to doubt its existence altogether.

Maria tuned the VHF to Channel 16 and called the port. Sure enough, we received an instant reply. We still could not see any signs of a pier or port facilities. Only with the binoculars, at a distance of four miles, we spotted the pier with a banana boat alongside. Encouraged by the friendly assistance of the radio operator, we neared the port where we were guided to a mooring buoy.

The beach is steep, too, and it is not advisable to anchor, nor is it safe to tie up at the pier. A very strong surge and undertow make it unsafe for small craft to do so. Larger fishing vessels anchored west of the pier for short times.

As I guided the boat to the mooring buoy, Maria and Charlie did a good job in tying up and I was glad we had not muffed it this time with so many people watching us from the pier.

The radio operator informed us that we would be boarded soon. He asked whether we had a Panamanian courtesy flag aboard as the authorities frowned on craft without one.

Oh, oh, we did not have one.

He told us he would send one over with the boarding party.

A few minutes later we were invaded by not less than six officials who swarmed aboard and into our cabin. I was overwhelmed: nowhere had we experienced so many important-acting people boarding such a small yacht.

There were two fellows in army garb, one official each for customs, immigration and health, and the port captain. They sat around the table filling out many forms and drinking the coffee we had made for them. The boat was searched from bow to stern. I had to hand my 22-calibre rifle over to the army men; it would be kept under seal and guard at the army post until we left.

All seemed fine until the man from the immigration looked into our passports and exclaimed, "No visas? Bad, very bad."

I tried to explain to him that according to our information from his country's Embassy, crew members of a yacht did not need visas to enter a port.

"Oh no," he said, "that is not right; you *must* have a visa; you better come with me to the Captain right now."

I felt a sinking sensation around my middle. All this seemed to spell more trouble for us. Dejectedly, Maria and I embarked with the boarding party into their launch and went ashore. Victor, the immigration officer, smiled and perspired a lot while he assured us that he would help us in all the dealings with the captain, that he was forced to report this minor irregularity and that we should not worry; after all, he was on our side.

He guided us to the army post and into the captain's office. A tall, handsome, black man sat behind a desk. He stood up, introduced himself, and asked if I preferred to have the conversation conducted in the English or Spanish language.

I told him that my wife spoke Spanish perfectly, but that I preferred to converse in English. He sat down, satisfied, and proceeded to give us a lecture about the laws of the country and the absolute necessity for every traveler setting foot on Panamanian soil to have a visa in his passport.

His English was flawless and surprisingly accent-free. A strangely uneasy current underlay the whole conversation. We did not know what caused it, whether it was his display of absolute authority or our irritation over a talk that seemed to lead nowhere. He made several phone calls and told us that his superiors had confirmed the fact that we did need a visa.

There matters stood.

He finally told us that it was late and that he could not

decide what to do with us, but that we were free to spend our money in town. He would let us know the next morning, he said, and then he dimissed us.

Early the next day, we walked the length of the pier into town and to the bank. Already many people filled the small room in long lines and we sighed at the prospect of having to stand there exposed to the cold blast of the air conditioner.

A teller saw us and motioned us away from the line to the manager's window. We were given priority in the exchange of our traveler's checks. I must state that in spite of the apparent harassment we went through with the authorities in Armuelles, we were always treated with respect and the utmost formality. Not once did we find an offensive or insulting manner in our contact with the many officials we had to deal with.

From the cold bank we walked out into the sunny street and felt the heat clamp down on us; it was like walking from a refrigerator into a hot oven. We made a stop at an ice-cream parlor and sat down to a cool drink to let our bodies adjust again to the outside world.

We found the tiny post office and sent our letters off. We asked the friendly lady teller at the window for directions to a market. Walking in the direction she had indicated, we found the commissary, as it was called, which is a supermarket operated by the company which manages the banana plantations, their packaging and shipping.

From there, we wanted to go to the fruit stands closer to the pier, but met Victor on the way. He informed us that we would have to come with him immediately to the next town, David, to get our visas. He had already hired a taxi for the forty-five-mile trip there and settled the price at twenty-five dollars for both ways. Needless to say, the bill was on us.

We left our recently bought wares in the care of a storekeeper and all three of us joined Victor in the car. In spite of the circumstances, we greatly enjoyed the ride to David.

While Maria conversed with great animation with Victor, Charlie and I admired the truly beautiful countryside.

The province of Chiriqui is not only the home of the Chiquita banana, it is also one of the most attractive and fertile regions of Panama. The two-lane road wound through lush meadows where well-fed cattle grazed, and through densely wooded areas. For the first time in my life, I laid eyes on a teak tree. I had worked a lot with teak and had always enjoyed the feel of this particular wood under my hands. For a short stretch, the road ran along the boundary of Panama and Costa Rica without any other division than a strip of grass. The houses on either side looked very much the same and the thought occurred to me that a housewife on either side could easily walk across the road and buy milk and eggs in another country and walk back with none the wiser.

Rolling into David, Victor confessed that we first had to go to the Central Intelligence offices for questioning. We wondered if we would ever see our boat again as he briskly guided us past the armed guards of the extensive complex of buildings. In a small office, we all sat more or less uneasily on hard chairs.

Victor, holding our passports, assured us repeatedly that it would be easy as pie, that the captain was his buddy, and that he would do all in his power to get us off easy.

By now, Maria and I were convinced that all of Victor's officious talk was somehow just a front, a role he had played many times before. Finally, he was called into the inner sanctum and we expectantly awaited his return. Our wait did not last long. He came storming out, a big smile on his swarthy face, and ushered us out to the waiting taxi.

"Did I not tell you?" he beamed. "Just leave matters to Victor and everything turns out alright."

"Now we must hurry and go to the Immigration offices to get the visas; I have already called that we are coming."

I resented having to trail after the energetic Victor, with our tongues lolling in the heat. Why we had to come along, I do not know. He did all the talking with the officials, anyway, and, as far as we could see, no stamps or signatures were placed into our passports.

Victor was handed a stack of small white cards and we left. He told us that, since we were here, we would make a sack of produce. His brother had a farm which he worked when away from his regular job at some government office or other. By the amount of produce stacked on the porch of the house, we thought that his enterprise must be a very successful one. We took advantage of it and loaded the trunk of the taxi with a sack of potatoes, onions, cabbages, carrots and beets, all for a very reasonable price. If Victor could, so could we.

We all felt extremely thirsty and hungry by now and Victor, of course, knew just the right place to go for a good lunch. That rascal! He had planned the whole thing so neatly and was so charming about it, that we could not be mad at him.

At the restaurant he took us to, we had a very tasty meal to which we also invited the taxi driver. The bill, including the beer, came to eight dollars for all of us.

It was past 1600 when we finally arrived back to Armuelles, where we still had to go to Victor's office. It was there he got down to business. He filled out the cards which he had brought from David and charged us for the documents—thirty-five dollars plus five dollars each for the boarding party—a total of sixty-five dollars. Another six and a half dollars went later to the port captain for the *zarpe*.

That evening, after an especially nice dinner aboard, we opened our 'casino' and settled down to a fierce game of rummy. It helped to take our minds off the adroit way in which we had been fleeced; I still was smarting when I thought about the $104.50 we had been forced to spend by the immigration officer.

The cards Victor had given us were meant for temporary shore leave of merchantship crews and were virtually worthless for us. He had told us that we would need them to go from the Panama Zone into Panama City, which we knew was humbug. Besides, the cards were good for ten days only and we would probably just then be arriving in Balboa.

We went to sleep to the murmur of the surf and the clatter of the conveyor belts filling the holds of the banana boat with tons and tons of cardboard boxes filled with green bananas.

The next morning we could observe just how involved an operation it was to tie up one of these ships to the pier. The ship had to maneuver itself between the pier and two huge mooring buoys which were placed parallel to the pier. The bow of the vessel, pointing seaward, was tied to the outer buoy, the stern to the one next to shore. The lines were handled from a motor launch with a crew of shore workers.

The launch then took the starboard bow and stern lines to the pier and the ship pulled sideways toward it. Immediately, the cranes with the conveyor belts are placed above the ship and the loading operation begun.

The packaged bananas are brought by train to the pier and are loaded from it directly onto the conveyors. We watched as, during a twenty-four hour loading period, the ship's waterline sank deeper and deeper until its holds were filled to the brim. These ships travel mostly up the west coast or, through the canal, to the east coast and on to Europe.

We found it strange that apparently nobody was swimming around this shore and before we ventured in for a dip asked why this should be so. We were told that the waters around the port were shark-infested and that we had better not try. At first we thought it to be just a joke, we had not seen any tell-tale fins, but who wants to take a chance? We refrained from a swim and used our trusty bucket.

Our main objective in entering Armuelles was to refuel, and Charlie and I set out with our jerry cans to the filling station. There was no fuel available at the pier for us. The station was not very far from the pier, but much too far to carry the full cans back. We loaded them into a taxi instead, which drove onto the pier to where our Avon was tied. Down the steps and into the Avon and over to the boat.

We emptied the cans and back we went for more. Unfortunately they ran out of diesel at the station and we would have to wait until the next day to finish refueling.

We still had to fill up with water from a faucet at the pier. We emptied the emergency supply we still had from our home port into the tank and Charlie rowed with the containers to the pier. Here he bobbed so much in the surge that he got more water into the Avon than into the containers. Evidently the man at the customs shed had seen his plight. He came with a piece of hose which he lent to Charlie to attach to the faucet and that made things much easier.

This had been a hard day for us. The second load of diesel we had had to carry the whole length of the pier. The taxi was not permitted to drive on to the pier while a train was stationed there and the loading still in full operation.

There was not much left to do but to pick up our *zarpe* from the harbormaster and my rifle from the army post. We would take care of that tomorrow; for today, enough of work.

Maria had finished hand-sewing a Panamanian courtesy flag, cut from fabrics she had taken along for this purpose. We had searched the stores of Armuelles for one of adequate size, but they were all too large.

The one lent to us by the radio operator was meant to fly from a ship's yardarm and was six feet by four and looked ridiculous hanging from our spreader. We had been advised to fly the courtesy flag from six to six sharp. Faithfully, we observed all the rulings which seemed so important in this country under military rule.

We took the big flag down and returned it to the radio operator, who had a nice long chat with us. He showed us his office and equipment, told us about his family and how well the children were doing in school, the usual sort of relaxed and noncommital talk one has with strangers.

As we came to the harbormaster's office, we discovered that he had left for David that morning on urgent business and would only return at two p.m. For a moment, I considered going back to the boat to fetch our diesel containers and finish filling the tank. We had about fifty gallons but I loathed the thought of having to carry the heavy containers once more along the endless pier. It would be even more difficult to load them into the Avon on shore. I feared that the boat would overturn in the surf and we could lose all the filled jerry cans.

Instead, armed with our cameras, we walked, for once without haste, through the town and took pictures. We had refreshments at an open stand with a large awning and small tables under it. We had just sat down when who should happen to come by?

Victor, of course. He immediately joined us, his whole being exuding benevolence. He was always well and comfortably dressed, and today he sported a particularly bright new shirt.

He ordered the refreshments and even paid for them!

Maria winked at me and Charlie and whispered in German: "I think Victor got his paycheck."

Charlie rolled his eyes up to the awning and I gritted my teeth to keep from bursting into loud laughter.

Victor asked us when we intended to leave. We answered that it all depended on the harbormaster's return and that I still had to fetch my rifle from the army post.

At that his tone grew confidential and he asked me if I would consider selling it to him. Only for a moment did I think that it would be a good idea to get some of my money back.

No, better not, I decided. I could not tell how devious Victor's mind worked. He seemed genuinely interested in the rifle and suggested that "there are ways."

I politely declined. I lied to him, saying that it had been a gift and that I could not part with it.

What I really thought about was the possibility of somebody observing me selling a weapon to a Panamanian and that I could spend the rest of my days in one of the country's jails. I was not in the least interested in my actions becoming an international incident.

We finally received our *zarpe* from a very apologetic harbormaster, who tried to do all he could to minimize our bad impression of Armuelles. He loaded us down with a whole boxfull of green bananas and wished us good luck.

I sent Charlie and Maria back to the boat and rushed to the army post. I had to wait for over an hour, for the captain was "in conference."

Just as my patience was about to give out, he appeared with the rifle, which was not handed to me but to a plainclothes man whom I followed into an army vehicle. Both of us were driven to the pier.

I called over for Charlie to come and pick me up. Only when he arrived and I had sat down in the Avon did I receive the rifle back from the man who had held it all this time. He remained on the pier until we had reached the boat, lifted the Avon on deck and cast our lines from the mooring buoy!

I wondered how on earth Victor would have managed to buy it from me under such close surveillance by the army authorities.

Be that as it may, with a sigh of relief we left one more port behind us, and crossed our fingers that we would not find too many more like it. We just did not have that kind of funds.

We now had a paltry 300 miles to go to Balboa. With the 4,200 miles we had behind us, our thoughts raced ahead, conveniently ignoring all the possible delays we could and would encounter.

Puerto Armuelles lies in a bay called Charco Azul, which can be translated, literally, as Blue Puddle. This puddle is full of islands, rocks and reefs, some with colorful names, like The Windows, Thieves, and Monkey Island. Names such as Pigtail River or Pork Hill vary with more saintly ones, popular in the southern hemisphere, where Sta. Maria Bay, or St. Lorenz entrance and Concepcion Island vie with the indigenous names like Chiriqui. This was the name of a mighty Indian warrior who had opposed the invasion of his region by the Spanish conquerors.

Southwest of the mainland coast, with its many bays and river mouths, are more and larger islands.

We were lucky to make Isla Coiba in daylight. We sailed along its western shore. The island is twenty-one miles long, mountainous and densely covered with vegetation. There are not many safe anchorages except in an inlet at Punta Hermosa on the west side. Landing can be made only with the permission of the Panamanian government as the island maintains a penal colony.

All we could make out were a few thatched huts and not a soul around. To the southwest of Coiba Island is Isla Jicaron. We made the passage between the islands in full moonlight.

From here on, we would have no more worries with islands. It was an entire night of motoring again, but the early morning brought the gratifying view of Punta Mariato.

The sun, coming up behind this high and steep shoreline, painted a glorious picture in gold and black for us. Dispersing the morning mist with warming rays, it caressed the sharp ridges and lit up the deep fissures, awakening the trees asleep in its shadows. A white line of breakers bathed the foot of the mountains, indented with small and quite inaccessible coves.

In the lee of the land we experienced another hot and windless day. We hoped to catch a fish for Igor, keeping close inshore, but not a single one seemed even interested in our lure. Maybe there are none around, the water is very deep here, the 100-fathom curve only two miles from the coast.

From Punta Mariato, the coast runs almost east to Punta Puercos and from here northeast to Punta Mala (Bad Point). How apt this name, we would soon find out.

I took advantage of this rather quiet day to change the oil in the engine. This is always such a messy job that I would preferably forget about it.

Due to the flat bottom of *Antares*, there is little bilge space, and under the engine this space is at its narrowest. Once I have managed to unscrew the bolt under the oilpan, the oil runs into the shallow drip pan below it. From here, the oil has to be transferred by means of a handpump into plastic containers, to be disposed of in the next port. See what I mean?

After this chore, I went overboard for a thorough cleaning. Maria and Charlie were reluctant to follow me; they found the water, which had turned from a deep and sparkling blue to almost black, as not particularly attractive.

They preferred to use the bucket and engaged in a water battle of major proportions. To judge by the noise they made, they were having a lot of fun.

At Punta Puercos, we encountered a good breeze which

brought us in sight of Punta Mala. I judged our position to be about ten miles from it, and, anxious to be away from it by daylight, we sailed with the aid of the engine in a northeasterly direction.

After sunset, the wind increased to a good twenty-five knots which made us slam hard into the steep and choppy sea. It was rough sailing, and I soon reduced our watches to two hours especially after Maria told me that she was not sure she would be able to hold the helm for her three hours.

She was clearly uneasy, more so as we were in the shipping lanes and a constant stream of merchant vessels was passing us on their way to and from Balboa.

No less than eight ships crossed our path during her watch. Toward morning, I tacked to the northeast, with the wind still howling out of the north.

At noon, we tacked again to the northwest and late in the afternoon we sighted land. It was decidedly too soon to have reached any shore below Punta Chame. This would have been such a fantastic run that I could not believe it.

Our argument as to where we were was settled an hour later as Punta Mala loomed ahead. The closer we came, the more ground we lost to the strong southerly current and we wound up five miles below the point.

I was tired and digusted and asked Maria for the chart My mood did not improve as she remarked that, according to the pilot chart, we would have done better to continue eastward and sail up the northwestern coast of Colombia with a favorable current. This was no time for "we should have's!"

We found a fairly well-sheltered, small bay and anchored in twenty-five feet of water. After a good night's sleep, I would feel more inclined to listen to suggestions from my first mate.

The next morning, though, was to herald one of our bleakest days.

Charlie announced that he wished to have a serious discussion with us after breakfast. Knowing Charlie well, I went unerringly to the heart of the matter.

"Don't tell me you want to leave us," I said.

Up to this point, Charlie had given no indication of having tired of our company or of sailing. But he confirmed my intuitive suspicion that he wished to return home from Balboa. And that was that, a thunderbolt out of the blue.

Charlie had made up his mind, and I did not try to dissuade

him. I just felt sorry that the voyage had not lived up to his expectations and that his patience with us had given out so suddenly.

We liked Charlie and would miss his company dreadfully.

Moreover, Maria and I would be faced with the decision of sailing on alone or seek a compatible crew in Balboa—if we ever got there. Enveloped in gloom, we eased out of our anchorage and motored along the shore until we passed that nefarious Cape Mala.

From here the shore curves around and forms the Bay of Parita. On our chart, a port was marked at a river mouth not mentioned in the *Sailing Directions*.

We had found that the book, which I had found aboard on purchase of the boat, was twenty years old. It had been a great help on many occasions. We had to make amendments though, as far as the "clusters of huts" and "small roadsteads" were concerned, as many of these had grown into major villages and towns.

Expecting that this would be so with Puerto Purio, we motored on and on. Nothing but a low and desolate shore with sand dunes populated by pelicans, was to be seen.

The water had turned to a muddy yellow from the many rivers which empty into the bay. The coves along the shore were evidently very shallow, strewn with black rocks which extended seaward from their respective points. Open to the prevailing north and northeasterly winds, we could not expect to find any sheltered spot for the night.

I was on my way to the cockpit to tell Charlie, at the helm, to stay a bit more offshore when, very suddenly, we struck a rock. Losing my balance, I fell over the table and Maria hit her back against the bulkhead which forms the enclosure of the head.

I suffered a few seconds of indecision deciding between aiding Maria or rushing into the cockpit. To ease the pain in her back, Maria had fallen to her hands and knees. I did not know if she was seriously hurt.

Looking up at me she told me, "Just get the boat out of here."

Charlie was at the helm, a bit pale from the scare. I took over from him and eased the boat out of the dangerous vicinity of the rocky spot.

After sunset, the wind came up again. We could see several

navigational lights and a brightly lit area somewhere among the hills close to shore.

We never found the port. It was dangerous to continue on this course so close to shore. After hoisting sails, we tacked once more due northeast.

The light of Punta Mala stayed for a long time with us. Only very slowly did it disappear below the horizon.

At 0200 we were becalmed and the next two hours would be the worst we had so far experienced. The Gulf of Panama is full of currents and countercurrents influenced by the Mexican and Peruvian flows and by the great difference in tides.

The boat was thrown about by the most violent tiderips I had ever seen. Sleep was impossible. We not only rolled in our bunks, we were thrown out of them! The noise of shifting and rattling objects not wedged tightly in the cupboards rose to an indescribable din. Waves slapped against the hull from every imaginable direction and vaguely, the question came to my mind—which would break sooner, our nerves or the boat?

By 0400 a light wind came up, and hastily we hoisted our sails. Anything would be better than the battering we had just been given.

In the morning, at 1000, I made radio contact with an outgoing vessel. It confirmed our position, obtained earlier by a sunsight, six miles north of Punta Mala. We sailed for twelve hours on one tack and twelve hours on another across the northerly wind. Our sight the next morning put us eight miles north of that well known point! Two miles headway in twenty-four hours!

We had still sixty miles to go to Balboa and we did not want to use the engine for fear we would run out of fuel which was mostly needed when it was time to motor into port.

In time, we certainly would have made it under sail to Balboa, but we had aboard a fellow who was growing increasingly fidgety and anxious to be off the boat.

Charlie was ready to ask any freighter which passed us for a few gallons of diesel fuel. This would have been uncalled for, since we were in no way in a distress situation other than from our own impatience. We had an ample food and water supply and could have lasted for weeks in that crazy place.

By noon we were becalmed and the waves had subsided considerably. I went overboard to inspect the hull and keels and make sure that the encounter with the rock had not done more damage than the blue and purple marks on Maria's back.

I could not find anything amiss and climbed back on board. Our VHF was tuned to Channel 16. We had left it on to monitor the conversation from ship to ship among the freighters passing us by.

I had left the mainsail up, to stabilize somewhat the rolling motion of the boat and to make us more visible, sitting in midtraffic as we were. Later in the afternoon, we listened to another yacht making a call to the Balboa Yacht Club.

The club did not answer but, before the skipper signed off, I broke in and called on the yacht. I explained my position and the skipper immediately offered his help. He could easily spare thirty gallons of diesel.

The *Scarlet Cloud* was a motor yacht served by a hired crew to sail it from San Francisco to its owner in Chicago. A ship which had just passed us had overheard our conversation. The officer on watch offered to help in giving the *Scarlet Cloud* our exact position and the course she had to follow. Another freighter, changing its course, joined in the effort to establish communications and lay out a course for the motor yacht.

The skipper of the *Scarlet Cloud* told me that they could only run at a speed of eight knots; it would take him about two and a half hours to reach our position.

The freighters had slowed down and seemed interested in our rendezvous. It was almost dark as we sighted the running lights of the motor yacht.

Meanwhile we had not been lazy. The Avon bobbed alongside, with six empty jerry cans in her bottom. I had never seen Charlie work that fast in pumping up the Avon. His spirits had visibly brightened at the prospect of reaching port in a foreseeable time. As soon as we made visual contact, the hovering ships went back on their course. I called them and thanked them for their help.

The *Scarlet Cloud* pulled alongside and Charlie and I rowed over to her. We were warmly greeted by the skipper and offered a drink. The yacht was a beautiful craft, with a crew of four.

Charlie helped one of the crew to fill our cans with diesel and, after they ad been lowered into the Avon, I motioned to pay for the fuel. But her skipper refused payment, which almost made me blush.

We had received so much help already that I was at a loss on how to thank him. The *Scarlet Cloud* stood by until we had transferred the fuel into the tank and were on our way ourselves.

The night was windless and we motored throughout, taking two-hour turns at the wheel. By early morning we sighted Punta Chame and Taboga Island.

A few hours later, the radio operator from the tower on Flamenco Island instructed us to anchor in the bay just behind the island, where we would be sheltered from the wake of the ships entering and leaving the canal.

It was not long after we had dropped anchor that the boarding officer from the Panama Canal Company came along in his launch. The formalities were minimal since we had been measured by the Coast Guard in Seattle for the transit of the canal.

This not only saved time but also the twenty dollar fee which is charged for the measuring by the officer. He was very courteous and called the Balboa Yacht Club for us to ask for moorage for our boat.

The club did not commit itself immediately. I was told to stand by on Channel 12. In the event of the club not granting us a stay, we would have to stay put in the bay until Monday. This sent Charlie into another fit of the jitters, which was only relieved an hour later when the club called us to its moorage basin.

Here Customs boarded us and again all formalities were rapidly taken care of. The Customs officer remarked on my boat-license, which had been issued for coastal trade. I had had in mind to do a bit of chartering when I had the boat documented, but found later that to be able to do so I would have to pass a stiff examination to get the operator's license required for that business. But when I discovered that the boat was not suitable for charter, I had given up the idea, but had kept the license. It did not seem to make any difference which one I held in home waters. The friendly officer left, saying that if I ever ran out of money I could do a bit of business on the side.

We sat back in the cockpit and contemplated the calendar. We had made it, eighty-five days out of Seattle and four weeks later than I had set as our goal. Oh well, nobody is perfect.

CHAPTER 5

THE PANAMA CANAL

The Balboa Yacht Club has no docking facilities except for fueling. As anchorage and dinghy traffic are impractical, the club provides mooring buoys and a twenty-four launch service. To attract the launch driver's attention, one must blow a horn or a whistle, ring a bell, scream, blink a flashlight, wave a towel, flag or arms anything short of jumping overboard.

When the launch comes chugging along, one can count on arriving fairly soon at the foot of the club's veranda. During our stay, there were about thirty yachts from places all over the world at anchor.

The club is a private enterprise and in no way obligated to give anchorage to transiting yachts. Usually a reservation and down payment are appreciated by the club secretary. Should this not be possible, a call, as the one made by our boarding officer, will grant a yacht a stay at the club's facilities.

The fees are ten cents a foot per day, the stay being limited to ten days. After this, the charges skyrocket to one dollar per foot a day and there are *no* exceptions. This greatly discourages any longer occupancy by guest yachts, which might extend their stay indefinitely, taking away mooring space from the members of the club or other transient yachts.

At the club office, we are provided with a copy of a hand-drawn map of Balboa and Panama City with the points of interest such as post offices, banks, marine-supply stores and markets.

The club is a place where crews from the four corners of the world meet. Here is their first chance to exchange their experiences or to tell their stories. The veranda is dominated by a long bar and at happy hour, a large crowd gathers around it. As we had arrived on a Saturday afternoon, we joined the session which was in full swing and engaged in casual conversation around the bar. One could plainly see that the place was humming!

To give Maria a welcome respite from the galley stove, we took a bus into Balboa and went to the local YMCA restaurant for dinner. This may not sound like much of a place, but we found the food excellent and reasonable in price.

To top the evening off with the brightest of highlights, we

walked to the offices of the phone company and placed calls to our families to assure them of our whereabouts and to hear the news from home.

We returned aboard, feeling a bit soused from a last can of beer we had at the club while waiting for the launch. We were reasonably happy and would have felt much more so had it not been for Charlie's impending desertion of the ship.

From Sunday morning on, he was busy washing clothes at the club's facilities and packing and re-packing his things. Maria and I lolled in the cockpit, watching the ships which passed us on the way to the locks or to the Pacific.

We could not quite understand Charlie's attitude and big hurry. He did not even show any interest in going with us through the canal, which is certainly a unique experience. We asked ourselves if it had been that bad, or if we had said or done anything outlandish to trigger his sudden decision.

Charlie gave only vague explanations and I am not the man to pressure anybody into saying what he does not want to disclose. His decision, we knew, would greatly influence the future of our voyage.

We had checked the large billboard at the club, where boaters pin messages and crews and skippers make offers for their services. We had not found anything or anybody that would meet our requirements and, in turn, had pinned a note on the board for a lineman, who would be needed for our transit through the canal.

The next two days were quite hectic. I had to get Charlie off our crew list, which in turn necessitated a dash into Panama City to buy a plane ticket; then back to customs and a side trip to the post office, where we were told that there was no mail for us.

This was a blow. We had expected mounds of letters from home as we had been diligently writing to all our friends and relatives.

In our wanderings in the streets of Balboa, we came upon a sporting goods store and went in. I found a reel of 100 lb. fishing line, lures, sinkers and leaders, all needed to replace the many we had lost. To our immense embarrassment, we discovered at the cash register that we were not allowed to make purchases at this store. It was a commissary in which only the employees and residents of the Panama Canal Zone were allowed to trade. A lady behind us offered to buy the articles for us and fortunately, the cashier had no objections to this transaction.

To reprovision ourselves, we would have to go to Panama City and haul every single thing by taxi to the club side in Balboa. We spent the rest of the afternoon raiding the market in town and returned, loaded with produce, meat and eggs.

Charlie was ready to leave. He had managed to pack his two seabags so that they would not exceed the forty-four-pound allowance on the plane, which meant that he had to leave a considerable number of things aboard.

After Charlie had left, Maria and I settled for a while in the cockpit, wondering about his sudden departure.

There was a lot of red tape to be taken care of to get permits for fueling and for going through the canal. This kept us hopping for the rest of the day from one bus to another, from one office into the next. By now we were getting to know Balboa very well; but we did not know that anybody else would know us as well.

I was, therefore, quite startled when a young man called my name on the street, frantically waving his arms. I could not recall ever seeing him before in my life. To our delight, the young man identified himself as a clerk at the post office. He told us that he had found our mail, a whole packet of it! This was the best news we could think of.

We detoured to the post office, picked up the mail, and then settled at the YMCA with a cold drink and read all our letters.

By evening, we had all our permits and had exchanged travelers' checks at the bank, as the money we expected to receive from home had not arrived yet.

In town we had found a money exchange office where we could turn our leftover currency from Mexico and El Salvador into Panamanian dollars, which are par with the American dollar.

Maria busied herself the next morning with a mountain of laundry at the club's washers, while I remained aboard awaiting my turn at the fuel dock. After another sailing yacht had left the dock, I made my way over, only to be overtaken by a huge motor yacht which got priority for being a member of the club. I stewed in the heat until it had filled up with 400 gallons of diesel. I topped the tank and filled six jerry cans, all in all taking on 125 gallons of fuel. This would get us somewhere.

It was not an easy task to return to the mooring buoy and to fasten to it all by myself. Due to the constant traffic in the locks, huge amounts of water are discharged into the shipping lanes and adjacent bays. With an outgoing tide, the currents created reach top speeds and I had to be quite nimble not to lose the loop of the buoy to which our line was to be attached. Missing it could mean my drifting and crashing into the boat moored behind.

I was very proud of myself when I had the boat securely tied up again.

Going ashore, I found Maria talking to a young German couple. Heinz and Inge had been on a grand hike which had taken them from the shores of Vancouver, B.C., down the west coast of the States and Mexico, through the countries of Central America. They were now on their way to Peru but had stopped at Balboa to visit the canal. Both were interested in coming along as linemen, desiring a first-hand look at the operation of the locks. We made a date for when we would be ready for the transit, feeling very fortunate to have found two linemen at one stroke.

The next two days were to be the hardest as far as work was concerned. We motored across from the club into a shallow bay where we anchored in six feet of water. We waited for the tide to run out under us to start the arduous work. No sooner had the boat settled into the sand than the starboard keel slowly sank into a muddy hole, making the boat list at a 30-degree angle.

This was not in any way serious. It just meant that we would be rather uncomfortable on board and that we could only clean the port side and one keel.

One look at the keels convinced us that it would take a major effort to have even one side of the boat clean before the tide came in again. They were so encrusted with barnacles that our scrapers were like toys against a concrete wall. Clearly, we needed more adequate tools. Maria wandered to a small restaurant on shore to see if we could borrow a shovel. They could not help us but suggested that perhaps the nearby gun club could. She finally came hobbling back with two garden spades, with which we could attack the fortress of barnacles much more effectively.

It was very hard work. We had quite a few curious onlookers, among them a middle-aged Panamanian who, after a while, came closer and offered to help. He told us that he had served in the National Guard, but that he had injured a foot at some time or another and had a six-month leave. His doctor had recommended that he walk barefoot on sandy soil to get his foot in shape again. He showed us his identification card and assured us that he did not want any pay, just to help us and to fill the time which seemed to weigh heavily on his hands.

Manuel was his name; he spoke no English but this was no obstacle for Maria. I watched them talk, there on the beach, Maria burnt brown with blonde streaks in her brown hair and Manuel, fairly tall with a huge bulging middle section, fair-skinned, with black hair and drooping mustachios.

His dark eyes were as soft and innocent as a child's. He told Maria that he would rush home and get a pair of shorts and be back soon. I was glad that we could count on two more hands for the job. It would speed up things considerably. We had no idea where Manuel lived, but assumed that it must be close by. It appeared, therefore, not very likely, as the hours passed and the tide began to come in, that he would ever be back.

When the water rose sufficiently, I moved the boat to another spot we had inspected and which seemed better suited to hold it upright. During the whole day we had not once stopped work except for a short break to eat a huge, juicy pineapple.

Maria was about to start making dinner when we saw Manuel waving on the beach. I could not help but remark that he had taken his sweet time and very conveniently returned with the tide high and dinner on the stove.

"Oh, don't be so suspicious," said Maria. "Go and fetch him aboard."

Manuel had returned bearing gifts in the form of a jar full of delicious pineapple refreshment, a bag of ice, mangoes and even a fish for Igor. He joined us for dinner, consuming prodigious amounts of rice, a situation Maria had luckily foreseen, for she had cooked a big pot full of it. Finding it too warm below, our visitor made himself comfortable in the cockpit and soon we all went to sleep.

I was awakened in the middle of the night by a loud, crunching noise and went immediately on deck. We had broken through the sand again and now the port keel was buried in the mud.

While climbing down, I philosophized that I had had enough foresight to anchor the boat at the exact spot where the starboard keel would now be free to be cleaned. By torchlight, I inspected our position, and since I was up and awake anyhow, I started to work on the keel. Neither Manuel nor Maria awoke even with the infernal noise I was making at such an ungodly hour.

Bobbing at anchor the next morning, we had another visitor—an American retired from his services in the Canal Zone. Retirees are not permitted to remain as residents of the Zone longer than six months after dismissal. Bob told us that he was quite unhappy about this ruling. He loved the country and would have preferred to stay. Of course, he could move over to Panamanian soil, but this would bar him from the Zone's commissaries. There was no way he could have both. When I told him about our difficulties in finding a suitable spot for our work on the boat, he immediately offered to show me where I could find a better one in the next small bay. I rowed over with him to inspect the site, where the wreck of a huge iron barge seemed, indeed, to offer enough protection from the currents.

I moved the boat for a third time, but all did not run as smoothly as I had imagined. After I had dropped the anchor, we drifted off a bit and were pressed against the sunken barge which was lying there. I let the anchor rope go. We could retrieve it when the tide ran out.

Meanwhile, I checked the rigging and found countless small jobs which required my attention. I inspected all running and standing gear to catch any signs of wear and tear, replaced a line here and tied down a shroud there.

Manuel, who had left in the morning, returned at low tide and pitched in when he found me crouching under the boat, scraping the barnacles from the inside of the keels. This was the hardest part of the job. The barnacles were not as big here as on the outside, but were just as sharp. They accumulated under the boat as we scraped them loose, and since we practically had to lie on our backs to do a proper job, it was a small miracle that we did not slice ourselves to pieces on them. Even so, we sustained a lot of small cuts which bled profusely and burned like hell when we went for a swim to clean off the sand from our bodies.

During this time, Maria had started painting the hull and was complaining that the anti-fouling paint was evaporating and thickening so rapidly that she was having trouble spreading it evenly. Manuel and I joined her in order to get the painting done as quickly as possible.

There were still more visitors to inspect our activities. A police officer from the Zone force walked over to have a look. In a soft Texan drawl he asked what type or make the boat was, because he never had seen one like it. I told him that ours was a ketch, built after an Ed Monk sen. design; that the twin keels have advantages over other boats; that we could beach her anywhere, providing there was enough tidal difference and a good sandy beach; that the flat bottom gives us more speed, even with our relatively small sail area of only 1,040 square feet. This fact, of course, also gives us greater safety in strong winds. Our mainmast is only thirty-eight feet above deck, very short for a boat of forty-five feet length. The keels are only twelve feet in length, though I would have liked them about six feet longer. We can beat into the wind very well, while making a lot of leeway, due to the little resistance she affords below the waterline. The hard chine prevents us from heeling too much, affording additional comfort in a cruising craft.

After the officer had left, I stepped back and looked my craft over and had to admit that it sure was a nice sight, especially with the newly painted bottom.

In the water and from a certain angle, I have always maintained that it has the look of a cigar box, a statement which has invariably brought loud protests from Maria. Be that as it may, we are rather attached to her plain appearance and try to keep the brightwork well varnished and the decks uncluttered.

The tide started to come in, and I had Maria in a nervous state as I was wading up to my knees, paint brush in hand, still touching up a few dark spots on the white hull.

Before we left for the moorage, Bob swam over once more. He came aboard, panting and shaking water from his ears and said, "Here, I brought you a present," and handed me a brand-new, three-inch-wide scraper. I was very surprised and pleased at this. After all, we were virtually strangers.

Manuel left us that evening, promising to join us early the next day at the club to accompany us into town and show us all the right places to get our provisions. To go shopping in Panama City is an adventure in itself. The district we went through is a maze of noisy, hot, overcrowded narrow alleys. Street vendors, selling everything from watches to Washington apples, records and trinkets, take a lot of space from the sidewalk, forcing passers-by to step into the street. One has to be quick to dodge the one-way traffic. To cross the street was to take a chance on one's life. From one of these streets, which we crossed with a certain amount of trepidation, Manuel guided us through a cavernous alleyway, dark and damp in the shadow of the high buildings on each side.

Sloping downhill, the alley contained a row of stands running in single file from top to bottom, where it opened upon the sunlit square of the public market. To gain access to the sunny patch at the end of this veritable tunnel was a slow process of winding oneself through a throng of people intent on the wares being offered at the stands.

Wallets, baby clothing, plastic buckets and cheap jewelry, shoes, notions and thousands of scarves hung from the roofs and awnings like fantastic colored flags from a mythical country. This sidewalk dimestore offered the same merchandise displayed in their fancier counterparts across the street, inside the buildings.

I could not help but gawk at all this and sometimes wondered if these sidewalk vendors really could make a living with their trade. I suppose they must, otherwise they would not be there. Frequently I envied Maria the easy acceptance of an environment so alien to me, the European turned American citizen.

But then, she had lived for long periods of time in South American countries and had mastered the language so well that the casual contacts with the people were, to her, a more rewarding experience. To me, but for a few exceptions, they always would remain strangers.

It was so with Manuel, who had taken a great liking to Maria, and I suspect for this reason was such a help to us. He would also make the transit with us. He had offered to come along as lineman, not as a favor to us, but as a special privilege for him. He had never been on or in the canal and was looking forward to it.

For the moment, he had showed us the way to an excellent meat market, where we drooled over appetizing cuts comparable to what we had been used to at home. To the meat, we added fragrant, freshly baked bread and mounds of produce.

Heavily laden, we arrived at the club, where Heinz and Inge awaited us. Using the club's phone, I confirmed our transit date and time once more with the port captain and we all set out to the boat.

Punctually, at 0800, the pilot stepped aboard. He immediately reported to the lockmaster via his portable radio unit and admonished me to keep our VHF closed down. During the transit, all ship-to-ship or ship-to-shore communications are prohibited. Pilot-to-lockmaster communications must at all times be free of interference.

An hour later, we moved into the Miraflores locks, the first step up to the canal. Ahead of us was the ship *Hope*, its stern dwarfed by the high walls of the lock. This first chamber is the highest one of the lock system, due to the extreme tide variations on the Pacific side of the canal.

Attendants atop both sides of the walls threw us lines with beautifully made monkey-fists at their ends. As each of these thumped onto the deck, we attached our own lines to them, which they then lifted and fastened to bollards.

The gates closed and as we rose with the water level, the lineman had to continually pull taut the slackening lines. Maria and Manuel worked the lines at the bow, while I kept an eye on Heinz and Inge at the stern. The pilot supervised us all, wandering from bow to stern and always concerned to keep the boat in the center of the chamber.

The chambers are not filled and emptied by pumps. Gatun Lake, a man-made, huge artificial body of water fed by the Chagres River, supplies the necessary water. This waterflow comes through culverts into the sides and bottom of the locks, filling them at a high velocity.

These immense quantities of rushing water create currents and eddies in the chambers which could cause serious damage to a small craft were its lines not handled properly.

As an added precaution, engines are kept running on idle to avoid any possible delays and ensure quick action if a line should part.

By the time we moved into the third chamber, about a mile from the first two, we felt like pros. Everything had gone well with clockwork-like precision.

We were now eighty-five feet above sea level. Leaving the last lock, we were now in the actual canal. This is called the Gaillard Cut, so named for the engineer who was in charge of it. The cut is a stretch eight miles long, hewn right through the mountains. Originally it was 300 feet wide, but with the freighters constantly being built bigger, it had gradually been widened to 500 feet. Both shores are lined with flourescent lights all the way. While we were motoring along it the powers above decided to unzip a big, pregnant cloud and let us have it.

My crew disappeared below while the pilot and I got the most thorough washdown we had had in a long time. After the first stiff formalities had been taken care of, the pilot revealed himself as a very funny and cheerful Panamanian.

Nonchalantly, he had taken off his uniform and sat beside me in shorts and T-shirt, undaunted by the downpour. He joked, "Please pass the soap, too!" each time Maria opened the hatch to hand us steaming cups of coffee or towels to keep the rain out of our faces.

When we reached the anchorage across Gamboa, we were sorry to have to let go of our cheerful pilot. The launch which came to pick him up brought us the news that the pilot who would take us across Gatun Lake to Cristobal had missed the train there and that we had a two-hour wait. This was just as well. I needed to dry out and wanted to do honor to the lunch which was spread on the table. The two hours passed in a flash, the five of us in very high spirits, sitting around the table and talking.

Our second pilot was the exact opposite of the first one. He came aboard, obviously displeased with the prospect of having to pilot a yacht. Later we would learn that many pilots dislike to be on yachts, while some look upon it as an all day picnic and love to take on these assignments.

The first question I had fired at me was, "Don't you have an awning? What if it rains?!"

I was hard put to answer that one. For one, our awning was meant to be put up only in port, since it takes too much of our view when underway and, besides, interferes too much with the mizzen sail.

Luckily for all of us, it did not rain any more on that day.

Asked about our maximum speed, I told him that we could go along at five knots.

"We'll never make it," he said. "But let's get going."

I tried my best to push the engine a bit harder and frequently had her going at six to six and a half knots, keeping an eye on the temperature indicator all the time.

Maria had her camera in hand as we moved through this extraordinary part of the crossing. Long-dead trees still raised their naked branches heavenward, mirrored in the quiet water. Densely covered with vegetation, innumerable islands dotted the lake, our wake lapping at their shores of rich red soil. A building on one of the islands caught Maria's eyes and she asked our pilot if this was a private house.

"No," he responded, "the Smithsonian Institute has stationed it here in the Gatun Lake to study fauna and flora and preserve the environment. From Cristobal one can make a tour by boat of the lake and the stations."

At a certain point, the pilot asked me if I would consider taking a shortcut. It would save us a good ten minutes, and it was just possible that we could reach the locks on time. If not, we would have to anchor and wait until 2300, at which prospect he seemed to shudder.

We went through the shortcut which, to us, was an added attraction. The narrow channel wound between islands which formed coves and nooks where trees hung over the water's edge and tall reeds swayed, whispering at our passage. We truly wished that we did not have to hurry so much.

We made it to the locks with a three-minute delay. A monstrous freighter tied at a pier, awaited our arrival. Going up on the locks, small craft followed behind the large ones. On the way back to sea level, we had to enter first, ahead of the large one.

Thus it was that we stormed, huffing and puffing, into the lock. Hardly had we secured our lines when the idling engine heaved a big sigh and relieved herself of some unwanted steam through a loosened hose. Dirty, boiling water sprayed all over the engine room and into the cabin.

Alarmed, the pilot bent his head over the hatch and, for the first time since he had stepped aboard, showed signs of good humor. He asked Maria if her pressure cooker had blown its top.

I had to work fast to get the hose refastened, refill the engine with cooling water and get it going again. I made it in time to jump into the cockpit and put her in gear as the gates to the second lock were just opening.

Without any further incidents, we went through the remaining locks. Gratefully, we dropped anchor in Limon Bay at the spot irreverently called the "mudflats."

It was Saturday afternoon, and as the pilot left he informed us that it was too late for us to get cleared by customs. We would have to remain for the rest of the weekend exactly where we were.

This unexpected necessity to remain aboard did not bar us

from taking the dinghy and smuggling Manuel back to shore. He knew his way around and would somehow hitch a ride to Balboa. We swam, slept and ate well and had the opportunity to get better acquainted with Heinz and Inge. They had traveled extensively, spoke several languages and were interesting company. This gave me the glorious idea of inviting them to join us on the way to Brazil. But first, I did want to get Maria's opinion on the subject.

She seemed reluctant at first, and her objections were valid ones.

"They have no sailing experience at all," she said. "And look at Inge. She is such a fragile, little thing; I really doubt if she will ever be able to hold the helm in a good blow."

"It would be better to wait and see if anybody in Balboa has read the note you left. I would much prefer, for your sake, to find an experienced sailor."

On the other hand, both of us loved to have young people around us and told our new friends to think it over and consider a rather lengthy detour to Brazil. They, too, had their own misgivings. The difference in our ages made them argue the point that they did not want to commit themselves to something that might turn out to be like "an outing with Mom and Dad."

Heinz, fiercely independent and individualistic, was taking advantage of his travels to work on a paper for a degree in anthropology. The prospect of having an opportunity to visit another country and several islands on the way, and for free, was too tempting an offer. So, after a consultation with Inge, they both agreed to join us.

Monday morning, we eased into our moorage at the Cristobal Yacht Club, our bowsprit nuzzling the parapet of the club's restaurant.

Our young couple took off for Balboa to get the rest of their luggage and settle the red tape with the authorities so we could put them on our crew list. They also had to cancel reservations with several travel agencies and would be gone for some time.

In Seattle, a fellow boater had given us the name and phone number of a canal pilot and had asked us to call on him and say hello. We had contacted John from Balboa and had made arrangements to meet him upon our arrival in Cristobal.

A short while after we had tied up, John drove up to the club and we met one of the most hospitable and helpful persons to cross our path in a long time. He was not only an impeccable host, but also a friend in need. He drove us to the nearest grocery store where we could complete our purchases of canned goods.

With four people aboard, Maria preferred to have a great variety of those. We would be at sea for uncertain lengths of time and would find many ports where such staples would not be available.

Later, we drove by John's house and picked up his wife, Jewel, and were taken to the Elks Club for lunch.

The rest of the afternoon we spent driving around the vicinity of Cristobal and got a rundown on many of the affairs of the Zone and the canal itself.

Our interest and attention alternated between the truly lush and varied vegetation bordering the roads and the realities of the political and racial undercurrents prevalent in the Zone. We, happily, had been oblivious to these matters for months now and felt a bit overwhelmed at the sudden onrush of the many new ideas, some of which gave us a lot of food for thought.

The history and background of the canal and the Panama Zone are very complex and not relevant to this narrative. However, we greatly sympathized with our hosts' line of thinking and offered our meager support to their stand.

CHAPTER 6

CARIBBEAN ADVENTURE

On May 28, 1976, at 0600 we left the shelter of Limon Bay and entered the Caribbean Sea with a bang.

We met with a good wind, which we did not mind; but we also met with a very short and nasty chop which we did mind—especially in our stomachs. Ten minutes later Inge turned green and was the first casualty, with Heinz close behind.

I was not feeling so good either and Maria hastily distributed seasick pills, taking one herself.

Generally and enviably, Maria does not get seasick, but with such violent reception after a long stay on land, she did not trust even her sturdy innards to stand up.

To top it all, it started to rain and I became cold and

miserable at the helm. By evening I still had not been able to shake a splitting headache and longed for a good rest. This was not to be.

As soon as Maria started her night watch, the combined fleets of all the merchant vessels in the Caribbean seemed to join forces, looming evilly over the horizon.

Some came close enough to breathe down our necks, leaving us understandably unnerved. With our crew out of action, neither of us got much sleep that night. Squalls with torrents of rain and blustery winds, followed by steaming calms, were our lot for the next two days. Our speed would vary from two knots to exhilarating runs of ten knots.

We sailed, we motored and we motor-sailed.

Luckily, Heinz recovered soon from his mal-de-mer and we could let him do a turn at the wheel now and then.

I pulled a tuna out after having lost one on a previous strike. I discovered that our new 100-lb. line could stand the strain, but that the leader had broken. I replaced it with a piece of the same line and the second strike was on deck in no time. Gleefully, we put the spaghetti away and had a sumptuous dinner of fish.

On her night watch, the third night out, Maria sighted a light and called me into the cockpit.

"Why must we always make a landfall at night?" she complained.

I was more surprised than annoyed. By our calculations, we should still have been four hours from sighting land. All we could do now was to shorten sails and tack to and fro until daylight.

Our chart showed the coastline south of Cartagena infested with reefs and shallows. Our best policy was to keep off as far as possible and not attempt going into port at night.

By dawn, we lost sight of the beacon and found ourselves utterly becalmed. To the southwest, a black squall hovered ominously, and I thought it better to lower the sails and have the engine going. The breathless silence which had kept our nerves on edge was broken quite suddenly as the wind roared over us. The sea churned, white and angry, slapping the boat violently from all sides.

Only with the engine at full throttle was I able to turn the boat into the wind. It must have blown at fifty knots with gusts of up to sixty-five. Then the rain set in, and I felt as if I were standing under a waterfall. The waves subsided completely under the onslaught of the furious downpour.

My eyeglasses afforded little protection from the deluge. I had to slip on my diving mask to be able to see. Our genoa, which we probably had not lashed down securely enough, rode up the forestay and fluttered violently in the wind.

Maria and Heinz rushed forward, and while Heinz clawed at the sail, pulling it down, Maria threw herself on deck on top of it to prevent it from escaping aloft again.

In that short time, the sail had ripped at the leach and several seams had burst open.

For two hours I fought to keep the boat headed into the wind.

If I had run with it, we would have lost our position and probably taken all day to get back near shore again.

As it was, we were just holding our position in the middle of this pandemonium.

The squall finally passed over us and two hours later we made out the high-rise buildings along Cartagena's shores.

Maria's attempts to make contact with the harbor authorities met with silence. She tried several channels commonly used for contact with radio operators. There was no answer, not even from the two vessels at anchor in the bay. We felt a bit ridiculous, skimming about in the bay, talking into empty space, receiving no feedback whatsoever.

Somewhere, somebody at the yacht club must have heard us. To our surprise, we were instructed to remain where we were until a pilot came out to guide us to the club.

For the easy, quarter-mile run, we had to pay twenty dollars! The club was just around the corner.

We were relieved of the tiring rounds to the different offices of immigration, customs and port captains. The Club de Pesca has an agent who handles all the necessary red tape for yachts arriving and departing from there.

We felt extremely welcome at the club, especially after Mr. Calderon, the agent, told us that the first three days' stay were on the club, free of charge. Fuel, ice and a case of coke were delivered directly to the boat. We found a sailmaker who repaired our genoa for ten dollars, all handsewn.

These unexpected niceties gave us ample time for a long visit into town. Cartagena is, in every way, a beautiful and remarkable city. Its old Spanish heritage is very much in evidence in its small plazas, kept cool and shadowy by gnarled, ancient trees. The houses in the narrow, cobblestoned streets are lined with carved, wooden balconies garlanded with ferns and geraniums, which cover the white-washed walls.

Amid this charming, old-world atmosphere, we came upon half-completed, concrete high-rise buildings in all stages of construction which had, apparently, been stopped for an indefinite time.

The large, red-tiled square at the waterfront is flanked by the old city wall with a gate, through which a never-ending flow of people streamed, milled and eddied into the square. A cathedral, a movie house and the market enclosed the rest of the area, open toward the bay. Here fish is sold from many boats, as well as produce brought from other parts of the country.

We ventured into the market but soon fled the heat under its tin roof and the smells of decaying fruits coming from the many ditches which carried the offal from the stands into the harbor. Rotten oranges, bananas and tomatoes, plus dead cockroaches passed at our feet in the muddy water on their way to the sea.

We found the stands in the square outside the market more appetizing and decided to buy here what we could carry back to the boat. As always, we found we would not be able to carry the load after all, and hailed a taxi. Once we were installed in the back seat, the car took off like a rocket around the next corner and we felt chills running up and down our spines as we dodged people, dogs, trucks and other cabs going just as fast.

Why they were in such a hurry, we did not know. Competition must have been fierce.

We raced along a narrow alley and the driver could not avoid hitting a fellow who had darted across the way. There was a dull thud and the sound of screeching brakes.

Maria closed her eyes in horror, expecting the worst.

The driver, pale and shaken, jumped out of the car amidst a wildly gesticulating and threatening crowd. It was amazing how fast they had gathered around us. He helped his victim, who stared dazedly about him, up from the cobblestones. Our driver put him into the front seat beside him and we took off.

Apparently he had not been hurt badly, but we gave the driver a few extra pesos to take him to a hospital for a check-up. He promised us that he would do that and apologized for the inconvenience. By his demeanor, it seems that such accidents are not taken lightly in Cartagena.

The club's piers are adjacent to the old city walls and these enclose a tiny and very charming restaurant, where a giant banyan tree spreads its branches over the tables.

The fortress itself looms not far from there, strangely reminiscent of an Aztec or Mayan pyramid. We climbed its endless stairways and battlements, peered into dank, narrow passages and wondered how, long ago, soldiers could wind their way through them.

From the topmost platform we had a breathtaking view of the city, the inland mountains and the Caribbean. This last reminded us that we must be on our way soon. Our crew would have preferred to stay much longer and make a visit to Bogota. So did we, but we had to explain to them that this was June and the onset of the hurricane season in the Caribbean, a valid reason to get going.

We had intended to hold close to the Colombian coast to Aruba, one of the islands of the Dutch Antilles group; from here, coasting along the Venezuelan shore in a loop to Curaçao. Some yachts take this trajectory, mostly by engine power, for they have to fight the trades and the strong westerly equatorial current.

As we picked up our clearance papers at the club's office, we were strongly advised against our intention of a coastwise run. Two very convincing reasons brought forward by Mr. Calderon made us change our plans.

"At this time of the year," he told us, "the sea conditions are extremely rough and dangerous close to shore.

"Furthermore, the threat of piracy is very real in this region, dominated by smugglers who will not hesitate to seize your boat, kill you and use your craft for their purposes."

Mr. Calderon spoke candidly about the inability of the government to put a stop to these conditions, as it did not dispose of the manpower or means to provide for an effective Coast Guard.

I did take his advice. There was no point in taking any chances, and we set out from Cartagena on a more northerly course. This route is the one taken by most yachts leaving from Cartagena or Cristobal toward Jamaica. I was facing a 900-mile detour to Curaçao, via the south coast of Hispaniola, from which we could sail south by southwest to the island of Curaçao.

On board was a fifth crew member, Oscar, black as night,

from independent Guyana and a resident of Georgetown. He had been stranded in Colombia, his money stolen in Bogota, his visa running out and no possibility to work and make enough to pay his way back home. We took pity on him and he wound up on our crew list.

Here, on the southwestern part of it, the Caribbean is at its roughest. At least, it was as we sailed north over it. The trades blew at a constant fifteen to thirty-five knots and life aboard turned into misery. The most uncomfortable swell made us sway drunkenly, throwing us from side to side in its unpredictable motion.

Pushing against the wind and making a horrendous leeway in the westerly current, we soon had the first victims of seasickness to contend with. Oscar disappeared below for three days, where he lay on a bunk alongside the engine. In the murk, we just could see the whites of his eyes as he lay there in his misery. Inge lay helpless in her bunk and only with much encouraging from her husband did she now and then emerge for a breath of fresh air.

Difficulties arose with our equipment and the crew. It was extremely doubtful that the sunsights I took at the time were of any use. The horizon was mostly obscured by the high waves or the flying spray.

To get the Greenwich time on our Zenith radio, I had to carry it above decks and then I got only very faint and indistinct signals. A passing cruise ship gave us a position ten miles to the west of our DR and I suspected that we were in the equatorial current and had to reckon with this westerly leeway.

In these seas, we had been forced to close all portholes. Even so, we still had a lot of water slopping over the decks and coming below through the mainmast. The bilges had to be emptied daily by now. The stove decided just then to give us a bit of a show, and instead of having a fire through the burners, some inadvertently-spilled kerosene ignited, filling the already rankling cabin with its stench and smoke.

I put the fire out with the extinguisher and bent to the task of cleaning the powdery mess left from it and then to repairing the burners.

I had just changed into dry clothing when, going to the hatch to examine one of the burners I had taken apart, a big dollop of seawater landed squarely on my neck and trickled down my back, drenching me thoroughly. That I was furious about such a small incident indicated that fatigue was getting the better of my nerves. I was tempting the odds, and the odds were slapping my fingers at every turn.

Conditions did not improve. They kept getting worse. Maria was bogged down by having to prepare meals for five people, three times daily, and frequently she had to bake bread twice a day. After Oscar recuperated, I relieved her from duty at the helm.

Inge was not much help to her. She tried, but had to give up her feeble attempt. She could not avoid being thrown against the handrail, getting a bruised nose and black eye in consequence. Tempers rose, and one day I inadvertently put my foot in my mouth by ordering my crew to go below and have breakfast. There were tears from Inge and grumblings from Heinz.

They told me that they did not want to be "ordered" about. It took all my diplomacy to get across to them that there just had to be some kind of discipline on board to make life easier for all. Heinz could not see the need for an orderly schedule of watches and mealtimes or rest periods. He thought that it was just as well for him to take a watch when he felt like it and for as long as he thought he could hold out.

He would also eat when he felt hungry, and read or sleep at his own convenience. The moment had arrived when a skipper must show who is master of the ship. I told both that if they wanted to continue the trip with us, they would have to adjust to life aboard and be able to take an order which could mean our survival or not in an emergency.

I know that both did not quite see it my way, but for the time being I had restored my authority. I wrote down a schedule for our watches and from that day on it was followed without question.

On that same day, the halyard of the mizzensail broke and I bitterly blamed myself for not having a spare one on the mast. Our mizzenmast is not stayed to the mainmast. Its shrouds run from its upper third only to the deck and that is its sole support. The tip swings free for about eight feet and in the crazy motion we were experiencing, there was no possiblity of climbing to retrieve the runaway halyard.

Without the mizzen, we had a very unbalanced boat on our hands and, for the moment, I could do little to improve the situation. I decided to heave to and sleep on it.

The next morning brought a brief lull in the wind, but the seas were as chaotic as ever. All five of us sat in the cockpit and held a summit conference. One of us had to go up that mast. Maria and I were too heavy. So was Oscar with his bulging muscles rippling under his dark skin. Inge was the lightest but the weakest and the most scared. It had to be Heinz.

I hoisted him with the boomlift for as far as I could and had him screw on an eyepiece for a block at about the same height as where the shrouds are fastened to the mast.

Since the mizzensail, even reefed, was now too big, we took it down and off its track and tried the storm jib instead. Still too big.

I did not want to cut, sew and change a good new sail. The only sensible solution which occurred to me was to tie the head of the sail in a big knot. This seemed to do the trick. It was the best I could do to gain some balance and steerage without endangering any of my crew. Looking over this jerry-rig we had accomplished, I was glad no other sailboat was in sight for miles!

The sail was loose-footed, with the clew attached to the end of the boom. This proved to be a mistake. Due to the compression force, the boom broke in half like a matchstick. This happened of course, in the middle of the night. I went topside to inspect the damage, fearing the worst for the mast. I had to lower the sail altogether and then lash the debris securely until daybreak.

By morning, I hoisted the sail after the broken boom had been removed from the mast. It was a frightening sight, watching the mast now curve like a bow, for the sail was now fastened to it only at the head and foot. This would not do.

With our combined forces fighting the flapping canvas, we wrapped the sail once around the mast. The sheet seemed to set best on the sternrail. This was much better now, but the mast was still being subjected to a lot of strain; this caused the freestanding part to whip like a puppy's tail.

In consequence, the radio antenna, fastened to it, shook loose, the top halter broke, the antenna dipped upside-down and hung along the mast. This took care of any further radio communications.

We had gained speed and better steerage in the constant easterly blow which howled monotonously in the rigging.

Maria said that she had never heard such a sound. I was

disinclined to agree.

"Wind is wind," I told her, "no matter where it blows."

Now, I am not so sure anymore. Come to think of it, it did have a peculiar, mournful up and down quality about it.

The days passed as we clawed our way to the northeast. It seemed years since we had left Cartagena behind. We still had the same unrelenting trades and the same strange seas which slapped us hither and yon with many waves washing over the decks and always finding a way below, further increasing our discomfort.

To cook, wash dishes or even shave, to do anything that required two hands, we had to tie ourselves to the handrails which run on both sides inside the cabin with the safety harness. On one occasion, when Maria failed to do so, she was thrown across the cabin, hitting the back of her head against the handrail on the opposite side. She collapsed onto the bunk, sobbing in pain, frustration and fatigue.

"I have had it," she cried. "I am sick and tired of this damn sailing business. I want to go home!"

I was anguished at this outburst and felt inadequate and guilty at the same time. I consoled her as best I could, made her take a tranquilizer and tucked her into her bunk. It was the least I could do for her.

The rest of my crew was very subdued. They had never known Maria to falter and did their best to help me through that night, which would be our last in open water.

The following night Oscar called me on deck. He had sighted land. I took over from him and briefly it crossed my mind what Maria had previously said about reaching land in the dead of night. In his slow and strange English, Oscar said to me, "It eez veery scaaary, the water is soo much quiet."

He was right. We must have come under the shelter of land. The seas had almost subsided and I experienced a glorious two-hour sail, with *Antares* gliding serenely under a silvery moon toward her ecnounter with an unknown shore.

Maria and Heinz excitedly came on deck and checked the shore for any sign of a sheltered bay or nook. There was none they could make out. We had to remain at a respectful distance from shore. Our depthsounder refused to register at this crucial moment, and I had to drop the anchor by my own judgment.

Helplessly I watched all the 300 feet of chain rattle into the depths, for the clutch of the anchorwinch had frozen solid.

As I stood there, surveying the shore, I thought that with this length of anchor rope we could not possibly go wrong. All of us had, for the first time in almost ten days, a long and uninterrupted sleep.

The next day at breakfast, Maria said to me, "You know, we have not done so badly after all. The Smeetons made the crossing from Portobello, Panama, to Jamaica in ten days.

"And Francis Chichester on Gipsy Moth 5 ran in five days from about the height of Cartagena to the Windward Passage.

"Is it not nice to be just in between?"

We had read the books those cruising and racing sailors have written and we greatly admired them. On this particular day, I would have wished to have the experience of one and the knowledge of the other.

Conditions had changed drastically from the night before. A sharp trade was blowing and a swift current ran west with it.

Today, I would just sit tight and wait until evening for the wind to calm down and then lift anchor. But yesterday I was impatient, a bit unsure maybe that the wind would not die down. In any case, we spent the better part of the morning fighting to get the anchor up. We ended up with a badly scuffed toerail, a bent stanchion and bloody knuckles. The anchor roller dropped into the deep, followed by my best and largest screwdriver.

I would have lost my eyeglasses also, had I not made a desperate lunge for them, just before they blew over the side.

For the first and, hopefully, the last time in my life, I cut the chain, sacrificing 150 feet of it and a Danforth anchor to the gods of the Caribbean.

Sailing was out of the question in these headwinds. Thus we motored along the shore, counting the villages and church steeples and making notes on the landmarks. We had no charts from Haiti and used as our only guide an old school atlas, a 1964 edition, which showed Jacmel as a seaport. Only in the late afternoon, when the shore started to curve southeast, could we pinpoint our landfall to have been across from Chardonniere in Haiti. We could consider ourselves lucky, a few more miles west would have put us squarely in the Windward Passage and we could have landed easily at Guantanamo Base in Cuba!

Briefly I had considered putting into Jacmel, to replace the boom and make sundry other repairs. At this news even Inge seemed to revive from her lethargic, horizontal position. In his euphoria, however, Heinz drove the boat too close to shore, putting it within reach of the breakers. We almost rolled over with the impact as one of them caught us broadside and dumped tons of green water on deck, filling the cockpit and drenching everything below.

Fortunately, Heinz kept his bearings and gave the helm a sharp turn, bringing the boat head on to the next roller. We rode that one out and were away from the danger zone.

The Haitian coast slowly unraveled before us. We passed Ile-a-Vache and regained the coast west of Cotes-de fer.

By now I had reconsidered my decision to put into Jacmel. The more I thought about it, the more uncomfortable I felt at the thought of not being able to communicate with the Haitian authorities.

Neither Maria nor I are proficient in the French language. I was not sure if Heinz would be of any help, as I could not judge the extent of his knowledge.

I felt that we had enough fuel to putter on to Santo Domingo in the Dominican Republican.

This change of plans had the effect of a bomb. Spirits around me hit rock bottom. More, I felt betrayed as Maria sided with the crew.

"You must understand under what stress they have been," she said. "I really feel sorry for them—they are so desperate to be on land which is so close by. It must be a torture."

Of course, I was acutely aware of their distress. Too, there had been very little privacy for me and Maria; now, with the addition of Oscar, as little for Heinz and Inge. Because they were so much younger, the lack of it may have instigated far greater pressures in them than 'old folks' could imagine.

They had also been supremely free to roam whole countries at their leisure. When and wherever they rested they had made a multitude of friends and acquaintances. The sudden change to the confinement of a sailboat, the close living night and day, always with the same faces around, was too great a contrast to adjust to without causing tempers to rise and nerves to fray.

Sailors, take heed: "Ye shall not take along landlubbers!"

We had made a grave mistake and we all had to live with it for the time being. Outnumbered and very much against my better judgment, I gave in and put into what we thought was Jacmel. Swaying at anchor in a small and sheltered bay, we were informed by passing fishing boats that we had come to Bainet, which is not a port of entry. The local authorities refused to give us clearance.

When we asked how far it was to Jacmel, someone replied, "About four hours." This information could be stretched either way, but we could not get any clearer directions. At that time we were not familiar with the Haitian's inability to cope with time and distance. These abstractions are meaningless to them.

We traded a shirt and a pair of shoes for two small fish and a lobster and lifted anchor at 1600. One headland after the other loomed over the horizon and we grew edgy with the approach of a thunderstorm. It drenched us and took visibility away from us.

It was almost night as we rounded the last cape and sighted a few poor lights glimmering faintly far inside the bay. Reducing our speed and with Heinz at the bow with our powerful searchlight, we slowly groped our way toward the lights.

There seemed to be some kind of pier and between it and shore we saw another sailboat at anchor. It was facing outward and had the mizzen sail set, probably to avoid swinging around in the small nook it had chosen. Not far from it, at the head of the pier, we dropped anchor and heaved a sigh of relief.

We had just finished our fish and lobster dinner, when we heard voices and a discreet knock on the hull. The port pilot came aboard and introduced himself. Marcel was his name and "please you must move your boat, it is not a safe spot to anchor," was what he said.

As we moved about in the darkness, I had the strange and distinct feeling that we were just moving in circles and coming to rest very close to the spot from where we started. Following Marcel's instructions with great misgivings, I put out a stern anchor.

"Please, Captain," he said, "that will be ten dollars for my services and, please, two dollars for the man who has rowed me out here."

Marcel promised to meet with me the next morning to arrange for wood for a new boom and to help us in the purchase of a few staples we were running short of.

Not long after Marcel had left, another boat with an outboard came alongside. Two young Americans came aboard, owners of the other sailboat, a trimaran, as it turned out.

Their first question was, "How did you make it in without hitting the reef?"

"Reef, what reef?"

We explained to him that we had no charts and had come in with the guidance of an old school atlas. The young man exuded youth, confidence and Haitian rum. He went into a long speech in praise of that particular drink, of which he must have consumed a considerable amount. He valiantly fought against the cobwebs in his brain and stayed with us for quite some time, giving us a garbled account of his life, profession and sailing adventures.

His friend sat with our young crew in the cockpit introducing them to the secrets of Haiti. Oscar, Heinz and Inge could hardly contain their eagerness to put to shore. I do not believe they slept much that night.

Marcel appeared the next morning with the purchases he had made for us, a basket brimming with the best he had been able to find. Maria opened a bag and showed me the tiniest chicken eggs we had ever seen. At first sight I would have thought them to be pigeon eggs.

I followed Marcel to shore in the Avon and went with him to a carpenter's hut to negoitate for a new boom. I had taken the broken one along, for size and shape, and had left the track as well as all the hardware on it to be used again.

On my way back, I stepped into the port captain's office to clear for our emergency entry into Haiti. I was treated with the utmost courtesy. Marcel, who spoke a passable English, was my interpreter.

Seen from the pier, *Antares* looked much like a gypsy boat. Maria and Inge were hard at work washing clothes, having already spread out all our bedding to dry. Only the larger items were sent to shore to a laundress. The price asked for the service was very high indeed.

By afternoon, Inge and Heinz had taken off for a visit to Port-au-Prince, leaving a sad Oscar behind. I could very well understand his sinking feelings as he watched them go ashore. We had provided him with food and transportation, plus shelter however wet and shaky that might have been.

It was beyond our means to provide him with entertainment also. I did however, give him enough money for refreshments at a dance he very much wanted to attend. Happily, he fished out his best jeans, vigorously combed his kinky hair and virtually flew ashore, not to return until the early morning hours.

That afternoon we made the acquaintance of Jerry Vink,

whose life was to be closely linked to ours in many ways. He had swum out to us, climbing aboard to give us a wet handshake. We took an instant liking to him, his boyish smile and open manners hiding effectively a man of strong character and will-power, with a mission in Haiti.

Before leaving, he invited us to visit him in his office and gave us directions on how to get there. For now, we had too many things to do aboard.

Maria was feverishly cleaning and scrubbing everything in sight, while I busied myself above decks, aided now and then by Oscar. I found that he would only get into action when I asked him to. He could sit or lie beside me watching me work and sweat my heart out, without ever lifting a finger.

Once, exasperated by this apparent indolence, I asked him why he could not lend me a hand. With great and earnest innocence stamped all over his face, he replied, "But you did not ask me to."

From then on I did a lot of asking, as one does with a child. It must have been an officer with great insight who wrote in Oscar's military discharge papers: "Needs constant and firm supervision."

The mizzen boom was finished in a remarkably short time and I fastened it to the mast and bent the sail on immediately. Painting could be done at some other occasion.

The halyard had been retrieved and repaired and the antenna refastened. For all practical purposes, we were ready to leave. Only our young German friends had not returned yet from Port-au-Prince and I could not very well sail away without them.

We waited one more day, I suffering with an acute case of impatience at the delay; I found it hard to control a mounting urgency to be off again.

We still needed a lot of easting before we could attempt a recrossing of the Caribbean Sea. I had calculated that we would have to refuel in Santo Domingo and sail on to the southeast point of Hispaniola from where it would be easier to reach Curaçao, in a south southwesterly run.

June 16th was overcast, but bright and slightly muggy. The bay in which Jacmel nestles, in the foothills of Haiti's impressive mountain ranges, is wide open to the south and southeast. The town is sheltered from the prevailing east and northeast winds.

However, the currents inside the bay are erratic and treacherous, made more so by a reef to the southeast of the pier. Two rivers empty their muddy waters into it, causing a great deal of silting. A hurricane, which almost devastated the town in the 1950's, also made the access to the port impassable. Since then, no ocean-going vessels have called here. The bay is considered one of the poorest anchorages on the south side of Haiti.

Tired of waiting for our crew, I suggested that Maria, who had not been off the boat yet, and I go together for a visit to Jacmel. We could take our cameras along and pay Jerry a visit at his office. As we rowed to the pier, we could not help noticing the heavy swell setting into the bay.

Outside, the trades must be blowing hard, judging by the mist and the ragged clouds above the sea. From the pier, we looked back at our boat. Nothing seemed amiss, so we took a picture of it and turned toward the end of the pier and the road leading into the town.

We found Jerry at his desk. He was obviously pleased at seeing us. He gave us a tour of the two-story building which houses his offices and showed us where he intended to install a dispensary, an infirmary and the other conveniences which were meant to provide him with the facilities to carry out his job.

Jerry was the director of the Jacmel chapter of the Foster Parents Plan in Haiti. He had arrived four months before and had succeeded in setting many plans in motion at which his predecessor had failed.

Full of energy and optimism, his enthusiasm seemed boundless. But by no means was Jerry a starry-eyed idealist. Having gained ample experience on a similar assignment in Asia, he had to face many difficulties here. Government officials offered great resistance to his efforts, and it was not easy to cope with the ingrained suspicion of the Haitians against any and all foreign influences.

From Jerry's office, we ambled to the nearest tiny cafe for a refreshment, closely followed by two self-appointed 'guides' we did not want. They had persistently attached themselves to us as soon as we had set foot on the pier. Across from the cafe, where we sat sipping a Coke, we watched the activity of the market. It is just a tin roof, held up by iron pillars over a slab of concrete. The guides pointed at it and repeatedly assured us, "This is the market." This pantomime was repeated over and over again; each time we glanced at a building or street, they would hastily step forward, point at it and affirm that this was a church, a restaurant or a tree.

Seen from the bay, Jacmel has the picturesque air of the old colonial times. Much of this charming appearance is due to the vegetation which hides the crumbling walls under nodding hibiscus, dark-green fronds of breadfruit trees and whispering palms. Close up, the town is a dismal sight. Nowhere had we met with such an overpowering sensation of decay and hopelessness.

A strange and depressing feeling came over us as we moved through the streets. A cloud of dust whirling above the roof tops in a sudden gust of wind made us uneasy at the thought of *Antares*, with just Oscar aboard.

We reached the top of the hill, where a shaded square invited one to rest and take in the sweeping view over Jacmel Bay. We moved to the parapet to have a look at *Antares*.

It was not there!

Dragging her anchors, she was being driven by the squally wind and the swell toward shore. In sudden panic, we flew downhill, through the narrow streets toward the pier.

Our two companions were still with us, shouting information to the inhabitants of Jacmel about the two white maniacs racing by.

With nearly bursting lungs, we reached the pier and jumped into the Avon. I rowed as never before, anxiety firing my muscles into frantic action.

Speeding broadside to the swell, we hardly noticed that we almost capsized with a heavy wave; all our attention was focused on *Antares*.

We reached her and for agonizing seconds we had to wait until a wave lifted us high enough to grab onto the lifeline and heave ourselves on board. We were just one boatlength from the first breaker and our only thought was to get the boat out of this dangerous proximity.

Oscar was at the stern, pulling in the line from the stern anchor, and I thought, fleetingly, that this was the right thing to do.

The next moment, Maria had turned the ignition key and the engine came to life. My hands flew to the throttle and I pushed her in gear. The brief and momentary relief which swept over us turned to desperation as the engine shuddered and died seconds later. Maria and I looked at each other, horror stricken, and instantly realized what had happened. One of the anchor lines had wound itself around the prop shaft.

Oscar, intuitively, grabbed a knife, jumped overboard and went to work. Soon he had company.

From shore, our guides of the afternoon had swum over, shouting already for knives from afar. While they dove in rapid succession, without any apparent results, I threw off my clothing and took the diving mask from a shivering and panting Oscar.

I dove down myself. It was hard and nerve-wrecking work. We had come into the first line of breakers and the sand which they whirled up made visibility practically nil. After more than a dozen dives I was able to free the propeller shaft from the tightly coiled rope, but it was too late to use the engine

The keels were already hitting the bottom at each passing wave. I looked wildly around, seeking anything which would stop the boat from its mad dash to shore.

A new danger presented itself as *Antares* was now being turned around parallel to the breakers and shore. Should we be thrown sideways onto the beach, the hull could sustain irreparable damage.

As no mechanical aid was available, manpower seemed to be the last recourse. I conferred with Marcel, who had joined us by now. He agreed to round up thirty men to help in an effort to turn the boat stern on to the breakers. Precious time was lost when he declared that first we would have to settle on a payment for the men.

I stared at him in disbelief, as he apologetically shrugged his shoulders, saying, "Only if I tell them how much you will pay, will they come and help."

This was a hell of a time to settle financial matters, but I had to agree to a certain sum quickly, before the boat was smashed ashore.

From the huge crowd which had assembled, Marcel selected the men who were to help us. Already, *Antares* was frequently teetering on one keel, with one side of the deck buried in green water. Each time this happened, a great cry and roar of laughter escaped from the crowd.

Not knowing why they should behave like this, I felt hurt and annoyed at this display of merriment at a moment when what I needed most was helping sympathy.

Unexpectedly, Jerry's head popped above the waves and he scrambled aboard.

After I had explained to him our situation and intentions, without much ado he jumped into the water and joined forces with the men Marcel had placed along the hull. With lines streaming from bow and stern to shore and secured around the solid trunks of palms, the boat slowly was pushed to a position perpendicular to shore.

As each wave rolled in and lifted *Antares*, with a great deal of commanding and shouting, the men heaved against the hull and pushed it a few feet away from danger. Twice we had to repeat this operation, when larger rollers came thundering along and we lost ground to the forces of the sea.

By late afternoon, with *Antares* solidly aground, energies were flagging. I had run out of workable ideas and was open to any suggestions.

We had come to rest, with the bow five feet from shore and a good 600 yards northwest from the head of the pier. Marcel came up with an idea of which I was highly skeptical, but I went ahead with it, as it was better than sitting and doing nothing. We tied all our available lines together and, with one end fastened to the cleat at the stern, we rowed the other end to the pier. Here, the line was led around a bollard and attached to the rear of a truck.

I put our engine in reverse and the truck started pulling. Soon its wheels were spinning, the cleat at the stern started buckling and, finally, the line parted. Marcel's idea had not been too bad, but it had been defeated by the distance to the pier.

I told him that if we could drop a couple of heavy anchors, directly behind the boat at about 200 feet and tie to it the line, we could possibly haul ourselves out by using our largest winch. The plan was put into action immediately, and at dusk Marcel, Jerry, Oscar and I took turns at the winch in a last and desperate effort to get us off shore. All the work to set the anchors, attach a pulley to it and lead the line from the boat to the pulley and back to the winch, was in vain.

I do not know if the line had snagged in the anchors or dropped off the pulley, but all we achieved was to pull the line taut to the breaking point. It was night and we had to give up for the time being.

I went below to where Maria, in quiet desperation, worked at the bilge pump. The terrific bumping the keels had suffered had loosened the hull bolts and water seeped in around them, flooding the interior of the cabin.

Jerry poked his head through the hatch and suggested that Maria should stay for the night at his home. At first Maria objected to this, but I convinced her that it would be best. We did not know what the next hours had in store for us. After they had left, Oscar and I settled for a restless night. We took turns at the bilge pump, frequently checked the lines to shore and to the anchor and had fitful catnaps in between.

The intervals filled my mind with all the if's, but's and should have's which commonly assault one in the aftermath of an accident. I also knew that all these considerations did not do away with the fact that we sat aground.

Worse yet, the way our situation was shaping up, there seemed to be no help or solution within reach. Unbeknown to us, however, several sympathizers were already at work planning a course of action.

At that time, as a gift to Haiti, the French government was completing the construction of a road between Jacmel and Port-au-Prince. Several French engineers were stationed in Jacmel and the next day they approached me with their plan. The only heavy equipment in existence close by was the roadbuilding machines the engineers were using for the completion of the road.

They proposed to bring in one of their bulldozers and push the boat from shore into deeper water. We could assist them by using our present anchor set-up and applying our forces at the winch.

I felt very touched by their concern and interest and agreed to do whatever was needed. What I would do with a leaky boat once in deeper water, I did not dare to consider at this moment.

Jerry and Maria came by in the early afternoon. Maria hugged me and told me that she had spent her time, since daybreak, sitting in Jerry's garden, unable to find the courage to come to the beach.

"I did not know what I would find," she said, fighting back the tears welling up in her eyes. "Will this really be the end of our voyage?"

I comforted her and told her of the new and unexpected help which had been offered to us. As we waded through the surf and climbed aboard over the bowsprit, Maria inspected the position of the boat and asked, "If they push on the hull, are they not going to rip the keels off? After all, we do have a 2,000 lb. drag down there with the 3,600 lbs. ballast of the keel buried in the sand."

I replied that this was a possibility I had considered myself, but then, "What do we have to lose? As it is, I do not know how long the boat will last where it stands now."

The bulldozer trundled in and as it was positioned fronting the boat, it was discovered that it stood a bit too high to reach the hull. The pressure would have to be applied against the bowsprit.

Maria, Oscar and I were apprehensively watching the preparations. The expectant crowd which had gathered ashore watched, just as interested. For them, this was a great show.

The bulldozer started up again and it bore down on us, pushing against the bowsprit. We did gain a few feet on the surf, and for a moment it seemed we would make it.

Then, the bolts which hold the bowsprit to the decks buckled and it snapped upwards. The stays to the mainmast swayed loosely and the boom from the stay sail crashed on deck. There was an instant of silence in which we surveyed the situation; we had not gained much and were three feet closer to the breakers now, absorbing the brunt each time a breaker rolled toward the beach.

It all seemed very hopeless and my spirits, in those hours, sank to their lowest point. Maria was standing halfway down the companionway, absentmindedly caressing the smooth varnish of the boom cradle above her head.

I bent down to her and told her that this was possibly the last straw.

"No," she said, "it cannot be; all the work, all the plans, all the love and the dreams gone, just like that!"

"We have to face the reality," I told her, "and accept the inevitable loss; we must look ahead and not to what has been. Tomorrow I must go to Port-au-Prince and get in touch with our families and contact the insurance company."

Just then, Jerry popped his head over the side and, cheerful as ever, said, "Come up to my house, all of you, and let's have dinner together. All is not lost yet." We were more than thankful for this distractiom and welcomed his never-flagging optimism.

Over a drink, after dinner we discussed our next moves. A message from one of the French engineers informed us that they had not given up their efforts to rescue *Antares*. A new and more elaborate plan had been discussed among them.

To put it into action, more men and materials would be needed. I would have to personally contact the director of their company to get his official permission, as well as a statement of agreement from the insurance company or from the American ambassador. This statement was needed as an assurance of payment for the additional materials and manpower involved in this major salvage operation.

The next morning, I took the plan to Port-au-Prince; it was the first of a series of more than sixteen flights I was forced to make to the capital. They were necessary mainly to make contacts and arrangements with my insurance company and to get in touch with persons who would, in the end, be instrumental in the salvage of my yacht.

Jacmel, a city of 30,000 sports just one public telephone. No private lines were in existence at that time. From the public phone, one could not begin a call. Instead, one had to wait until the operator in Port-au-Prince opened the line for an incoming call. At this time, the Jacmel operator would ask to hold the line open for whomever wished to call a number in the capital. If, by chance, a connection was made, any clear understanding was defeated by the antiquated system which garbled the voice to unintelligible scratchy sounds. To place a call to the States would have been an impossibility. During the first days of our forced stay in Jacmel, I was naive enough to give this phone set-up the benefit of the doubt.

One morning as Marcel and I sat on a bench waiting in the office and conferring about matters at hand, I casually glanced into the sunny street. A fellow was coming up the hill with my cap on his head. Now this headgear was my prize possession, the best one of the lot. I gave way to my momentary impulse, stormed into the street and planted myself in front of the guy. "What are you doing with my cap?" I asked him, at the same time whipping the cap off his mop of hair and putting it over my pate. He was startled and speechless. He did not understand a word of what I had said to him and lifted his hands as if to ward off a blow. I had no intention whatsoever of hitting him, but I must have looked fierce enough to scare the wits out of him.

Marcel, who had followed me, not knowing what this crazy white man was about to do, talked to the fellow in a rapid succession of inquires. He turned to me and explained, "He says he bought the cap for a dollar from another man. You want me to take him to the police?"

"For heaven's sake, Marcel, let him go," I replied. "I'm glad to have my cap back."

Marcel made a flicking motion with his hand and barked an order at which the man scurried away and disappeared around the next corner.

At one time or another during our grounding, someone had stolen the cap. If the startled fellow would have been brought to the police, he would have been in jail for a long time. Courts are very slow and there is no bail in Jacmel.

The French engineers would not be able, after all, to realize their rescue plans. My insurance company, meanwhile, had contracted the services of an American company stationed in Port-au-Prince at that time. This company was engaged in the construction of two new piers to accommodate the many tourist cruising ships calling at Haiti. The insurance company sent a driver to Jacmel where he inspected the position of the boat and after a short while assured us that *Antares* could easily be refloated in a short time. I wished I could have shared his supreme confidence.

By now we had removed all our belongings from the boat and stored them in Jerry's bedroom. He had invited us to share his house with him and stay for as long as needed or until our fate was decided.

All in all, we would spend a bit over six weeks under one roof together. We will forever be indebted to this young Canadian for his generous gesture. Unselfishly, he gave to us much of his time, support and assistance. To us, this was a highlight, a solace amidst the see-sawing emotions which gripped us at that time. Not only the sudden grounding and its consequences but also the forced stay in a country in which we could not understand the language, much less the strange behavior of its population, deeply influenced our thinking and emotional reactions.

As it turned out, *Antares* was not so easy to get into deep water as David had anticipated He brought over, from Port-au-Prince, first a five-ton truck and a wire rope. He built a harness around the boat to pull on the whole hull rather than a cleat only. From the harness, that wire rope was led through the pulley we had already anchored 200 feet out at sea with four big anchors. When everything was ready, the truck snapped the wire and Dave had to give up at that point. A couple of days later, he was back with a brand new and stronger cable. After it was put into operation, the truck which pulled it only spun its wheels deep into the sand and *Antares* was not moved an inch. Next thing Dave came up with was a compressor and a suction pipe. He went into the water and tried to suck the sand away from the keels. But the breakers brought with one sweep more sand in than he could ever suck out in between the waves. The cable was now fastened to a palm tree with a hand operated device. I had no say in the salvage operations, as the company had taken over full responsibility. They had also brought on board two gasoline operated pumps to keep the water out of the boat. Next, Dave brought a bigger compressor and a three inch suction pipe, but had not more success than with the smaller one. After that I did not see him for a week. He stationed two of his men ashore who were alternately operating the pumps. Otherwise, no further action took place.

At the end, nature gave a helping hand. We had now a full moon; at this time the tide rises about one and one half feet higher than usual. We pulled on the "come along" and, inch by inch, *Antares* slid more into deep water with every breaker which passed under her. After twenty-three days, she was floating again, if only two waves off shore! What a wonderful sight to see her gently moving with the long waves again. Ahead of us now there were many things that had to be done. First, we had to bring *Antares* into a more secure place. As there was no tug or any other motor boat in Jacmel to give her a tow and because the engine could not be bought back to life, the only way to move her was to row out an anchor and pull in the chain. After that, another anchor had to be moved out and the process repeated. Slowly, in this tedious way, step by step, we anchored her where she was reasonably safe. The salvage company agreed to leave the pumps and the two men on board for another two weeks. After that it was up to us to keep *Antares* afloat and proceed on our own. We had to get help from the Dominican Republic as there was none available in Haiti. For this reason, on my next flight to Port-au-Prince, I took Maria along. She would be of great help if we could find someone from the Dominican Republic as Spanish is their language. The flight over the mountains took Maria's breath away. Seldom had she seen such beautiful scenery. Therefore, the stark contrast between this short flight and the realities which presented themselves after landing in Port-au-Prince was one of our most depressing experiences.

Maria had seen much poverty in the South American countries, but what she saw here surpassed anything she had ever experienced before. To reach the offices of the construction company, we had to walk across a wide flat, just inshore and across from the new piers. Here, an accumulation of dismal huts, built with an assortment of discarded materials and held together by the mercy of God, sweltered in the heat of the bright forenoon sun. We had to press handkerchiefs over our faces, not only because of the indescribable stench which hung over all, but against the fine, white, powdery dust whirled up by the cars and trucks roaring past. This dust slowly drifted down, settling on tin and cardboard roofs and onto heaps of garbage by the roadside; here pigs, with backbones and ribs sticking almost through their coarse skins, snuffled desultorily in their search for an edible morsel.

The peasants of Haiti do not feed their domestic animals. Not having the means to still their own hunger, the very concept of feeding their animals is alien to them.

The picture looks quite different if one arrives on one of the modern luxury liners. The pier is right in the heart of downtown. One will see the legislative building with its huge, modern office buildings, consulates, banks and so forth. The novelty stores are there and in the few places where one can get food and refreshments natives play music on their drums and guitar-like instruments. If a visitor does not look closely, he may be impressed with the city. There are mostly bus tours arranged and the visitors are taken to Pattonville, which is built on the hills of the southeast. Here are the houses of the rich people and everything looks beautiful. Modern shops and hotels are next to big mansions, remains of a bygone era.

Back to our problems, we did contact the consulate of the Dominican Republic. We were advised, then, to contact the attaché of the Office of Commerce National. There we met Senor Ervin de Leon. He welcomed us very warmly and immediately made several telephone calls to Santo Domingo to the naval base and commerical shipping agencies. Things looked promising and we had hopes again.

We stayed overnight in one of the big hotels and found out that the prices were as high as the hotel building itself. For the two of us, we paid $56.00, dinner and breakfast included. On my previous overnight stays, I had been in a French *pension* where it was only $14.00. After we had arranged everything in Port-au-Prince, we went to the airport. There we learned the bad news that they had overbooked our flight and that we would have to wait for two days. We had two alternatives: we could try to get a ride with one of the few cars going over the new road or take the bus. Maria was for the latter choice.

The 'bus' turned out to be nothing more than a truck with a wooden roof and a row of wooden benches below it. It offered little or no comfort.

We had been advised to take our seats early as the tickets were sold on a first-come, first-served basis. We installed ourselves on the first bench immediately behind the cab. The hours stretched interminably as we waited from two to seven o'clock, surrounded by the milling crowd and the waves of heat; worse yet, a sweet, cloying, nauseating smell of decay permeated the air.

Finally, we took off with a load of about eighty people, wedged tighter together than sardines in cans. Some hardy souls perched on the roof, among numerous bundles and crates. Moreover, the truck could not take the new road, at the moment closed to all but vehicles with special permits. After leaving the comparatively good blacktop road leading out of town, the truck went onto the dirt road which goes over the mountainous terrain and winds around hilltops innumerable times, crossing the two rivers which had looked so appealing from above.

If part of the trip had been during daylight hours, it would not have been such a torture. At least we would have been able to appreciate the landscape, which now, in the darkness, was only illuminated by the headlights of the truck.

As it was, we became more and more painfully aware of the narrow bench we sat on and which, for some obscure, sadistic reason was upholstered with what seemed to be a fill of some kind of rocky material. Thus, the total seating area was reduced to perhaps five inches. We sat nine people in a row, not counting the baby the woman beside Maria held in her arms, tightly wedged against each other. There was not much space left to stretch our legs, as bundles and baskets had been heaped at our feet.

We were the only non-Haitians aboard and were thus subject to comments and curious glances from the rest of the passengers. They did not seem to mind in the least as the truck groaned and creaked, swaying through the night on what was little more than than a track through the wilderness. We made many stops, twenty-two to be exact. I counted them—as well as the fifty-four times we crossed and recrossed the rivers tumbling from the watershed toward the sea.

We often left our bench on these stops to stretch our cramped legs or to disappear briefly behind the bushes. Even so, our buttocks were numb and our backs were beginning to feel the strain.

At one time, Maria put her head to my chest and cried, telling me that she felt like an animal being transported to the slaughterhouse. "How can people, human beings, accept such treatment," she sobbed. "I would gladly walk the distance, instead of being subjected to this."

I was almost tempted to remind her that it had been largely her idea to take the bus. I had intended to take our chances and to hitchhike along on the new road on which government and private vehicles made their way to Jacmel. It would have been infinitely easier on our morale.

It was getting toward midnight when, once more fording the shallow river bed, the truck stopped in the middle of it. At first we thought it was an engine failure; but the driver shut off the lights and, putting his head on his arms across the steering wheel, calmly went to sleep.

The passengers stoically accepted whatever the driver decided to do and slept also, with their heads on each others' shoulders. After about fifteen minutes of this, I stepped down from the truck and sloshed ankle deep in water to the driver's window.

At that moment I was furious enough to take over the steering myself.

I knocked on the glass and told him to get going. He had charged us double the amount of the regular fare anyway, and I felt I had a right to be taken to my destination as quickly as possible. He protested feebly that he was tired, but I was adamant that he continue. I may have infringed here on Haitian custom as nobody voiced support to my demand. To the passengers, mostly Haitian peasants, time had no meaning.

But since there were no protests either, the driver sighed and turned the ignition key. By 1:30 we got off the bus and painfully made our way home through the deserted streets of Jacmel. The distance from the Haitian capital to Jacmel is a scant thirty-five miles, as the crow flies.

The next morning, David, the diver from the salvage company, plugged the several holes where fittings had come loose with underwater cement. He was not able to do the same with the keels. The keels have flanges and these are bolted through the ribs to the hull. The bolts had ground the holes bigger, so water entered through them. It was, however, impossible to plug these leaks from underwater because of their inaccessibility. For this reason, we had to continue pumping until we would be out of the water.

Since the rudderpost was bent at a 45-degree angle from its original position, we could not steer her, not even if our engine had been operable. Oscar, who had been assigned night duty during the first days of the grounding to keep the bilges from overflowing, had overslept one night and the water had risen two feet inside the cabin. The engine had been flooded with seawater and our Frieda sat there, a hunk of rusting iron junk. I had little hope of ever getting her to perform again.

Therefore, it was with joy that we celebrated the news transmitted to us by Mr. de Leon that he had been able to secure a tow for us to Santo Domingo. He could not tell us the exact date of the arrival of the shipping agency's vessel, but cautioned me to be ready, as it could put into Jacmel any day.

We transferred our belongings back aboard *Antares* and I stowed most of them in the head enclosure on the starboard side. This was necessary to offset some of the list she had to port. The ballast from the keel plate on the starboard side had come loose and was forever buried in the sand off the beach.

Jerry shared in our happiness, even if it did mean our separation. We had become good friends and through him we had learned much about Haiti and its stormy history. He loved the country and was deeply committed to his work there. He had told us that his work could not be expected to bear fruit before two or three generations had passed. Right now, all he could do was to teach the people how to help themselves and instill in them the concept of cooperation. It has always seemed to us that the only time Haitians got together and did anything as a group was at their voodoo ceremonies.

We had never attended such a ceremony, nor did we wish to do so. But we had pondered its significance as we lay awake at night, the drums throbbing incessantly from sunset to dawn.

Just below Jerry's house was a string of small houses, tucked into the bottom of a ravine. One of these houses must have been a houngfor, a voodoo temple, where ceremonies were celebrated regularly. At that time we understood little or nothing about this religious cult. Tourists who witness the showy demonstrations put on for their benefit may get a completely distorted concept of its significance.

Today, we have come to realize that voodoo, with its African roots and strong interlacing with rituals borrowed from the Christian church, may very well be the only spiritual source of strength from which the Haitian peasant can draw. It allows him to withstand and survive his present excruciatingly poor standard of living. It was thus, also, that we could not begrudge them the many small thefts which had occurred, or the many feet of nylon and dacron lines which had been cut in the dead of night.

Oscar had made many friends, especially among the younger Haitian ladies, but even he had felt a certain depression and was glad at the prospect of leaving.

Heinz and Inge, who had returned to Jacmel two days after the grounding, decided to remain in Haiti for a while. They had been thoroughly shocked when they had walked onto the pier to discover the boat stranded at the beach. In a way, as Inge confessed later to Maria, they felt a bit guilty and responsible for the accident. Indeed, had it not been for their delayed return, we would have left Jacmel long before that. I must confess that, for a while I, too, thought along this line.

But in time I came to realize how unfair it was to put the blame on anybody, including myself; it was a foolish and senseless train of thought which only helped to dodge reality. The sum of our actions or inactions had brought about our present situation.

Maria assured Inge that we bore them no rancor or blamed them for any of the things that had happened. They quietly set up their tent in the garden and shared with us for two more weeks the ups and downs of hope, frustration and despair.

After that, it became evident that we would not be able to continue our trip in the foreseeable future. It was even doubtful that the boat would one day be pulled off the beach. By maritime law, I was still responsible for my crew and guests who had been aboard and was bound to house and feed them.

Fortunately, Heinz and Inge were financially independent and had already made arrangements with the German consulate to stay for the time being in Haiti. Once they had been taken off my crew list, I was no longer responsible for their well-being.

They moved to Port-au-Prince, where they joined a group of young people engaged in the kind of work Jerry was involved in. We never met again and often wondered what became of them.

Jerry had acquired the habit of checking *Antares'* situation with the binoculars each morning. He was more worried than we about the possibility that she might drag the anchors and wind up on the beach again.

On this eventful morning, Jerry turned to us and with a broad grin announced, "I think your ship is coming in!" We joined him and watched, fascinated, as a small freighter made its way slowly into the bay, passed the reef and tied up opposite *Antares*, on the pier. It was July the 29th and our stay in Haiti was coming to an end.

The next few hours were filled with frantic activity as we packed our last things in two seabags, unceremoniously throwing together underwear, pots and pans, toothbrushes and sneakers.

We did run out of wind when the skipper of the freighter told us that he did not intend to leave before eleven that night when wind and tide were at their lowest.

Antares had been brought alongside the *Elvia* and was being readied for the tow. Chains and lines coiled about her decks as seamen busily arranged a sort of cradle to which the towline would be fastened.

The heavy swell and current at the pier caused further damage to our boat as it was mercilessly smashed against *Elvia's* iron hull. The fenders had burst like balloons and two stanchions bent inwards. I could see how sometimes rescue operations did a lot of additional damage to a vessel already suffering from disrepair.

By noon, the departure hour had been moved ahead to two in the afternooon and this set us again into frantic motion. Maria hustled us from store to store. She wanted to make sure that we would have enough food for easily prepared meals. It would not be easy to cook as the interior of *Antares* was stripped bare of many of the conveniences we had been used to.

Once more, and for the last time, Jerry herded us to his house and presented us with a full meal. Rose, his housekeeper

Las Hadas—one of the most beautiful resort hotels in the Bay of Manzanillo

Our very first Dorado

For yachts moored at the Balboa Yacht Club, this is a daily sight—liners moving towards the locks of the Panama Canal

View of the modern day section of Cartagena, Colombia

Jacmel Bay

Antares stranded and helpless on the Haitian shore at Jacmel

Antares in tow, swaying drunkenly behind *Elvia*

Charlotte Amalie, capital of St. Thomas, U.S. Virgin Islands

Floating market, in Williamstad

Our faithful mascot, Igor

and cook, had been working at it for the whole morning. Maria hugged her in parting. They had shared the tiny kitchen for so long and though they could not speak to each other, they had gotten along famously using the universal sign language.

It was time to leave. We were taken to the pier in Jerry's Land Rover and we climbed over the decks of *Elvia* and down to *Antares*. The lines cast, we slowly moved away from the pier; then the lines which held us alongside the ship were loosened and we dropped behind, our bow tethered to *Elvia's* stern.

Good bye, Jerry, thank you for your help and your friendship and the many things you taught us. We won't forget, and hope to meet you someday in much happier circumstances. We waved until we could see him no more.

Jacmel seemd to have put her prettiest dress on. The light of the afternoon sun was bright and in the clear air the town seemed to bid us a coquettish farewell.

CHAPTER 7

SANTO DOMINGO AND THE DOMINICAN REPUBLIC

On Saturday, July 31st, 1976, we entered Santo Domingo harbor and came to rest alongside *Elvia*. To the people sitting at the sidewalk cafes under multicolored umbrellas, we must have been a sensational sight.

To us, it seemed as if we had left Haiti 200 years ago and returned to the present. Behind us lay forty-six hours of constant pumping, little sleep and much worry. I had no idea and no means of knowing if *Antares* had sustained any structural damages during her grounding. If so, the strain of the towline would have been disastrous.

Right now, she was a frightful sight, with her dirty decks, leaky bottom, sagging stays and lifelines, and her several broken stanchions. To complete this bedraggled appearance, a large piece of her fiberglass covering had come loose and flapped about just off her starboard bow. It exposed the wood underneath and *Antares* gave the impression of a lady of doubtful reputation who had gotten into a fight with some rowdy elements and had lost all her dignity with the exposure of her petticoats.

When we came to a standstill in quiet waters, the leaks

seemed gradually to let less and less water come through. In all probability it was the muddy river water which did us this unexpected service. The Santo Domingo harbor is built in the estuary of the Rio Ozama on which now floated a collection of water lilies toward the sea. The skipper of the *Elvia* told us that it had rained hard in the mountains upriver and that this was the cause of the heavy silting. In any case, we were happy that the constant pumping was now reduced to a twice-a-day job.

Soon the owner of the ship came aboard and we shook hands with José. He was to become our 'anchor man' in the Dominican Republic. For now, he told us, we would have to remain where we were as it was Saturday and only on Monday could the technicalities with the authorities be settled. However, he lent us his pick-up truck, driven by his aide who went by the name of Cooky. He drove us into town and seemed, at first, at a loss as to what to do with us. Our first stop was at the sidewalk cafe, under the same umbrellas we had seen as we zig-zagged behind *Elvia* into port.

Here, with refreshments in front of us he visibly started to brighten up; not only because we had bought him a beer, but because of Maria's easy way of conducting the conversation toward matters of town and country. During their talk, Cooky soon realized that what we needed most right then was to dash quickly to the nearest market to replenish our supplies. He drove us to the city market at breakneck speed along Calle Conde, the city's main commercial artery.

At the market, we almost fell over ourselves at the sight of the abundance and good quality of the produce, meat, fish and fowl. It was almost closing time and we literally grabbed left and right at the wares, unmindful of what they might cost. To our delight, the prices for fresh food were surprisingly low in Santo Domingo.

Cooky deposited us and our purchase back at the boat and told us that José would come by the next afternoon.

Sunday morning, Maria and I walked into the city in search of a phone. After many turns and questions for directions to it, we found the offices of the telephone company. The guard at the gate motioned to the two street phones in front of the building and told us that we could place our collect calls home from them.

We felt a bit foolish as we found later that we could have placed these calls from any of the public phones in Santo

Domingo's streets. We had been so used to having to place calls from central offices that this possibility had never even occurred to us.

José came along in the afternoon and took us for a typical Sunday afternoon drive through Santo Domingo. José is a rather stout man, short of figure. So it was no surprise to us when with a wide grin on his round and placid face, he confessed that he loved to eat!

This candid attitude stretched beyond himself to his countrymen and we have never heard him remark negatively or derogatorily about any other person. He is a man full of a quiet energy, constantly on the go and a shrewd businessman to boot. I believe that this Sunday drive was not only for our enlightenment, but also to provide an opportunity for him to size up and get to know us better.

We must have made a good impression, for after the two-hour drive he invited us to his apartment to meet his wife. His youngest daughter was there, too, holding in her arms her brand-new baby which, to us, apppeared to be an exact replica of the proud José.

From his apartment, we all drove to a suburb, to the house of a friend of the family. I don't know at what point José had decided to take us under his wing, but the introduction to Laura and Franco must have been already part of his calculations.

Tall glasses of coke and rum appeared and the conversation, very naturally, turned to our adventures and present predicament. By the end of the afternoon, it had been decided that we would rent one of the two apartments adjacent to Franco's house.

José would be in charge of finding an outhaul for *Antares* and hiring the workmen which would effect the repairs. All these arrangements had come about rather quickly and left us a bit breathless.

For Maria, it had been a *tour de force*, as she had been interpreting to me all afternoon and could not always keep up with the lively exchange. José obviously believed in rapid decisions but it took another two weeks before we found a place where *Antares* could be put on land, surveyed and repaired.

Several possibilities for drydocking had been considered, discussed and discarded.

José and Franco seemed to know just about everybody of any importance in Santo Domingo; not only in what business they were but, also, their political background and all the very complicated family ramifications that seemed so important here.

In the meantime, Maria and I had sufficient time on our hands to roam the immediate vicinity of the city. Around the port and to the west of it we found the old city walls, in places intact, in others restored and landscaped. Most of the streets in the inner core of the city are the original thoroughfares, with their cobblestones laid down centuries ago.

Columbus' son, Diego, lived here and governed the colonial town. His house, an impressive mansion, has been restored and is open to visitors. It is completely furnished with original period pieces; all the paintings, Gobelins, as well as the utensils for daily use, are authentic.

Adjacent to the house is a small museum in which we admired suits of armor, wood carvings and priceless ceramics of Spanish manufacture. Here, too, are two seachests which accompanied Columbus on his voyages of discovery—one of them of tooled rawhide, and another with the most beautifully executed wood inlay. His desk, chair, stool and money box top this fantastic collection of 15th and 16th century art. House and museum stand on the outer limits of a square with a fountain and a statue of Isabella of Spain, the patron of Columbus.

Across from where we had tied up to the pier was an immense tree. Chained to it was an anchor. and a plaque nailed to the tree proclaimed that it had belonged to one of the ships of the great Italian discoverer.

In the course of our wanderings, we had come, one day, upon a cool ice-cream parlor, where we had the best sherbets and liquid concoctions made from the many tropical fruits so abundant in this country. It was tucked away from the main pedestrian traffic in a quiet short street. Although we very often searched for it through the maze of narrow and ancient streets, we could never remember its location and came upon it always by chance.

All these amenities were highly enjoyable, but each time we returned to *Antares* we became more and more aware of the urgency to start the repairs.

Finally, a site was found for her, one which seemed the best and most convenient for everybody.

While we moved our belongings into the apartment, the boat had to be towed, once more twenty miles farther east to the Club Nautico, close to the Port of Boca Chica in the Bay of San Andres. This move not only involved a bout with Dominican bureaucracy but, also, the tedious task of hauling all our things to the Customs House. Here all sailbags, bundles and cartons had to be emptied and every single item made ready for inspection. This took the better part of a day. At times, we thought the three inspectors would never finish. When, finally, the sign came that we had been cleared, our belongings could be put back into their containers. We loaded everything high on José's pick-up truck and drove through the gates of the freeport. For the time being, we had to leave Oscar behind to watch over the boat.

I joined him next morning at the pier where the *Elvia* was already prepared for the four-hour tow. Once in the open and in motion, the accumulated silt which had plugged the leaks so effectively was washed out. Oscar and I were hard put to keep up with the inflow of sea water and had to pump continuously until we reached the docks of the Club Nautico in Boca Chica.

At the club, a marine surveyor who had flown over from Puerto Rico awaited me. I had requested, from my insurance company, an inspection by a professional, first, to have an official list of the many repairs which had to be performed and secondly, to be very sure that the hull of the boat was still sound and the intended repairs a worthwhile undertaking.

To my relief, the surveryor made a very thorough examination, writing a detailed report to the insurance company. Before he left, he assured me of the soundness and strength of the hull of *Antares* which had so well withstood the grueling conditions to which she had been subjected. With my mind at rest on this point, I left for the apartment. *Antares* was now high and dry, resting between palm trees on land. I put Oscar in charge of the boat, not only as a watch but, also, because our landlord had made it clear to me that he did not wish him to live on his premises.

This was a rather delicate situation, which we had some trouble accepting. We did not want to hurt Oscar's feelings as we, among ourselves, had never experienced any racial prejudice against him. To us, he was just a twenty-three-year-old irresponsible child in need of supervision. In our absence, he liked to show off an authority he did not have and he frequently put his foot where his tongue belonged. This attitude brought him many quarrels with the workmen at the club. One night, he even wound up in jail, from where we had to bail him out. Motorcycles were Oscar's first love. Apparently, he had owned one in his home town and had worked as a mechanic in this field.

He made efforts to find work in Santo Domingo in this line but, as a visitor, he could not apply for a working permit. I offered him payment if he would apply himself to help in the restoration of the boat. Unfortunately, by now, his relationship with the rest of the Dominican work crew had deteriorated so much that I had to make a final decision for him. I bought Oscar a plane ticket to his home town in Guiana. He left us, probably with a bit of mixed feelings for now he had to confront two ex-wives, a pregnant girl friend and several offspring on his return home.

Such are the responsibilities of a skipper toward any and all crew members aboard his yacht.

For the first week, we settled into a very domestic life in our apartment. The furnishings were sparse but adequate. A bottle of rum, ashtrays and matches, which we found moving in, revealed Dona Lupe's thoughtful and loving nature. Often she greeted us with an ice-cold papaya milkshake when we returned, hot and tired, from our daily work at the boat.

After a few token visits to the club, it had become apparent that my presence and supervision of the work was indispensable. And after Maria had worked herself through the gigantic task of washing every single item of clothing which had been stored aboard, she went most every day with me to the club. Not only did she join forces with me in the work but, as an interpreter, was invaluable in communicating our instructions to the carpenter and the foreman in charge.

I was very soon at odds with this man. Moreover, the language barrier was not the real obstacle which created our misunderstandings. His working methods were, most of all, what gave me frequent reasons for a mounting dissatisfaction, and I soon found myself losing my cool with him.

Maria and I compared him to a nervous crow, as his skinny body darted and hopped from one job to another. He seemed to be in a constant state of hysterical motion, starting and never finishing any of the jobs on hand. He scattered tools and woodshavings around him, which he never bothered to collect at day's end; not once did he clean up after himself before leaving. Being an orderly and meticulous worker myself, he kept me in a never-ending state of quiet rage, for he stubbornly used the right materials on the wrong places and vice-versa.

Always and regularly, he decided to start on a job for which the spare parts had not yet come. This, of course, gave him the opportunity to put the blame on somebody else. His working hours were as erratic as his methods and some days he chose not to come at all. I cannot say that our relationship was a happy one. Maria and José had a hard time controlling my patience, worry and ruffled feelings.

The manufacture and repair of the metal parts, José had jobbed out to several workshops he had under contract for the repair and maintenance of his own three ships which comprised the small fleet of his agency. Since these ships had, understandably, priority over our boat, some of the parts we needed were slow in being delivered. We soon realized that the term *manăna*—tomorrow—did not necessarily mean the next day; it could be next week or next month even.

To gain access to the keel fastenings from the inside, most of the built-in interior in the main cabin had to be removed. Felix, our carpenter, gleefully applied himself to the work, armed with a crowbar and a gigantic screwdriver. He ripped and tore anything apart which would not immediately yield to his frantic attempts. Demolition was a better description of the character of his work than construction.

We constantly had to keep an eye on him; even Maria started to have mixed feelings about him when she discovered that he had been mixing paint and resin in her prized Tupperware.

One morning I surprised him in the act of spreading contact cement, instead of bedding compound, on the keel flange, prior to joining it to the hull. He looked defeated and got quite angry when I told him that this would not do. I was beside myself at the thought of having heavy underwater fittings joined with a material unsuited for this purpose.

Moreover, as far as I knew, the new keelbolts, luckily, had not been delivered yet.

His outburst had the effect he had hoped for. The whole work crew of the boatyard watched and listened as he gesticulated wildly, telling everybody how difficult it was to please a yacht owner who was so particular and picky. He ranted on and on, hopping about, invoking the help of the heavens to witness his plight. He gave a good show, but if he had hoped for sympathy, he did not find any.

The rest of the workers called him *Mata Patos*, a term used to designate a person known for laziness and shoddy work habits. Everybody returned to his job while Felix was forced now to clean the drying contact cement from the rough metal surface of the keel flange.

Maria and I wound up cleaning and repainting the boat's interior. It was she who hauled me up to the mast to work on the rigging. Together we sanded and varnished all the brightwork above decks.

Our work was not only hampered by the delays with the spare parts and the antics of Felix, but also by the frequent thunderstorms which brought torrential rainfall from August to the end of October.

Just about this time, Maria received the sad news from Brazil, that her father had passed away. I knew how very painful this news was for her, for their relationship had been particularly close.

At one time I had proposed that she fly to São Paulo for a short visit, but Maria had declined, knowing this would mean sacrificing a large portion of our savings. We were not prepared for such an expense. I desperately wished now that she had taken the trip. There was so little anyone could do to relieve her quiet grief.

Maybe it was good that just then José invited us to take a trip to Puerto Plata. He had been planning on it for some time and I hoped that it would help Maria in distracting her from the present depression.

We had no idea what was in store for us as we sped in an air-conditioned bus through the green landscape. The Dominicins seem to be bent on turning their countryside into one huge park. Wooded hillsides with stands of evergreens surprised us when we saw them intermingled with groups of royal palms. Fields of rice, sorghum, tobacco and sugarcane appeared as we neared the city of Santiago. Situated in the *Cibao*, the agricultural center of the Dominican Republic, it is the second largest city to Santo Domingo.

The bus stopped here briefly and José went out to stretch his legs a bit. He returned with a bag full of fresh meat pastries. These pies, which are deep fried, have a feather-light crust which melts in the mouth. The filling adds just the right amount of spice and fragrance to it. We found them to be highly addictive. José constantly delighted in introducing us to the many tasty regional dishes; his waistline was living testimony to his fondness for them.

An hour later, we rolled into Puerto Plata, an old but very pretty and neat colonial town. Jose's sister, Lita, was to be our hostess. She had, like José, an enterprising mind and ran a tiny restaurant on one of the main streets of the town. At the "Yellow Canary" she served us a superb lunch. If you should ever come to Puerto Plata, don't fail to stop in; it will be worth it!

José found no difficulties in borrowing a car from his brother-in-law, husband to his oldest sister, Judith. After our royal lunch, he did not intend to waste much time, but took us immediately on a sight-seeing tour. By cable car we reached the summit of a 3,000-foot mountain, landmark of the port. During the Trujillo era, the dictator had a military outpost on this mountain-top, housed in a concrete fortification. After his demise, the citizens of Puerto Plata erected, in defiance of his terror regime, a giant Christ statue. It stands on top of the above-ground cupola of the former bunker, now a hollow sounding shell which we did not care to visit.

We were much more delighted by the surrounding area, today a beautifully landscaped park with benches, brick walks and a fountain which the gardener turned on for us to photograph. The high point, though, was the sweeping view over the truly beautiful hilly countryside—stands of royal palms, the deep green fields of sugarcane and, to the north, the Atlantic Ocean.

To the west of the port, we made out the contour of the reef which guards its entrance. Testimony to its dangers was the white sliver of a Greek freighter stranded there a year ago. It had attempted to enter the port during the night, without a pilot's assistance.

The port is open to the northers in winter and to the northeasterly trades which at times bring heavy rainfall to the region. The temperatures are very amenable; Puerto Plata is much cooler than the ports on the southern side of the island.

José's bag of tricks seemed to be bottomless. He drove us, the next day, to Sosua. In this small town he stopped at a crossing where one of the streets bears the name of his only brother.

"Here," he told us, "my brother was killed in ambush by Trujillo's men for no other reason than having voiced displeasure with the regime."

"My son is now the only male descendant to carry on the family name. I have sent him away to study in the States and in Canada. Our university, like so many in the southern countries, is a hotbed of political dissent. I don't want him to come to grief in a silly political dispute. It is enough that one member of the family wound up as a shooting target."

José bears no rancor. He is realistic in his retrospective view of his country's struggles and sometimes disastrous changes in government with their subsequent economic ups and downs. As did many other Dominicans, he and his wife chose long years of exile during Trujillo's reign. Most of these exiles lived and worked in the Miami and New York areas. Many of them have returned now, hoping that the government of President Balaguer may achieve some economic stability and return freedom to this beautiful country.

We drove on to Sosua Beach, a well-protected half-moon bay, white sanded and lined with tall and ancient trees. This bay is one of the most attractive spots on the northern shores and will, in future, be full of American vacationers. Already Puerto Plata and surrounding areas are preparing for a major influx of tourists. Hotels, shore cabins and even an international airport were even then almost ready to receive vistors from all parts of the world.

On that Sunday morning we had the beach almost to ourselves and enjoyed hours of relaxation, swimming and walking along the sandy beach. We sat in the shade of the trees, talking and sipping the delicate water from green coconuts. Dominicans sometimes add a shot of rum to these coconuts and the combination of flavors is exceedingly refreshing.

José enjoyed these hours as much as we did. He derived an obvious pleasure from our admiring comments and endless questions. His love for his country is limitless and he quoted Columbus in saying that the island of Hispaniola was one of the most beautiful places in the world. We could not help but share in some measure his feelings for it.

On the drive home, as we passed a large field of sugar cane, he told us of how he had invested in these fields and lost a substantial amount of this investment when the price of sugar dropped suddenly, influenced by a fickle market.

"But," he said, "there is always enough money for a good meal."

Parking beside a roadside stand, José invited us to have a taste of the regional grilled pork and a glass of beer. Feeling hungry after our long swim, this seemed a heavenly idea.

We gobbled hunks of deliciously juicy and tender meat, so well cooked and seasoned that we did not mind a bit that we had to eat with our fingers. (Would it be a bad pun to say we made pigs of ourselves?) Meanwhile, José and the vendor chatted amiably. They knew each other. But then, José knew everybody and everybody knew him. This was his home town, here he had grown up and married, and here he wanted to retire.

We met José's wife visiting her mother, a tiny, fragile and delicate person, presiding over a large plantation home. In her garden, she cultivated innumerable varieties of rare ferns and ornamental plants. These were sold to homes and gardens in Puerto Plata and Santa Domingo.

She was aided by several employees who clung to her with an open display of loving and solicitous devotion. Many of the servants in Dominican homes have retained the same employment since childhood. This may smack of exploitation or, perhaps, a form of slavery. The truth is, though, that for the poor peasant with a house full of children, it is an honor and a blessing when one of his offspring has the luck to be chosen and taken into a more affluent home. Not only will the child's duties be light, but he is assured a good home, clothing, regular meals, health care and most important of all, a school education.

We have witnessed on many occasions how well these children are treated, for they form an integral part of almost every family's daily life. There may, indeed, be exceptions to the rule. But in each society one may find elements that will take advantage of any opportunity to gain from cheap child labor. I do not think, however, that such situations are tolerated here for long.

Parent and child at all times have the right to visit and spend time with one another. I believe there is much to be said for a people who love and protect their children and youth as the Dominicans do so well.

We visited many of José's relatives and friends in Puerto Plata. Everywhere we received a friendly and sympathetic reception. More than once we were asked if we did not want to remain in the country. We had been here for so long already!

Maria and I came very close to giving way to a momentary impulse and considering seriously settling indefinitely in the Dominican Republic. Had it not been for the need to return to the States, and our rapidly diminishing savings, we might have done it. Especially at this point, when the death of Maria's father had taken the urgency out of our intended visit to Brazil. Besides, *Antares* was not ready yet. Much still needed to be done before she became seaworthy once more.

Maria and I had much to talk about on our return trip home. We savored the last two days once more, recalling all we had seen and experienced, from the visit to the park atop the mountain to the swimming pool filled with sea water. Set at the edge of a reef, and with an ingenious array of culverts and pumps, the water in the pool renews itself continuously. Public and private clubs share the same elaborate care in construction and concern with providing an attractive setting

We also commented on José's generous offer of this marvelous trip. He was sincerely committed to the idea of having us take home "only happy memories." We certainly were filled to the brim with those, down to the tiny cup of strong and very sweet coffee which was served during the trip, a courtesy of the bus company.

We returned to Santo Domingo happy and tired, finding that our section of town was, once more, the victim of a blackout. This happened periodically in Santo Domingo as the public utilities could not keep up with the city's rapid growth. Water and electricity were often in short supply.

Therefore, many of the suburban homes have huge, underground water tanks. And each household has an ample supply of kerosene or propane lamps, enabling it to cope with these temporary crises.

About two weeks before *Antares* was put back into the water, Maria and I moved back aboard her. I knew that the move was a bit premature but I hoped to speed up the completion of the repairs if I could be at the boat at all times. However, there were some disadvantages to living on a boat, high and dry on land. For instance, the dishes could not be done aboard and the use of the head was out of the question. In my mind, I still can see Maria in the middle of the night, speeding across the club grounds toward the restrooms!

We did though, in some measure, speed up the completion of the work. On the following day the engine arrived, back from some obscure repair shop. I looked her over and found that she was in dire need of a protective coat of paint. I set to it immediately and the next day she was hoisted into the engine compartment.

This was no easy undertaking. I needed all hands available to help. With an array of ropes and pulleys fastened to an adjacent palm tree and running from there to the main boom of the boat, we labored for two hours, until Frieda finally rested again on her blocks. Welcome home, old girl!

It was a great day for us as the lift transported *Antares* to the water's edge and slowly lowered her to her proper environment.

The subsequent days proved to be of a most frustrating nature. Frieda came to life, grunted, coughed, spit and quit on us, repeating this performance over and over again. We discovered that much of her distress was caused by a large amount of water which had collected in the fuel tank through condensation. It was then decided to pump all the old fuel out and refill the tank with fresh diesel. After this was done, one would think matters might have improved. But now we had to turn our attention to the batteries, the alternator, and the whole electrical system.

I knew very well that the two mechanics found themselves often at their wits' ends for they were not professional men. But I did not want to hurt José's feelings by saying so. He was always fiercely protective of the workmen and never brought himself openly to admit the ineptness of some of his protégés.

We did, finally, manage to get Frieda going and went for a trial run in the lagoon. The speed was not all I had wished for. I found that the engine vibrated at higher r.p.m.'s, though we did move fairly well at about three or four knots. I wished I had been able to take the boat out into the bay, but this again would have involved us in a battle with the port authorities.

Each yacht is required to have a special permit even to put her nose out of port. I was satisfied with Frieda's performance and returned to the dock where José was awaiting my verdict. He cast an admiring glance at *Antares* and said, "By God, it is a beautiful boat you got there." Then, "Do you think everything is o.k. now?"

I answered that I thought, it would for the time being. In any case, I could consult a mechanic in San Juan, Puerto Rico. Maybe I could find out there what I could do to improve Frieda's performance.

As long as we had lived at the apartment, we had never been at the club on a weekend. From Monday to Friday it was rather quiet with only an occasional visitor taking his boat out. Saturdays and Sundays the club came to life. Car after car pulled into the grounds. All club employees wore sparkling, impeccable white trousers, T-shirts and tennis shoes. It became a familiar sight to us, as early each Saturday, two of them carefully raked the sand, put up the umbrellas and set up the lounge chairs in a neat row.

To achieve a militarily perfect formation, one of them held a line attached to a tree in front of the club house. The one holding the line taut directed the other to place the chairs along it. It took them a long time to finish it to their own satisfaction.

Most yachts had a regular attendant who, during the week, looked after the craft. Men scrubbed and polished endlessly on these boats. Perhaps once a week, they cleaned the bottom, and they were always available to supervise any repairs for which an outsider had been hired.

These men held privileged positions which they guarded jealously, and they formed an effective patrol at the club. As long as we were guests of the club's facilities, we never suffered a theft or unauthorized boarding. At night, two armed guards patrolled the gate and the grounds. We seldom, if ever, felt the need to lock the boat in our absence.

These week-ends also gave us the opportunity to get acquainted with several of the regular club members. There was a small group of sailors, and it was natural that our interest brought us closer together. Most members of this group had foreign backgrounds and came from Germany, England, Cuba and Spain. Most Dominicans had a preference for motor yachts, which they used mostly during the fishing tournaments, of which several are held annually.

One Dominican family owned a ferro-cement sail boat which the skipper had built himself. They did not do much sailing, except for short trips to La Romana or San Pedro de Macoris, the two ports east of Boca Chica. But the couple and their two children enjoyed their weekends at dockside tremendously.

Very often the whole 'gang' congregated on one of the sailboats, a twenty-four foot one, and it seemed like a miracle that it did not sink with all of us perched in the cockpit and on the cabin top. The owner, a gregarious skipper, handed beer and coke bottles and platters with snacks through the hatch. Those were relaxed days, spent in friendship and close camaraderie.

There was always much excitement when the big yachts returned with their catch; a crowd always gathered around the scale to watch the weighing in. The largest fish we saw was a marlin which tipped the scale at 280 lbs.

The sunfish competitions were an all-day event for everybody. This race was held inside the lagoon and was perhaps the most attractive because the colorful sails dotting the blue-green waters offered such a pretty sight.

Our departure date was nearing. We were anxious to continue at this point for the time of year was just right for it. November marks the end of hurricane season, and the Caribbean Sea at this latitude has calmed down a great deal.

We took on provisions for just a week. I figured on a four to six-day trip to San Juan in Puerto Rico. I intended to reprovision there, especially on canned goods. These are available in Santo Domingo, but the government has put a one-hundred precent duty on all imports, and since most of these goods are imported from the States, Spain and Portugal, it would have meant an unnecessary strain on our resources were we to purchase them here.

We invited Joe and Marty to a last, quiet dinner aboard. Joe, working as a pilot for an airline, flew between Santo Domingo and Miami or New York. He had purchased for me, in the States, some of the boat fittings I had been unable to find here.

He and his wife were putting the finishing touches on a thirty-five foot sailboat parked on the front yard of their home. From Joe's numerous marine catalogs I had selected a knotmeter which proved later to be one of my poorer choices. For the occasion, Maria had prepared dorado fish rolls simmered in a tangy, lemon-curry sauce. The dish was a success. And the leftovers came in very handy at a later date, as we shall see.

Two days later, at dawn on November 2, we cast off our lines. The port officer had brought our departure papers and inspected the boat to his satisfaction. Once out in the bay, we hoisted sails to a light offshore breeze and watched the sun, rising like a gold coin, out of the water. At long last we were on our way again!

This short trip to San Juan also proved to be a test for both of us. We were alone for the first time. Would we be able to handle the boat day after day, just the two of us? I still had not given up all hope on our self-steering. With *Antares* out of the water, I had carefully measured my handiwork, done in the dead of winter at home, and I had found out that the brackets were not mounted dead center on the stern. After I had corrected their position, I was convinced that we now could count on some help from the vane.

For the moment, I was more concerned with Frieda. Not quite an hour out of port, I had not been able to raise the oil pressure above twenty pounds and the r.p.m.'s left much room for improvement. So, I was not overly surprised when the engine came to a grinding halt Maria took over the helm and I went below into the engine room.

I spent all morning there in a fruitless attempt to get Frieda running again. By noon I had to give up my efforts as Frieda came to a last grating stop. I had come to the end of my knowledge and patience. Time for decisions: should we go on or turn back?

By now Maria had brought the sails around, the wind had changed to a breeze and our speed was three to four knots, course 105 degrees true toward Saona Island. So, the decision already had been made. Maria was perfectly happy at the helm and told me she could take the whole day if need be. I then turned to a few other small jobs, such as the compass and running lights. I was amazed how quickly corrosion had set in, doing damage to the electrical system. Even the hinges on our eyeglasses were giving us problems as the metal began to deteriorate from the action of the salt.

Since we were coasting, we could keep a close check on our position. By mid-afternoon we had made forty miles. The log on the knotmeter, however, had an accumulated mileage of only twenty-two. In fact, I had expected this sort of thing to happen. The device was a mechanical one, which transmitted the speed via a coil to the read-out panel. Due to its construction, I had been forced to guide the coil in several loops to the instrument in the cockpit, a method which proved highly unsatisfactory.

For our first day out, I had put in a lot of work. For the time being, I decided to store away my tools.

By sundown we had passed the western point of Saona Island. The wind fell very light and by 2100 was almost gone. The island is about fourteen miles long. We struggled along its coast for the rest of the night and part of the next morning.

With a breeze, we then turned north by northeast and by 1500, Saona Island fell below the horizon.

During my watches I worked to set the windvane, and at times imagined that it was performing quite well. I settled down to repair the clew of our genoa, which had been torn off so long ago when we had crossed the Caribbean from Cartagena to Haiti. We had repaired all the other sails ourselves, after we had searched in vain for a sailmaker in Santo Domingo. But because I felt that the repair on the genoa should be done by a professional, I had left the job for San Juan. Now, in view of the light winds and the failure of the engine, we would need that sail. I gathered enough materials on board for a makeshift repair and worked on the sail until the light began to fade. The night still brought very light winds, but enough to keep us moving at the rate of two to three knots.

At 0600 on November 4th, Maria woke me with the news that land was in sight. This was very encouraging. By our charted course, which we had maintained all night, this could be Desecheo Island, about twenty miles from Mona Island. However, by noon we were becalmed, and I resumed my work on the genoa.

At 1500 a merchant ship passed very close to us. Maria went below and established radio contact with it. The crew seemed very interested in us and we held a lengthy conversation. In parting they gave us our exact position. It was very discouraging; fifteen miles from Mona Island! This was another one of those tricky spots where the currents are strong enough to upset the speed of the boat in light winds. We had steered and made headway only to the east.

Dejectedly, we sat in the cockpit and considered the alternatives left to us. None looked too promising. We would meet with headwinds and currents any way we turned, except west. But, our real problem was that we had not provisioned for a lengthy sail to get to San Juan. And though it was not impossible to get there by sail only, Mona Passage is not easy to negotiate because of the strong southerly set of its currents. On the Dominican coast, there are no aids to navigation and the Puerto Rico side is full of shallows.

Around Cabo Engaño alone, our chart showed not less than six wrecks. Considering all the facts, it seemed to me that to return to Boca Chica was the safest step to take. The freighter was long since gone, and we still rolled in the glassy swell. This was the best time to go for a swim.

I donned my diving mask and went overboard. All around me and close to the surface, a school of dorados circled the boat. This was too good an opportunity to miss. I went back on deck and rigged the line with an artifical lure. The fish came and nudged against the bait but, disdainfully, swam away.

"Pity we don't have live or fresh bait," I said to Maria.

"I have a few fishrolls still on ice," she replied. "Want to see if they'll go for it?"

It sounded ridiculous, but what did we have to lose? There were a dozen fish below us, apparently hungry enough to get caught on anything but a phony squid. We put the fishroll on the hook and lowered the line into the water.

The bait was taken so quickly that it caught me by surprise. I did not react fast enough and the fish made off with it as it shook loose of the hook in two mighty leaps.

"I think they like your fishrolls, Maria. Have you got another one?"

"Just one," she replied, "and you'd better catch something with it. We are sacrificing Igor's dinner."

This one we firmly secured with thread around the hook, and by golly, this time we were prepared. A big one made a dash for it, dispersing the smaller ones which had been making a cautious approach. I gave him some line as he took the hook, but kept it taut and hauled him in. Maria, ready with the catcher, scooped him aboard.

"Noboby, absolutely nobody, will ever believe this fish story," said Maria, looking down at the eight-pounder flopping in the cockpit. I had to agree that this was probably a first in fishing history.

During the night a good easterly blew under a lowering sky and we reached speeds of ten knots. I felt a bit uncomfortable, for I expected to see the Saona light any minute, and decided to lower main and genoa.

With staysail and mizzen I had a better control of the boat. To my amazement I sighted a high headland instead of the low coast of an island. This must be Punta Espada, fifteen miles north of Saona. I tacked the boat and hove to with just the staysail sheeted amidships, and lay down in the cockpit for a rest.

We must have made some headway, for after a short while, looking up, I made out a low shore line to our starboard. I called Maria and together we hoisted main and mizzen. The wind had let up a bit and we steered south to where we could see the flashes of Saona lighthouse, with the coast still below the horizon.

By 0400 the wind had blown itself out, and we crawled along the coast. We made Catalina Island, across from Macoris by nightfall.

Only the next day, by midmorning did we ghost up to Magdalena Point, the east point of the Bay of San Andres. We remained off it until, by 1700, a breeze favored us and we could make the dash across the bay to the harbor entrance of Boca Chica.

As soon as we came around into port, we were in the wind shadow of the little island in front of it. It was very doubtful that we could even reach the pier of the yacht club under sail. In the end, a small fishing boat with an outboard towed us the last 300 feet to the club. Here, the port officials were already expecting us. Several of the club attendants already on their way home, had turned around and come back to take our lines and to find out what had happened to us So, quite unexpectedly, we found ourselves the recipients of much attention and sympathy. Only by 2100 did the last of the officials leave. Alone, over a cup of coffee, we discussed the events of the last five days. In conclusion, Maria and I agreed that we had been happy alone at sea and we were able to handlle *Antares* by ourselves.

José, whom I had called, came by the next day and promised that the engine would be looked after properly. This was on November 7th. On the 10th, a mechanic came, took the injection pump out and disappeared with it.

A day later, two men worked almost eight hours to get the pump back on the engine. José, his aide Cooky, and a third mechanic joined forces until they had Frieda going in a rough sort of way. José then suggested we leave the dockside and take the boat out, if possible, into the bay. He had the necessary papers on him for the trial run. Maria and I felt this to be a premature move, but yielded to Jose's request.

We moved slowly away from the dockside and I thought that the easterly wind was driving us faster than the engine which was running at 1600 r.p.m.

Coming abeam of the port pier, I tried to push the throttle forward to gain speed. This had the immediate effect of stopping the engine cold. And, while the three mechanics clustered around Frieda, like surgeons around a patient, Maria and I rushed to hoist the sails.

But *Antares* is slow in gathering headway and there was that island again taking the wind out of our sails. Both of us started to get anxious as we drifted toward the narrow harbor entrance. The engine, meanwhile, had made a few turns but then died completely. The head mechanic put his head through the hatch and apologetically said, "We cannot get her going again."

By now the strong current had pushed us toward some big rocks and with a sickening crunch, we came to a hair raising stop.

What followed next was something resembling a slapstick comedy act. Only we did not feel like laughing for it was not funny at all. Jose´ yelled at a group of boys swimming nearby, unaware of our situation, to go to the port captain's office and request the launch to come out and pull us off. One of the boys took off at a run but the rest swam to the boat's side.

I had lowered the dinghy, intending to row an anchor out and pull ourselves off. But three of the boys tried to climb into it at once and overturned it.

Cookie, who had jumped overboard, shouted for me to lower the anchor to him, that he would swim out with it. But he went as far as ten yards from the boat and had to drop the anchor. It was, of course, too heavy. At that distance it was quite ineffective to help us.

By now, people at the club had been alerted to our predicament and two motor yachts came roaring to our aid. However, Jose´ and Cookie became engaged in a shouting match with the crews of the boats while I stood helplessly by, unable to make myself heard above the noise of their engines and the shouting men.

Lines were thrown over and fastened to the stern cleats. The motor boats then pulled together and gave us such a mighty yank, that I feared keels and rudder would be ripped off on the rocks. Indeed, on the way to the club's dock I found that the rudder did not respond to the wheel and hauled the auxiliary tiller out of the hold.

But before I was ready to attach it, the motor yachts abruptly dropped the towing lines. Without steerage, *Antares'* momentum brought her right into the piling of the fuel dock, wrenching the bowsprit loose. On the rebound, the stern swerved around and away from the pier. By the skin of our teeth, we just managed to get a line on shore and finally came to rest at our mooring.

José, pale and visibly shaken, went ashore and distributed gratuities to the multitude of men who claimed to have helped rescue us.

The mechanics did their mysterious things to the engine, took the injection pump out again and left with Cookie and José. Maria and I worked in silence, hosing down the decks where the mechanics had left the oily imprints of their hands and the seats of their grimy overalls. Actually, both of us were more shaken by this grounding than we liked to admit. And I realized how really fresh the scars still were from the recent grounding in Haiti.

After a diving inspection, I found the hull and keels undamaged. The rudder post, though, was bent and the shoe which connects it to the skeg was torn off. *Antares* would have to come out of the water again. Worse yet this delay meant that we would have to shelve the trip to Brazil.

José had pressing business matters to attend to in Venezuela and Puerto Rico which he had been putting off on our account. So we did not see much of him for the next three weeks. Mechanics came and went sporadically, taking Frieda's various parts off and going away with them. But, for us, there was not much to do. I attended to various small jobs on deck and worked on the motor of the anchor winch. This caused me some aggravation as I could not find the reason for its erratic function. However, I did repair the damage to the bowsprit, took the runner from the staysail off and replaced it with a block. The stern light which had broken off when Cookie had tried to hoist himself aboard on it, was refastened and the electrical connections checked out.

While I wrestled with fits of impatience, Maria calmly accepted the situation. One evening after dinner, we sat together with charts of the Caribbean Sea in front of us. "Look," she said, "there are so many islands and places to visit. Why don't we take it easy on our way home and take a look at the Virgin and Windward Islands? You know as well as I do that the time has run out for us to sail to Brazil."

I knew and regretted the fact and acknowledged Maria's request for a more leisurely trip. It would be a hard beat, from here to the Virgins, but from St. Croix it would be much easier to sail on a beam reach south. Then we could turn west and sail to Curaçao, for once with the wind and currents in our favor. It all depended on how fast we could set sails again.

But, since neither José nor the mechanics were in a great hurry to get things done, we settled down to enjoy life at the club. We swam every day to keep in shape and on those days when the wind whipped up the lagoon too much, we went into the pool for a swim and did pullups on the diving board. On weekends we joined our friends and on one Saturday I was invited to crew on a sailboat during the annual race. I was more than delighted to oblige for I had never raced before. Needless to say, our boat came in first.

We went over to the reef on one sunny day and I worked at the oars. All I saw of Maria was her rear end; she was endlessly leaning over the stern of the Avon, inspecting the landscape below through an aquascope. "Lot's of fish here," she reported, "and the sea urchins are getting more numerous and much bigger, too."

We left the dinghy on the shore of the small island and walked across it. On the other side, the surf roared over the reef, just yards away from the island's shore. Here, an American motor yacht had met with disaster when it had attempted to enter the port without detailed charts to guide it, at night time. It had finally been pulled off after divers had chipped away from the coral heads from under it. When it was towed in two days later, we felt extremely sympathetic towards its owners. They and their boat in many ways resembled us when *Antares* had limped into port. The yacht was not a complete loss, it was being repaired at the club's boatyard, but work seemed to be proceeding just as slowly as was ours.

The port and part of the yacht harbor had been dredged. For weeks, tons of pure white sand had been flushed through 2-foot diameter steel pipes along the shores of the lagoon, creating a wonderful beach for sunbathers and swimmers alike. To make this recreation area more accessible to the public, several big blacktop parking spaces also were built. These new sand masses yielded a great variety of shells which Maria collected in ever-increasing amounts. Naturally, we had opposite views on this matter. To me it seemed a bit boring to zig zag along the shore in a bent over position which only strained my back. My interest in shells was perfunctory, while Maria's increased with time and eventually became almost an obsession. Yet, I could not deprive her of the long walks along the beach in search of a prized specimen. She not only collected shells, but met people. Two or three teenaged boys were always at her heels, curious as to her doings. They had long talks about our trips and about life in the States and where she had learned the Spanish language so well.

As pleasant as all this was to her, it left me for prolonged hours alone aboard with a mounting desire for food. When she finally returned by nightfall, tired but radiant with her new treasures, my empty stomach gave her a rumbling reception.

Invariably she would ask, "Why did you not make yourself a sandwich?" Good question. Why had I not? The truth is, Maria is one of those women who manage to thoroughly spoil their man. And there is nothing I like better than being spoiled by my girl. After dinner, and only then, would I be persuaded to admire some of her interesting finds, while she washed and polished the lot before storing them away.

Unexpectedly she found an ally, when Chris came to the club one nice day. He had crossed the Caribbean single-handed on his thirty-foot trimaran, presently berthed in Santo Domingo harbor. We agreed with him that that was not a place to stay for any length of time.

The manager of the club had granted him space to anchor and had brought him over to us. We informed Chris that he could get any basic foodstuffs close by and that his boat could not be in a safer place. Then we invited him to have lunch with us and Maria soon found out that he also was a 'shell nut.'

I groaned inwardly as they discussed cones, moonsnails, conches and olives, for this meant more search expeditions and more shells aboard. But Chris was such an all-around nice young fellow that before he left, I had promised him to come to Santo Domingo the next morning and help him sail over to Boca Chica. Unfortunately, Chris and I wasted three hours the next day to get a permit for me to join him. The port authorities turned a deaf ear to our request and he had to leave alone. He set sail at noon and came into Boca Chica at 1700. A good run, considering that he had to beat all the way until rounding Cape Caucedo, where one turns north and is on a beam reach for the last mile into port.

Over dinner that evening, Chris told us that he had been sailing for several months in the Caribbean, sometimes alone and sometimes with friends who came over from the States.

Right then he was fresh out of sailing companions and longed to make a trip home and spend the Christmas season with his parents in New York. I told him to store his valuables with us (such as radio, binoculars and R.D.F.) and I promised him that we would check his boat periodically in his absence. By the time he left, *Antares* had been again lifted onto land. It was December 6th. Exactly one month before we had returned from our first attempt to leave the Dominican Republic for good.

The rudder and rudderpost were taken off and away and I looked after the truck on which they had been loaded and wondered when I would see them again. But, the mechanics were not the same men that we had before. These men knew what they were doing. They turned the engine upside down and found it in dire need of new cylinders, pistons and piston rings, as well as a new gasket for the oilpan.

Meanwhile, the skeg was being repaired by a new carpenter and though he was not much faster than Felix, at least I could see that a neat and clean job was being done. Much to my discontent, in measuring the skeg, I found that Felix had made it a half inch narrower than the original. In fact, the whole skeg had been hanging from just two of its fastenings. Felix had not been able to get the other two all the way through the center beam and had instead covered the holes with wooden plugs.

It was now necessary to fashion a special U-bolt to give the skeg more support. A row of tedious little jobs had to be done as we discovered faults, one lead to the next, uncovering the shoddy handiwork Felix was capable of when no one was looking.

On Christmas Eve, the rudder and rudderpost were returned. The rudderpost had a suspicious looking bulge where it had been bent, and I had grave misgivings about it. The man who had done the job told me that the welding had been done to "reinforce" it. But the measurements I took proved that it would have to be slimmed down to fit into the rudder well.

I was determined to get the boat into the water that same day. As we had been so long on land again, the bottom had to be repainted with antifouling, for prolonged exposure to sunlight destroys its properties.

Maria went over to a group of club attendants and announced, "We need three men to help paint the bottom. Ten dollars each for whoever comes."

"Hey, I said three only," she shouted, as the whole group

started to move toward the boat. They settled the issue among themselves, and the work proceeded at breakneck speed.

By 1700, *Antares* was back in the water. Maria gave me a kiss and said happily, "It's the best Christmas present we could get."

I put Frieda in gear and we moved to the only moorage left in the club. A few yards away from it, Frieda blew her top and sprayed dirty water over the whole length of the cabin. We barely managed to get a line to the pier and avoid a collision with the many yachts berthed close by. This incident made me furious at our bad luck, and I cursed all Dominican mechanics under the sun.

After my anger was spent, I felt depressed and dejected. The club was now silent and deserted; we were the only people there except for the two guards at the gate. Maria slipped away and returned with a handful of poinsettias. She arranged them around a white candle she had decorated with some tiny shells from her collection. With a blue tablecloth under it, the arrangement gave the whole cabin a festive atmosphere. At dinner she tried to console me, but I was still brooding over our misfortunes, and it took me a long time to accept the situation.

My mood did not improve when I noticed my bare feet getting wet under the table. I checked under the soggy carpet and found that water was seeping in through a keel bolt that had not been properly fastened.

"Merry Christmas, Felix."

On Christmas Day, I let Maria sleep in and prepared breakfast, as I usually do when we are in port. By 0900 I was so hungry that I snapped a tape into our recorder and turned the sound up. Maria came to with one of Beethoven's rousing symphonies even happier than with a kiss from me. Indeed to awaken her early in the morning can be a dangerous mission, for the morning hours are not her best ones.

That day, the club was filled to capacity. We had guests on board and visited with other yacht owners on their vessels. All in all, if not our happiest, this Christmas had been a peaceful one.

On December 28th, the mechanic and I worked on the engine again, seeking the origin of a strong vibration which set in each time we put it to a higher r.p.m. We did not succeed, for we did not have the proper tools to check the alignment with the propeller shaft. Nevertheless, we had to go for a trial run. We could not leave without making sure that the engine could pull us out of a tight spot. Frieda was not exactly purring, but she did run reasonably smooth. Soon after we left the dock, I lost steerage completely and we anchored quickly before landing on the mudflats adjacent to the club.

I went below into the crawl space under the cockpit to inspect the cables. I thought I might have done something wrong the day we worked so hard to get back into the water again. I was more and more puzzled, as I could not find anything wrong with the steering assembly.

Then I went overboard and checked the rudder. I found it very loose and could easily move it by hand. Apparently, the rudderpost had broken at the point where it had been bent before and then welded over. I had feared that this might happen.

Bronze is a tricky metal to work with, especially when a large piece is being heated and welded. If not properly done, the metal breaks down and loses its strength. Then, the slightest stress applied will cause it to break.

I was thankful for one thing—that the fault had been discovered while we were still in port. We would have had a hard time of it had it occurred at sea. We motored very slowly back to the moorage, steering with the rudder of the windvane.

That evening, two days ahead of schedule, Chris returned from New York.

"Boy, am I glad to be back," he exclaimed. "It's cold up there and no one can imagine the rat race." We could, and welcomed him back.

Chris unloaded his bags and started pulling out some of the things we had ordered—a complete set of charts from Panama to San Diego, a battery charger and needles for sail stitching.

We offered Chris the leftovers from our dinner, which he was not too proud to accept. As we sat talking, I mused about how a day gone sour could end so calmly and peacefully.

The next day we where hoisted on land for the fourth time and I had a hard time getting the stump from the rudderpost out of the well. I went with José to town and we arranged for the manufacture and delivery of a new stainless-steel rudderpost.

The coming of the New Year we celebrated on *Antares*, still high and dry on land. Chris joined us to carve up a ham he had brought for us from home. By midnight we had downed several drinks and we sounded our foghorn for want of any other appropriate noisemakers. We toasted to a happier 1977.

On January 6th, almost at day's end, were we swimming again.

The next day, Chris and a friend of his who had arrived from New York, sailed away to explore the shores of Haiti. Chris had told us that if he lived frugally, he could keep sailing until June. His departure made me feel itchy to get going—and Maria also wished for a fresh wind and sea. Not that we did not like it here, but we had become so fond of the lagoon, the club and the country as a whole, that we felt only a quick getaway would save us from our growing roots.

Therefore, on Sunday the 9th, we announced to our friends at the club that we had it in mind to sail on the 11th. As usual, we had been boat-hopping and were now, all twelve of us, perched on Toni's twenty-four footer. A heated discussion ensued about the right place to go to give us a farewell dinner. We could not stop the whole plan—they all had made up their minds and settled finally on the Club Español.

We had a marvelous evening at this club, where we consumed a paella in which the rice disappeared among the pieces of seafood, mainly lobster. We toasted with a Spanish wine, and the following speeches just about set us crying. The good-byes were not made easily. But good-bye it was, as we pushed off by midmorning on January the 11th.

We let Frieda run for two hours to charge the batteries and set our course, confidently, once more toward Puerto Rico. Our speed was not as good as on our previous run and we found January to be much cooler than November, especially in the late afternoon, when with a dying wind, we turned to Frieda for help. She flatly refused it. When I went below to check on her status, I found the bilge full of transmission oil. Surprises never ceased, and there was nothing else we could do but drop the anchor. For a moment, even Maria lost her cool and shed tears of frustration.

Two boys in a small fishing boat with an outboard came by, curious as to why we had anchored at such an unlikely spot. They evidently wanted to show us the way to a better anchorage a mile or so to the east. Maria explained to them that, for the time being, we could not move away and asked them to take her along to shore. They soon disappeared from my sight and I remained alone to chew off what was left of my fingernails.

Long after nightfall, Maria returned and told me she had managed to talk to José and tell him our new situation. There had been no phone where she had landed. It was just a small village, seven miles west of San Pedro de Macoris. She had had to hire a taxi which drove her to a hotel four miles farther along the shore, from where she could place a collect call to José.

"They must have been a bit shocked as I walked into the lobby, but the receptionist was quite nice. I do not look too elegant," said Maria, looking down on her shorts and T-shirt. "José will send a mechanic around tomorrow morning."

We settled down for a terribly rocky night. Sleep was impossible, not only because of the terrific noises, but also with the fear that we might yank loose and drag the anchor. Only toward morning, with a slight offshore breeze, did *Antares* settle down and we sleep for a few hours.

José kept his word. A little after 0800 he was on the shore opposite us. He hired a boat to send the mechanic over. By 1300 Frieda was back in shape and we climbed into the Avon to get the mechanic back on land. I left Maria in charge to cruise back and forth and come as close to me as she dared to pick me up.

I was halfway to the beach when I heard Maria call. The engine had stopped again. I had a hard time catching up with the boat, as the offshore wind drove her out to sea. When we finally came aboard again, Maria insisted on keeping the mechanic with us and having him run the engine for at least two hours to make sure we would not be in the same spot again after he left.

The nerves of both of us were getting frayed with one scary emergency after the other, and this was all we could take without falling apart at the seams. But the mechanic was an older and knowledgable man. His manners were polite and calm, which helped us considerably in getting over our case of nerves. He fished another bolt, which had not been properly tightened, out of the bilge and found others just about to drop off the engine. Only by 1600 did we feel satisfied. I took the mechanic back to shore.

During the night and the whole next day we had a northeasterly blowing. The seas were very uncomfortable. We worried about our position for we had only been able to sail east instead of into the Mona Passage. With the heavy overcast, there had been no opportunity to take sunsights.

On the 14th, just north of us, we sighted Cabo Rojo, the tip of Puerto Rico. The wind blew directly from there. We clawed into it with the help of Frieda for a whole seven hours. We had just passed Boqueron Bay at 1500, when Frieda decided on a rest, and quit.

Tinkering here and there and getting dreadfully dirty in the process, I cajoled her into running a bit longer. Across from a nice sheltered bay, she blew another cooling-system hose and we called it a day.

By now the wind had calmed down and we dropped our anchor a quarter mile from shore in thirty-six feet of water.

The V-belt from the alternator was in shreds, due to its poor alignment, and I had to replace it with the old one. The broken hose could not be repaired. I used a piece of regular water hose instead.

I crossed my fingers that my make-shift repairs would hold until we put into Mayaguez. The engine would not run for long without a new V-belt and we decided we could clear customs there.

We cruised until almost 1500 among the shallows along the port entrance until we could tie up at the pier of the free port. We were as good as home, on American territory.

The customs official came along and at first everything was fine. But from the moment I told him we had spent five months in the Dominican Republic for repairs, his attitude changed and he became very businesslike and almost hostile. He informed me that all repairs done in a foreign port are subject to duty and that I owed the U.S. government about $9,000 in taxes. He phoned his superiors in San Juan and informed them of our arrival there.

My head was spinning with all this news and I began to feel bitter about the reception. I put the new belt on and we motored up to Añasco Bay and anchored for the night. Columbus had anchored here on his third voyage to the New World and he, too, had had his problems. I cannot quite remember if he could solve his, but after a refreshing dip to wash the sweat and oil off my body, I felt better.

After all, the man from customs was just doing his duty. If only he had not been such an eager beaver about it! He made me feel like a long-sought-after criminal on whom the law finally could clamp down. Firmly, I resolved not to let it bother me and to wait until I could unravel the mystery with customs in San Juan.

The next morning we started out with very little wind; but it was a glorious day, warm, sunny and very clear. From Punta Borinquen we turned east and hoisted the sails to a breeze from the east northeast. We sheeted them as tight as we could, because Frieda needed all the help she could get. Now and then I had to make a dash below and frantically pump fuel into the filter as she started to slow down and cough. Otherwise she behaved very well and we had time to admire the coast. From Punta Borinquen, for several miles east of it, is a stretch of rugged coastline ringed by reefs and flat topped rocks, called Las Quebradas (The Breakers). The long Atlantic swell rolled and broke thundering over these rocky formations. I would hate to be close to this place in an onshore storm. Today, it was safe to keep a quarter mile from it and enjoy its wild beauty.

We intended to stay overnight in Arecibo, the only anchorage on the way to San Juan. The afternoon was already slipping into early evening as we closed into shore to what we thought was Arecibo.

Nope, we had goofed. Arecibo was still eight miles away and anxiety time was here again. The sun was dipping toward the horizon and the wind had practically left us. I doused the sails and Maria and I just dreaded to think that we would have to put into port by night. In a cruising book, we had found a good drawing and directions for entering the port. But we began to doubt its accuracy as we searched for a glimpse of the light which our chart told us was supposed to be there.

Our luck did not run out. A fresh offshore breeze came up and I hoisted sails again and we raced toward the port at eight knots. At least that is what Maria reported from the bow, where she stood with the binoculars scanning the darkness ahead. I could not make out anything except for a few bright lights, and I hoped that she was right. It was so dark over the water that we almost ran over the buoy we had been searching for for the last half hour.

Minutes later we motored around the breakwater and anchored in a cove the size of a handkerchief. The lighthouse from Arecibo is no longer in operation; it stares with blind and broken window panes into the night.

We left at dawn, not wishing to incommode any port officials, and had an uneventful run to San Juan. The harbor entrance to this city is very impressive with the old fort guarding it from the top of a high cliff. We had our cameras quickly on hand, only to discover that tourists on the battlements had theirs trained on us. We are going to wind up in a lot of photo albums and dark drawers for the next twenty years!

By 1500 we had tied up to Pier 8, where José has his main offices. We found him at his desk, busy as ever. He was very pleased to see us and immediately arranged a moorage for us at one of the local yacht clubs.

CHAPTER 8

PUERTO RICO AND THE VIRGIN ISLANDS

We had a lot of plans for Puerto Rico, and expected to stick to the promise we had made to ourselves; namely, to take it easy.

"Let's not rush in and out of places," Maria had pleaded. "Now we do have the time and should get a bit better acquainted with the ports we visit."

"As soon as we have things settled with customs, I promise you, we will take a bus and go south and visit Ponce and all the other nice places along the south shore."

Since I had to renew the documentation of my boat license, my first step was to go to the Coast Guard offices. The officer there looked at my license and raised his eyebrows. "Did you know you were cruising in foreign waters with the wrong license?" he asked.

"No," I told him, "as a matter of fact the customs officer in the Canal Zone even congratulated me on having it."

"Well, this one authorizes you only to cruise in American coastal waters."

I told him that I had not been informed of this at the Coast Guard station in my home port. I had mentioned there my intention to cruise to South America and had asked if it made any difference which license I held. As I had not been advised to change it I had taken off, assuming that the papers were in order.

Apparently it was not too late to change the license now. I left the Coast Guard office with the new documentation. *Antares* was now a pleasure craft and not a commercial vessel, in which capacity she had never been used.

With this documentation I went to the customs offices where the inspector received me personally. I explained to him why and how we had been forced to make the repairs in the Dominican Republic and the circumstances of our grounding.

He nodded to all this and said, "Just make out a written report and deliver it to me. I do not believe there will be any difficulties in clearing your vessel."

But the relief we experienced hearing these words was short-lived. On returning to the club, we found that two men from the customs offices were waiting for us. They told us that we should present ourselves to a customs inspector the next day. It was urgent. Though both of us raked our brains we could not come up with anything concrete which might throw light upon the subject of this summons.

There was plenty wrong, we found the next day while we were sitting across from the desk of a stern looking inspector. As a matter of fact, the whole thing smelled to high heaven.

My actions of the previous day must have looked very much like a clumsy attempt at tax evasion. The inspector could not think otherwise, for he had the report from his subordinate in Mayaguez, where I had entered American territory with the old license. I had come to his office with a brand-new one, changed from commerical to pleasure craft. I still did not see the difference.

"Why have you changed your license?" he asked.

"Because the Coast Guard officer here advised me to," I replied, and explained to him how the whole thing had come about.

"I am sorry, Mr. Hauser, but you did enter with the wrong papers," he said, adding that any vessel traveling with a commercial license was subject to report and pay duties for any and all work done in foreign ports. Even a yacht came under this law unless it could prove that the work was indeed an emergency repair, and nothing new had been added to the craft, such as radio or other electronic equipment which had not been aboard previous to the emergency.

"What will all this do to me?" I asked.

"U.S. Customs requires a set of invoices for all repairs, materials and the man hours expended on your boat. These should corroborate your earlier statement of $18,000 expenditure for these costs. Meanwhile, I must ask you to post a bond of $10,000; otherwise, your yacht may be seized by customs until the 50% duties on the repair price has been paid."

He added that the documents then would be sent to Washington headquarters, where it would be decided what the fate of *Antares* would be. "And," he added, "please, Mr. Hauser, stay in port. Do not leave under any circumstances."

Could there be any more cheerful news? It was a pathetic twosome that left the customs offices. It was almost as bad as losing the boat on a reef. We did not have $10,000. We did not know anybody who would post bond for us.

On our way home, we stepped into Jose's office and unburdened ourselves to his partner. We sought some advice, hoping that a shipping agency could tell us which way to turn. Jose's partner calmed us down to a certain extent and told us that the agency might consider posting the bond for us if things went from bad to worse.

Of course, he would have to consult José about it. He was scheduled to be back in San Juan on the next Tuesday. This left us three days to worry and chew off our fingernails. It spoiled the whole weekend on which we had intended to be exploring the town and surrounding beaches. On Saturday afternoon, two young sailors from Oregon rowed over for a visit. Their boat was at the other club across the bay. The two young men told us that they had recognized *Antares* from the articles they had read in the boating magazine. We were grateful for this distraction, for our spirits had now reached rock bottom.

I remembered the marine surveyor who had inspected *Antares* in Boca Chica. I called him at his office and explained the dreadful situation I had gotten myself into. I asked him for a copy of the report he had made for the insurance company.

The next day he came by and brought the copy with him. He had been interested in us and the boat and wanted to see how well the repairs had been made. In Boca Chica, while we had been waiting for the boat to be lifted out on land, we had had the opportunity to get better acquainted. We had talked for two hours about my experiences in Haiti. He had given me his business card before leaving and had asked me to contact him when in Puerto Rico. As far as he could see, there was really not much to worry about.

"I know the customs inspector personally," he told me. "He is a fair man. I am sure that there is no case against you. I'll call him and tell him what I know. Perhaps it will help to clarify the situation."

This statement kindled a tiny spark of hope in us.

On Wednesday we conferred with José, who politely declined to furnish us with invoices and statements. Instead, he suggested that we use a copy of the contract which had been drawn up and signed by both of us. All repairs and costs were clearly stated in the contract. He saw no valid reason to subject his office staff in Santo Domingo to sorting out all invoices and statements from his files there. It remained to be seen if the American authorities would find this contract an acceptable substitute.

At the customs office, the inspector's secretary leafed through the documents I had with me and the report of the grounding we had written ourselves. She looked up at me and said, plaintively, "But you have no bond and there are no invoices."

"That is all we have," I told her. "A higher authority will have to decide if these are valid."

She then took the voluminous folder to the inspector and had us wait outside. While we waited, sitting in the cool shade of the gallery around the inner courtyard, we talked about what to do if the boat would be taken from us. Either way we looked at it, it would be a raw deal. Any boat, left anchored and unattended in tropical waters for any length of time, will slowly rot away. We had seen enough yachts along the way, in Mexico, in Panama, even here in the bay.

But to raise the required sum to pay for the duties, both of us would have to return home and work for at least two years. By that time, our boat could be almost a wreck. We had no illusions about the future when we were called once more before the customs inspector.

To our surprise, he was jovial, positively friendly. "I have checked your reports. They satisfy the requirements of U.S. Customs," he said. "Your statement about the license I believe to be an honest mistake." He made a little speech about maritime law and then handed me the documentation papers. "Your boat is cleared. You can go wherever you please."

Numb with relief, I pumped his hand in thanks. We floated, more than walked, into the sunny street. I could have hugged the whole world in my euphoria. I took Maria's hand and marched into the next store and bought some things for her.

Then, we did as the tourists streaming from the cruise ships do. We walked through town and had lunch in a restaurant which had once been the inner courtyard of a patrician home. Tables and chairs invited us to sit under flowering vines. Gigantic ferns grew around the fountain in the center of the patio. Floors and walls were covered with blue and white tiles. There were flowers on all the tables. Two multicolored araras on their perch talked and chased each other with raucous cries which drowned the music coming from the loudspeakers.

The parrots grew more vociferous by the minute until a waiter, impatient with their shrill and scandalous behavior, poured a glass of cold water over them. It must not have been the first time they got such a drenching for they immediately settled down to groom each other, uttering low cooing noises. We could hear the music again and smiled. We smiled so much our cheeks ached!

We went to the fort overlooking the harbor entrance and leaning over the battlements, watched the waves break over the reefs at the foot of the cliff. We looked at the Atlantic and along the coast to the east where we would soon be sailing to Cabo San Juan and across to St. Thomas Island. It felt good to be free of trouble again.

After what we had been through, all the many tedious, little jobs which still loomed ahead receded into their proper perspective. We worked above and below decks, interspersing the days with trips into the old part of San Juan. Our chronometer had stopped and we carried it along for two days, going to every watch repair shop with no positive results. We had to wait until we would be back home. With our alternator, we did somewhat better. A repair shop would rebuild it for fifty dollars, but I found out a new one would cost only seventy-five, so I settled for the new one. I discovered a well-stocked marine supply store where we could buy those items we were unable to get in Santo Domingo. We bought 400 feet of 5/8 line, 200 feet anchor rope, four new fenders, battens electrical bulbs, bolts and numerous other items. In the end, the owner gave us a free ride back to the boat because we never could have carried the whole load.

The old part of San Juan is very well preserved the way it was built centuries ago, but the shops themselves surely have changed. The souvenir stores are bursting with valuable displays from all over the world. Most attractive, however, are the innumerable jewelry stores for which the town is famous. Their products are sold duty free and, therefore, every tourist is shopping here. We, too, enjoyed browsing through all these beautiful displays and I found a nice ring which I bought for my youngest daughter who was to graduate in the spring. We had to find an optometrist as the frames from both of our eye glasses had broken hinges due to the corrosive forces of salt water. We were lucky. We found a well-stocked store where we could get new frames for our glasses. Now we had to buy our provisions.

There was a supermarket not too far from the boat. One of the cab drivers stationed in front of the store took us under his wing. Not only did he help us move the groceries back to the boat, but he also drove us to other stores scattered over the new section of the city. There we could buy leak-proof batteries for the radio and propane bottles for our spare cooker. The driver also knew the shortest way to grocery stores in the suburbs where we could get kerosene. While our containers were being filled, he drove us to his own house right around the corner. His wife brewed for us a strong, sweet coffee. We sipped from tiny, delicate china cups. This was a comfortable and most enjoyable rest. The cab driver was very proud of his wife and their two children, and it made him happy when we commented on his nice family and house.

The buses in San Juan are particularly inexpensive as one can ride from one end of town to the other for about twenty-five cents. We, therefore, used them for sightseeing, taking one long drive out to the airport and another which followed the contour of the beach. We did not see more of the island because somehow both of us felt we should be sailing on.

On January 30, as we were just about to cast off, Don, one of our friends from Oregon, came rushing along the dock. Panting, he told us that his boat was overflowing with fruits they had picked on a trip inland. On a visit to relatives, they had come away with so many oranges and other citrus fruits that they were afraid they could not consume them all before they rotted away. Maria went with Don to their boat across the channel and returned with a bag full of fruits. We were grateful for this gift, for most of the fruits sold in the market were, indeed, very costly.

St. Thomas lies about eighty-five miles east of San Juan. To sail to it, we had the wind right on the nose all day long. Frieda helped us along but demanded much more of my attention than I would have liked. By 2100 she had brought us into the lee of Palomino Island, where we anchored for the night.

When we left our cozy anchorage next morning, we were tired of being a slave to a piece of machinery. We made very little headway most of the day, tacking across the wind and against the prevailing westerly current. The winds fell light during the afternoon and rain clouds hovered over the glassy waters.

A quarter mile away from us, we sighted a whale as it rose high and splashed with a mighty bellyflop back into the sea. Its enormous fluke struck and whipped the water into a white froth, then it spouted several times and sounded. We learned later that the area around the Virgin Islands is a breeding ground and one can meet, at times, whole schools of whales.

We had come close to Culebra Island and we started to look for an anchorage, for I did not feel up to sailing in the dark among the many islands, reefs and rocks in the area.

It will always remain a mystery to us how the heavy and clumsy square-rigged ships of the Spanish discoverers had managed in these uncharted seas. They must have been superb sailors. Today, armed with detailed charts and with aids to navigation, we still feel uncomfortable in close waters like these.

A nice little bay with a sandy beach looked very inviting as it opened up. So we sailed in to spend the night there. However, a sign, planted among the shrubbery above the tide line, warned us that this was U.S. Navy territory and that anchorage was prohibited. With a rain squall approaching, we moved on to a less promising spot along the shore and anchored in a nook where the coral heads barely showed above the water. It was not a very safe place, but we had no other choice. Maria, as always, was eager to explore the shore in search of shells, and talked me into lowering the dinghy to bring her over to the narrow strip of beach.

The hoisting and lowering of the dinghy had always been hard work for us; therefore, I decided to try out a new method I had been thinking of for quite some time. I rigged a sling with the painter of the dinghy into which I hooked the snap shackle of the main halyard. Maria now winched the dinghy off the cabin roof and as it swung free, I guided it over the life line, Maria slowly lowering it into the water. In a matter of seconds, it was bobbing alongside.

I could have kicked myself for the many times we had heaved it over the side, almost breaking our backs in the process. It was so easy with the aid of the halyard and such a logical thing to do, that I could not understand why we had not hit on this simple solution before.

During the night I grew worried as the wind whistled over us, coming down from the hills. I slept fitfully and got up several times to check on the anchor. By 0700 I could stand it no longer. We lifted anchor and moved on.

Out of the shelter of Culebra Island, the wind gave us an enthusiastic reception. The seas were whitecapped and choppy. Frieda labored miserably. One could say she suffered from an attack of seasickness, for she vomited fuel into the bilges at an alarming rate. For the moment I could not do much to alleviate her condition.

With the staysail and mizzen up, we were making the grand speed of about one knot. At this rate it would take a week to reach St. Thomas, about thirty miles away.

And to add insult to injury, a yacht pulled out of Culebra harbor with all sails set and engine at full throttle. It soon passed us on its way to Charlotte Amalie. I looked after it with envy and down at Frieda in disgust. For the rest of the day I had to be at her side, nursing her along, as one thing after the other broke down, came loose or refused to budge.

By late afternoon, with all sails set now, we tacked away from Sail Rock, a bare, huge rock about five miles from St. Thomas. We reached Cabo Virgenes where the current ran so strong against us that it seemed we were not making any progress at all. Maria, at the helm, was tired of the conditions. She pushed the throttle all the way down, and *Antares* shot forward and soon reached a speed of six knots.

Minutes later I just caught a glimpse of Maria as she stuck her tongue out at Sail Rock. We had finally passed it, as well as Cabo Virgenes and had come into much calmer water in the lee of St. Thomas.

Frieda ran much better at these higher speeds, but had a fiendish tendency to overheat quickly and blow her top. Maria, with hand at the throttle and eyes glued to the temperature gauge, slowly pulled her back to the usual speed of two knots.

Below, there had been no perceptible vibration and I asked Maria how things looked topside.

"Boy, all my teeth are rattled loose," she answered.

At dusk we anchored in a small and well-protected bay off Water Island. We liked it so well that we remained there for two days. Then we motored around the island and, with all sails set, rushed through the Haulover Cut into the bay of Charlotte Amalie, the capital of the Virgin Islands.

Swinging at the hook, we looked over the many yachts vying for space in the crowded anchorage. They ran the gamut from the old and traditional to the newest and most modern, down to the derelicts, creaking with age and neglect. Some of them made us wonder what miracle held them afloat.

Our first stop in town was, of course, the diesel engine shop. I had taken along the manifold on which I had patched a dime-sized hole with Marine-Tex. I knew that this makeshift repair could not last long, and left the part at the shop to be redone. The welder did a good job. After I had put it back in place, the mechanic came aboard to find out what he could do to improve Frieda's performance. He found that the fuel pipes had nicks and that the couplings were not tied. The filters had to be renewed, and the connections to the injection pump were leaking. In one forenoon he had it all very well done, and from here on we had less trouble with the engine.

To have these repairs done, we had to go to the pier which belonged to the Holiday Motel. They charge ten dollars a day with electricity extra. For us it was worthwhile. We filled up our water tank and charged the batteries with our 12 V charger. After two days, we went back to the anchorage from where we commuted by dinghy to the same dock. For the privilege of having the tender tied to their pier at a charge of three dollars we could use the laundromat and the showers.

Charlotte Amalie is a pretty town and, like all the rest of the Virgin Island harbors, is very much geared for the tourist trade. Liner after liner disgorges a multitude of people who have come here for a respite from the cold winter at home.

We have always found the out-of-the-way places more attractive and far less expensive. Of course this is a matter of taste and personal perference. For some, the conveniences of a marina and the crowds at the bar or restaurant are by far more important than the solitude of the quiet little bay. But this is one of the nice things about cruising these islands. There is something for everybody to enjoy, according to taste, style and pocketbook.

Until now, we had denied ourselves many pleasures and had refrained from buying anything not strictly necessary for our immediate daily needs. Indeed, *Antares* and Frieda had both been insatiable in their demands and our budget had suffered accordingly. In Charlette Amalie we indulged ourselves, for we could not resist the low prices of the duty-free alcoholic beverages. In general, we do not drink much, especially not hard liquor, which requires ice and mixers to make a really good drink. We favored the shelves lined with brandies such as apricot, cherry, orange and various other sweet nectars. For the colder latitudes we would be sailing to later, we set apart a bottle each of whiskey, rum, vodka and gin. Maria laid in an ample supply of cigarettes, which, being duty free also, cost so much less than anywhere else.

We went to visit Bluebeard's Castle, which is an old tower, all that remains of the notorious pirate's nest. Today, a hotel has been built around it, and one cannot go too close to the tower, because it houses the bridal suite of the hotel. We wondered what Bluebeard would have thought of this arrangement in the remnants of the old stronghold of buccaneer times.

We climbed back into the taxi which we had hired for a sight-seeing tour, and had the driver in a state of irritation, for each time he pointed out an island or bay, we knew the names already.

On the top of the highest peak of the mountain range was a restaurant where all tourists stopped and most every one ordered a banana daiquiri, a specialty served only at this place. I could not find out what went into it but it certainly tasted delicious.

Back in the car we got into a thunder storm. The rain was so heavy that the visibility went down to a few feet and the driver pulled to the side and waited until it was over. It stopped raining as suddenly as it had started. A beautiful rainbow now showed over the sea. We thoroughly enjoyed the trip and thanked the driver who had made many stops so we could take pictures and had pointed out numerous points of interest.

The city is very clean and the back alleys between streets are well planted with all kinds of bushes and flowers and are open to go through. Often, one can enter the shops also from the alley entrances. We browsed through the many shops, which were always very interesting. What surprised us most was the fact that here, on St. Thomas, apparently was one spot in the U.S.A. territory where the colored people had reached equality. We met shop owners, restaurant proprietors, harbor master, post office director, fire-engineers and many others, positions all held by black people. To us it seemed that here was one place where a black man stood on the same level with a white man.

The time had come for our departure fom this lovely port. We were spending more money than was good for us, so we fled the temptations of St. Thomas and sailed on to St. John. Here we spent a night in Fish Bay and sailed on to Salt Pond Bay.

We dawdled in this place for two days, resting, swimming and walking along the sandy shore. Maria, in her steady quest for shells, was a bit disappointed. There were not many worth taking along.

All these bays are good anchorages with good holding ground, mostly of sand and coral. The water is so clear that one can see the anchor twenty feet down. This is one of the best features of the islands, where diving is one of the most practiced sports.

We had read up on the bays of St. John, and Maria suggested we visit Hurricane Hole, reputedly one of the best shelters in foul weather. We set out for it but somehow overshot the entrance and found ourselves in the Drake Passage. There was Tortola Island on port, and to starboard a string of small islands with the unlikely names the buccaneers of long ago had vested on them—Scrub, Fallen Jerusalem, Beef, and Dead Man's Chest. But our detour was worth it. Drake Passage was dotted with sails from end to end. It was one of those perfect sailing days, the wind just right and the seaway kind.

It was too late to sail all the way to Hurricane Hole, and instead we anchored in Round Bay. From here, one can sail straight south to Christiansted in St. Croix, across thirty-five miles of open water. For this crossing, we had hoped, and more or less expected, to find northeast or east winds but, especially for us, it blew from the southeast!

And how it blew! There was not another sail in sight as we beat our way south. Under these conditions, we could not help making some leeway. Around 1300 I had Frieda going for us to hold our course better and charge the batteries at the same time. Later, when the wind eased, I shut off the engine. We hoisted the genoa and for the rest of the way we had a marvelous sail.

We sailed into the harbor with Gallows Bay to port. It was crowded with yachts. But by the time we had made up our minds where to drop anchor, we had passed the bay. We had to make a tack to get back. Just then we lost the wind. I rushed below to Frieda, who remained absolutely silent. My heart skipped a beat. Something was awfully wrong again.

Maria, at the helm, was getting nervous and told me to get the anchor ready.

"We cannot anchor here," I answered her. "We are in the middle of the fairway."

"Well, I prefer the fairway any day to the rocks. We are twenty feet from shore," she said, rather exasperated.

I dropped the anchor, and felt like throwing Frieda after it. We stayed put for the night, a few feet from shore and from the gaily red painted Fort Christiansted.

Early the next morning, the pilot boat came by and the crew ordered us to move out of the way. I explained to him that I had to wait for the morning wind to come up, as we had no engine power.

An hour later we ghosted along and had to do many tricky turns and tacks to make it to the anchorage. In narrow quarters *Antares* is not easy to handle, for she needs a lot of searoom to maneuver in light winds.

This was going to be a troublesome anchorage to us. The bottom is muddy and our Danforth anchor did not hold so well. The owner of a neighboring boat complained we had bumped into them during the night and, tired of resetting the anchor every day, we finally sailed up to a mooring buoy and tied up to it. It was quite a long way to row to the dock of the marina, but we felt the security of the buoy very reassuring.

This time I found that it was the starter which was the troublemaker. I disconnected it from the engine and brought it to a repair shop. For once, I was fortunate enough to have come to the right place. The owner of the shop offered to rebuild it, which represented a saving of one-hundred dollars as against buying a new one. As he was a busy man, I would have to wait a week for the repair and we had to settle down to a quiet life aboard.

Maria's preferences run to walks along the beaches, but to both our sorrow, my back was troubling me so much that I could walk only short stretches. The pain became so agonizing that I had to sit down every fifty yards and wait until it subsided to a more bearable level. So we had to limit our tours to the immediate vicinity of the port, where we could, at any time, sit on a bench or go into one of the countless small restaurants for an ice cream or a coke.

One day we took a bus and ventured to Fredericksted. We found both towns, away from all the quaint little shops, not very attractive. St. Croix once had been the center of sugar production for Denmark as well as other European markets. Today, not much is planted on the island. Except for a few citrus fruits and bananas, all produce is imported and excessively expensive.

Apart from all this, we saw plenty of very happy folks with peeling noses and flaming shoulders, enjoying their vacation in the hotels, bars, shops and swimming pools. Trimarans and glass-bottomed boats take loads of visitors to Buck Island, which is a recreational area. No buildings can be erected on it. The reef extending for miles around the island is a marine sanctuary and ideal for diving and underwater photography.

As most tourists do, we paid the fort of Christiansted a visit, and on another occasion went to the town's tiny museum housed in a building which has served at different times as residence, church and government office. The receptionist, an elderly and chatty lady, enlightened us on one point about which we had been puzzling. There is a vast difference in attitude and standard of living between the natives of St. Thomas and those living in St. Croix. According to her, St. Thomas, because of its topography, could not be as successfully used agriculturally. Instead, it developed as a shipping and commercial center. Its population enjoyed a better education and greater wealth. After the sugarcane boom collapsed, the freed slaves on St. Croix inherited an island with a decaying economy, and they reverted to a more primitive lifestyle. The once sumptuous plantation houses crumbled and the land was left untilled. While St. Thomas still could boast of a certain prosperity, St. Croix languished in obscurity. "Today," she concluded, "the people of St. Thomas still look down their noses at the natives of St. Croix."

In view of what we had so far experienced in the Virgins, we reconsidered our intention of sailing along the Windward Islands. We did not look forward particularly to checking in and out with Dutch, French and British port authorities on each island. Besides, February was almost gone and we had thousands of miles to sail. By June we should be clear of the Baja coast before the *chubasco* season set in. A *chubasco* is a Mexican hurricane.

Maria was in agreement with me that we should sail from St. Croix, directly to Curaçao. And so, on February 25th, we set sail from the easternmost point of St. Croix where we had anchored overnight and shaped our course to the south southwest.

CHAPTER 9

CURAÇAO

Sailing across the Caribbean Sea to the Dutch Antilles was something we had been looking forward to for a long time. Since we had come east through the Panama Canal, ages ago, all that we had been doing was beating into winds and fighting against currents.

Our moment of glory had come at last. Sailing was rough, but fast and exhilarating. I was so happy and excited that I could not sleep. All three of us suffered in some form or another on the two first days at sea. For me it is insomnia; Maria has a problem with constipation and the cat got seasick.

Maria and Igor recuperated on their own, letting nature take its course. As to my problem, Maria suggested a good dollop of rum in my after-dinner tea. I can recommend it. I slept like a log.

The temperatures were, to us, rather cool and only during the noon hours could we steer on our three-hour watches without the protection of jackets and long pants.

Gradually the trade winds increased and with it the pressure on the helm. Still, both of us felt reluctant to reduce sails. On our second day out, and before I went below for a nap, I told Maria to loosen the sheets of genoa and main if the pressure became too hard for her to handle. She grinned at me and taking a strand of hair out of her face said, "O.K., Skipper."

When Maria calls me that, I know she is happy. When she says "Aye-aye, SIR," she is annoyed with me. In our life together, I have learned to gauge her moods by the different names she calls me, some of them not exactly flattering.

Lying in my bunk, I listened to the water rush along the hull. and with Igor curled up alongside I settled in for a few hours of sleep. It was not long before I heard a rending noise, the clatter of hardware and the fluttering of canvas.

The genoa had ripped off at the clew again. I swept blanket and cat aside, went on deck to lower it and hoist the staysail.

The change did not seem to impair our speed at all. Maria told me that she had just reached out, a second before the sail tore off, to loosen the sheet. "What a pity, I was a second too late."

We loosened main and mizzen sheets, which diminished the pressure on the helm, and had a smoother ride.

The seas had increased with the wind also and we had ten to twelve-footers following the boat; nothing alarming, except for a few crosswaves which gave us a good wallop now and then.

I was not to be able to have that nap after all, for coming into the cabin I stepped onto a soggy carpet. The forward head was overflowing. I went to stuff a tennis ball into the neck of the drain to stop the nuisance. A crosswave made the boat lurch and, with my elbow, I shattered the light bulb of the fixture on the bulkhead. For months afterwards, we fished glass splinters out of the bilges.

But that was not all. Walking through the main cabin, I lost my balance once more and, flailing with my arms to find a handgrip, I banged against the stove and knocked down our glass coffee pot. We prized that particular pot simply because it had survived so many attacks on its fragility. It was a minor miracle that it had lasted that long. We gave the remains a burial at sea.

When the sailing is hard and things start flying around our ears, we brace ourselves and ask, what next? And there is never a long wait. That night the compass light gave up on us and I could not get it to light again. We steered by the stars, checking our course now and then with the aid of a flashlight.

Unfortunately, I had handed Maria the one with a built in magnet, which is supposed to hold it against metal surfaces. That magnet did horrible things to the compass. Maria had a few anxious moments at the helm until she discovered what was causing its wild behavior.

Having had ample warning that day, I should have taken heed and lowered the main sail, or at least reefed it, but I did not. In the dead of night, one of the sheet fastenings on the boom broke. This sudden release from the restraining sheet made the boom jump high and lodge between the backstays of the main mast. The strain on the gooseneck was so hard that it also cracked and broke.

I had hours of hard work to take the boom down, put the mainsail away and secure the boom on deck. With the storm main up, staysail and mizzen, we still made satisfactory speed.

It was time we slowed down a bit anyway, for on the next night Maria awoke me ahead of schedule with the news that she had sighted a light straight ahead. As I came on deck, she said, "It must be the light on the northern tip of Curaçao." Our chart did not give the rate of the flashing light and I asked Maria how she knew that it was on Curaçao.

"Well, what else could it be? We have been steering toward it for the last three days," she answered, with typical feminine logic.

I am a terrible doubter. We had a reasonable DR, but for the last twenty-four hours I had been unable to take a usable sunsight. As far as I was concerned, this could be Bon Aire or Aruba or the Venezuelan coast. The light was just above the horizon and, depending on its height, we could be anywhere between two to ten miles away. There was not much to do but to slow down and wait for daylight.

At daybreak, the mountain ahead could only be on Curaçao as it is the only one of the Dutch Antilles with elevations above 1,000 feet. Maria had been right, we had hit Curaçao right on the nose.

We hoisted all sail we could and ran for the leeshore of the island. At last, we found ourselves in calm waters. The wind funneling down the hills screamed over us and put *Antares* on her ear every few minutes.

There were still twenty-five to twenty-eight miles to be sailed, first in a southerly direction and then southeast as the island curved around from Bullen Bay, until we could put into Willemstad.

We never made it.

Up to Bullen Bay, our progress was good and we anticipated being in port by 1700. Staying close to Cape St. Maria, we only received the full impact of the wind as we cleared the point and put into Bullen Bay. It was bullish. The bay was filled with flying mist blown from the top of the short and steep waves. Our headway became slower and more painful with the increasing fury of the wind. I put Frieda to work and lowered the mizzen to put a reef in it. As I rehoisted the sail, it tore a two-foot gash along the reefing points. I had to lower it quickly again before it blew itself to shreds. Without the mizzen sail we would be too handicapped to sail on. We turned about to seek shelter in St. Jan Bay.

In a snug little dent in the coast I let the anchor down. It was incredibly quiet and peaceful here, only the twisted bushes on the top of the hill had their leaves ruffled by occasional gusts of wind. A herd of goats climbed on dainty hoofs about the steep and rocky hillside, their intermittent cries the only sound to disturb the heavenly silence. The air was still and warm, the tranquility absolute. We lowered the dinghy and I rowed to where I had put the anchor down. Through the incredibly clear water, I could see it had set properly. But I also noticed the ripples of currents and counter currents which could make us swing around and into the coral heads closer to shore.

I had Maria secure a line to a stern cleat, the other end I took into the dinghy. Eight feet from the boat was a group of rocks above the waterline. I fashioned a sling on the line and draped it around one of the rocks. We left the line slack—it was just an added security measure in case we should drift about. We checked the line while we cleared the decks. It was quite alright.

After we had taken the mizzen sail off the boom and inspected the damage, we put the work off for the next day. We felt we had earned a rest.

Maria went overboard with my face mask and soon forgot about time, the rest of the world and dinner. Enchanted, she dogpaddled back and forth discovering the wonders below the surface. Multicolored fish flitted among corals or hung motionless among seaweeds of the fantastic undersea garden.

As she toweled herself dry, she mused about all the things she had observed and said, "I can understand now the divers' enthusiasm about their sport. I sure wish we could afford some diving gear."

"How about a cup of hot coffee and some dinner," I asked, to divert her from these dangerous wishes.

"Aye-aye, Sir," was the answer.

The next morning, Maria settled down with the tear in the mizzen, and I kept my appointment with Frieda. By now, we knew each other well. For the rest of the trip the engine would cause us much worry and anxiety, as it always seemed to give up on us when we needed it most. From what I have heard and read so far, this seems to be an inborn characteristic of most marine engines.

Around noon, a car appeared on the road into the cove and

four fellows climbed out of it. First they honked the horn, then they shouted. When they started waving to us, we could no longer ignore them and I rowed over to shore. They were Customs and Immigration officials, just checking who, what, where and when and if we needed any help.

"No," I said. "We are fine and expect to be in Willemstad by tomorrow." They seemed satisfied and drove off again.

I joined Maria and helped her with the stitching of the mizzen sail. We finished with the last fading light of the sinking sun. The work had taken much longer than anticipated.

The next day, by 0900, we were on our way and making good progress; the wind seemed to have lost some of its bite and we hoped to make it to Willemstad this time. We crossed Bullen Bay in one-hour tacks. As the wind increased again, those tacks became almost impossible to accomplish and I started to jibe the boat instead. Though we took the utmost care not to let the mizzen boom come about with a bang, it ultimately crashed against the shrouds and broke neatly in two halves.

I was not about to give up and run for shelter. I took the sail down and put the boom on deck, where I aligned it with one of the aluminum whiskerpoles. I lashed both together, from end to end, hooked the gooseneck back onto its track and rehoisted the sail.

To do all this work on a heaving deck took some time, and meanwhile we had lost some ground. We fought on doggedly and in the late afternoon almost made it to Willemstad. A half mile from port we had to tack away from shore, for the wind was blowing with insane force straight out of the channel from the port entrance. It was infuriating. There was not a safe bay in sight that we could reach and anchor for the night.

Tacking away from the city, we watched as all the lights came on in the streets and houses along the shore. We were so close to it and yet, at this moment, out of reach.

What we did not know at the time was that we were fighting a strong northwest current which sets around the island's shore and, enforced by the winds, reaches a speed of two to three knots an hour.

If we had come via Bon Aire and sailed around the southern end of Curaçao, it would have been child's play to enter Willemstad. Maria had a fit of anger at this embarrassing situation. In her opinion, we were the most stupid sailors afloat.

I did not want to argue the point right then and chose to

remain silent. All we lacked was local knowledge. It was no use to fan the fire, for I had to concentrate on getting us into port in one piece. Maria went below, and after a while I could smell dinner cooking. She came up to take over the helm and apologized for the acid remarks she had made earlier.

"You had better eat now, it looks like it is going to be a long night for us."

I heaved a sigh of relief to find that she had gained her composure again.

It did turn into a very long night. We were not the only ones zig-zagging across from Willemstad and waiting for daylight. Several tankers, freighters and tugboats loomed in the wind-swept darkness, barely moving, but enough to give us one scare after the other when they unexpectedly turned and made straight for us.

By daylight we found we had lost ground and stood now about three miles from port. At 0800 I had radio contact with the harbormaster's office and asked him for advice on where I could sail from our present position. He asked me if I could make it under power.

I told him that our engine did not have enough power to make it against the present conditions, and that the current was driving us farther out. He then told me to hold as close as possible to shore, he would send a pilot launch out and have us towed in.

I was a bit surprised at his offer, but agreed to stand by. Only after an hour did we sigh the launch as it sped toward us, throwing spray high over its bows. When it came close enough, it first circled us, deftly avoiding a collision.

One of the crew threw me a line which I fastened to the bowcleat.

I kept Frieda running and remained at the helm to keep us aligned behind the launch. It might be revealing as to the sea and wind conditions prevailing on that day, that the launch toiled for over three hours to tow us safely into port—not into Willemstad, for it could not fight effectively against the current. It had to take us three miles north of it into the Hilton Inn marina. A guest who was on the dock and helped secure our lines, glanced at *Antares* and remarked, "Had a bit too much wind?"

"You can say that again," we answered in unison.

It had taken us, from the north end of the island to this

marina, almost as long as crossing the Caribbean from St. Croix to Curaçao!

We remained here for two weeks, tied up to the ferry dock, which has a sign with the following legend—DO NOT TIE UP AT DOCK. KEEP OFF AT ALL TIMES.

Apparently no ferry service was in effect at the moment.

We met with many of the guests at the Hilton Inn and though most were happy vacationers, many complained of the never-ending wind. The hotel is built in the shelter of several hills and we at the dock, sheltered by both, listened to the moaning in the rigging by day and by night. It seldom let up for a few hours and then only during the night. It got on Maria's nerves and she welcomed every opportunity to be away from the boat, which was not too frequent.

Extremely strong currents swept the small bay and our lines chafed dreadfully as there were no adequate cleats on the dock and they had to be fastened to iron railings. Nevertheless, we took the good with the bad and our stay here was a very pleasant one.

The harbormaster came by in person to check that we had been berthed adequately and brought all our mail along. I had written to him from Puerto Rico to expect us in Willemstad and to hold our mail until we got there.

A few days ahead of us, another yacht, with the same name, had pulled into Willemstad and he had questioned the skipper closely, for he assumed it was my boat with a different owner. Since theft of yachts in the Caribbean is not uncommon, he had grilled the poor fellow until he was satisfied that it was not the *Antares* he had been expecting. I do not know how the skipper of the other *Antares* felt about all this, but I was grateful to the harbormaster for his alertness, for had my boat been stolen, it would never have gone beyond Curaçao.

A customs official ambled by the next day and once cleared, we could leave the hotel grounds and have a look at Willemstad. It is a neat town, with old houses painted in soft pastels and very, very clean. The port is almost landlocked and on one of its side channels, right along the street, a dozen or so boats are tied up. These come from Venezuela, laden with fresh produce, and supply much of Willemstad's population with their wares.

In every port we found one or the other item which was within our reach. In Curaçao we bought several cans of butter and meat products; in other ports these were offered at ridiculously high prices. Eggs were of good quality, but when I bought a pint of milk in a carton, I hardly could drink it. It was reconstituted powdered milk.

On Monday we had an appointment at the harbormaster's office. I had to sign a report he had to write about the use of the pilot launch for the tow it provided us. I was a bit concerned and had braced myself against a huge bill for this service. To my immense relief, it did not cost me a nickle.

"It's all in a day's work," the harbormaster said.

My good fortune kept holding out for at the same time one of the chief engineers from the Shell Company was present in the offices. He offered to make me a new gooseneck for the main boom. He also provided me with several addresses of lumber yards where I could find the wood for a new mizzen boom. Unfortunately, all of these places were rather out of the way for us, precisely six miles out of town toward the opposite direction of our anchorage.

Taxis are expensive, buses rare, and on foot it is too far to carry lumber. I hauled out our folding bikes and set off for these faraway lumber yards. Maria had offered to come along, but she was out of practice. First she fell off the bike and scraped her knees, right in front of the hotel guests. I knew that she was just dying with mortification, but I had to admire her aplomb as she quickly got up and mounted the bike again.

Once on the road, it was another story. She labored hard uphill, and once over it, found that she had to pedal downhill because of the strong wind. She could not keep up with me since the cars, zooming along, terrified her. In the end she had to give up when a tire went flat. I waited for her, sitting on the curb of the sidewalk. When she came close, she was out of breath and conceded defeat.

"Just look at my thighs," she exclaimed. "They are trembling like jelly. Am I ever out of shape."

I fixed the tire and we agreed that it would be better if she turned back to the boat.

On my return four hours later, she admitted having pushed the bike all the way to the hotel. Poor girl, she could outswim, outrun and outwalk me anytime, but on the bike I was tops.

On this trip I had managed to carry along on the bike the wood for the boom, twelve feet long, a box with a new kerosene lamp, and assorted groceries which included a dozen eggs.

The boom had been roughly cut to my specifications, but I still had a whole day of hard work to finish it. My tools were a small ax and a tiny plane. While I toiled at the dock, Maria sat in the cockpit checking the sails and stitching many of the seams and all the weak points she could find.

We had a lot of onlookers that day. Some stopped on their walks to chat a while with us.

From the commodore of the Halifax Yacht Club, we received a standing invitation to come and tie up any time at their club. People from Seattle and from the four corners of the world stopped by, some just curious and others, sailors themselves, with their own stories to tell.

Another yacht, one of those beautiful sailing machines, had come in during the night and tied up ahead of us. *Victoria* had originally been fitted as a racing yacht. For now, its owners, a Brazilian and his wife, were on a sailing tour around the world. We exchanged courteous greetings, but did not go beyond those, for the owners had rented a room in the hotel and we saw little of them.

From a talk to Gerry, a young fellow from South Africa who was the yacht's crew, I discovered that *Victoria* was on her way to San Diego. Perhaps we would meet again.

The days slipped by pleasantly. We made another trip into town, this time taking our cameras along. From the hotel, the bus takes ten minutes to Otrabanda, across from Willemstad and separated from it by the St. Anna Bay, the harbor entrance. This bay, or channel, is spanned by two bridges; the Queen Juliana (185 feet above the water) is for car traffic. At the mouth of the bay is the Queen Emma, a floating pontoon bridge, which carries all foot traffic between Otrabanda and Willemstad. This bridge is engine propelled and swings open for the passage of vessels leaving or entering the inner harbor, the Schottegat. At those times, two ferries operated by the harbor of Willemstad are put into service and take over the foot traffic.

We combined our picture-taking stroll with a tour through some of the shops. Most of the clerks, we found, were rather indifferent to the presence of shoppers. It may be just that they are accustomed to the large numbers of tourists in search of bargains, or just that they have a naturally aloof attitude. All spoke English and Spanish but the native population's language is a strange mixture of the Dutch, English and Spanish, called Papiamento.

That evening we took advantage of a free movie shown at the hotel. We had seen one the previous week which was supposed to be a comedy but it had failed to tickle our funny bones. This one was a serious movie and had us in stitches to the very end. We had been the only ones left at the end, for the other five spectators had long since drifted away.

As we returned to the boat, still laughing, we found Igor sitting primly on deck close to his favorite porthole, bravely watching over our home. He had greatly enjoyed the stay at a dock, where he could go ashore and get reacquainted with Mother Earth.

That night, Maria was awakened when a dripping-wet cat plunked down on her stomach.

"Why, you stupid cat, have you fallen in again?" she exclaimed, turning on the light.

Maria's bunk was soggy and Igor, blinking self-consciously, had all the appearance of a plucked chicken. He purred loudly and appreciatively as we toweled him dry. We recalled the time he had been in the drink in Boca Chica. How he had gotten himself into that tight situation, we never would know. All I can tell is that I was awakened in the middle of the night by a miserable-sounding howl in the distance. I discovered that Igor was not aboard, a fact which filled me with the gravest misgivings. It took me a long time to find him, perched in the most precarious manner on the bracket of the outboard engine of a boat a few feet away from ours.

Remembering this episode, it was no wonder that on the following night, both of us were startled by his familiar-sounding cry. Some of the late guests of the hotel bar witnessed a strange sight as two half-naked nuts ran along the dock shining a flashlight into dark recesses and calling "kitty-kitty-kitty."

Igor, himself, sat quietly in the shadows, obviously amused at our behavior. After all, he had just been learning a bit of Papiamento from a Curaçao lady-puss.

Antares was almost ready to sail. All that was missing was the gooseneck for the main boom. The engineer who had taken the old broken one as a sample came by one afternoon and unwrapped a beautifully-tooled replica made of monel, courtesy of the Shell machine shops. I was almost speechless: it would have cost a fortune anywhere else.

The engineer waved away my fumbling 'thank you's'. He was a sailor himself, and knew what it meant to me. He even helped me to check and mount the alternator on the engine, which also had given me much trouble lately.

Somebody, at this point, might ask, "Why not throw away that troublesome piece of machinery and buy a new engine?" The answer is simple. I knew that Frieda was still basically a good engine. Her shortcomings stemmed from the inexpert handling she had been subjected to by amateur mechanics.

I am an amateur myself. I hate engines, but I depended on this one and I was getting, free, a full-fledged course on diesel-engine repair! It was trial and error, that's for sure, but in spite of all the abuse Frieda suffered at my hands, I kept her in running condition to the very end.

CHAPTER 10

A NARROW ESCAPE

Sailing time was here again.

As the harbormaster handed me our departure papers, he asked me to send him word from Cristobal of our arrival there. "If I do not hear from you in a week or so, I'll start asking questions." He was serious. He really meant it. I shook hands with one of the nicest and most efficient harbor officals we were to meet on the whole voyage.

By 1400 I had the engine going and the sails ready to be hoisted. It was already March the 17th and high time to be shoving off. I loosened the bowlines and *Antares* put her bowsprit around and away from the dock. Holding on to the stern railing, with still one foot on the dock, I asked Maria to put the engine in gear, then I climbed aboard and let the last line slip off.

In the next few seconds nothing much happened. We were drifting slowly away and Maria, looking over the stern into the water, exclaimed, "Oh, my gosh, I think the propeller is not turning!" There was no danger of bumping into any obstacles for wind and current were offshore.

"Quick," I said to Maria, "let's hoist the main."

The sail unfolded, filled with wind, and we were off. Glancing back, the hotel and the marina had already assumed that toylike appearance things have when seen from the distance. This had been an unceremonious departure. Good-bye,

Curaçao, hello Caribbean.
For the next hundred miles we had to steer a northwesterly course. With east southeast wind and the now favorable current, *Antares* clipped along six to seven knots. The main, for the moment, was enough sail.

The island of Curaçao very rapidly disappeared from sight, not below the horizon but more from the fact that its arid hills are of a light tan color which blended with the flying mist; soon its contours became invisible. Seas, as expected, were rough so to improve the balance, I hoisted the staysail, sheeting it tightly amidships.

By 2100 Maria sighted a plane flying into a landing pattern above Aruba, eighty miles west of Curaçao. This small island, part of the Dutch Antilles, is about seventeen miles long and lies in a northwest to southeast direction, roughly eight miles north of the Venezuela coast.

By 0500 the next morning, the last light on the northern tip of Aruba had slipped below the horizon. During the night and all morning, the winds had been moderate and the sailing good. At noon I estimated a 110-mile run, not bad at all.

We shaped a southwest course which would keep us at a respectful distance from the Colombian coast. In the afternoon, as the wind started to pick up, I took the staysail down. The bolt rope at the foot was coming loose and we had enough sail up anyhow and continued with just the main.

On March 19th the sun rose, a pale and sickly yellow, like the winter sun of the northern latitudes. The horizon was obscured and misty with flying spray. It would be difficult to take a sunsight today. The sailing had not been so good. With the main alone, the boat was not well balanced, and steering had not been a pleasure.

As soon as Maria was up to relieve me, I hoisted the stormtrysail and fastened it to the staysail boom. Then I went about to put a reef in the main. I hated doing it. Not only was it hard work but the result was never quite satisfactory, for the main sail had by now acquired a substantial belly. When reefed, she formed pockets and wrinkles, no matter how tightly I pulled the outhaul.

With the mounting wind and seas, it was vital to have an adequate sail area—too much or too little could be equally disastrous.

With the reefs all in, I finally could start to rehoist the sail. It fluttered violently, caught in the shrouds on port; then the boom came over and the sail lodged itself between the starboard shrouds. I lowered it again, halfway, to free it but as I started to winch it up once more, the halyard shackle came open and ran up to the mast top! I used the spare halyard to hoist the storm main as I had given up the idea of using the main sail. I stowed and secured the main while Maria had a hard time keeping the boat on course during the change of sails. My experiment with the trysail on the staysail boom was not a success. I bagged it and hoisted the number two jib.

"That's much better," shouted Maria from the helm as we rushed on like a bat out of hell.

I was thoroughly worn out by then. I had been working without interruption for the past three hours. But rest was still not in sight. A ship approached, crossing our bow, and I dashed to the VHF. The reply was instantaneous and friendly. After signing off, I charted the position I had been given. This saved me from a balancing act on the cabin roof to take a sunsight which, under the present circumstances, would tend to be of doubtful accuracy.

Too fatigued even to eat, I sent Maria below for a rest and settled down at the wheel. Bascially, and in spite of the tiredness, I was enjoying myself. *Antares* handled well in these seas, the stern lifting easily with the waves. We surfed a bit along with the crests and settled gently when the wave had passed under us. More and more I came to appreciate her performance.

By 1500 Maria took over from me and I finally could stretch out on my bunk. I could not sleep, but dozed off and on. It was difficult to find a restful position, for my body seemed to ache all over.

I awoke with the impression of a sudden and tremendous impact. The air trembled, filled with a deafening, crashing noise. I heard Maria scream, and jumped from my bunk, only to be thrown violently against the bulkhead. My first thought was that we had been hit by a ship or other solid object in the water. I clawed my way to the companionway and climbed on deck.

"What happened, what was it, why did you scream?" I asked her.

Her voice was weak and uncertain. "A freak wave," she answered. "We nearly pitchpoled. I thought we would die right here and now."

Maria was trembling and tears were trickling from under the rim of her sunglasses. I could see how deeply shocked she was and told her to go below and rest for a while. I steered on, still looking about me for that solid object I thought we had struck.

My mind grappled with the concept of a freak wave and I tried to come to terms with it. Generally, one expects such waves in the *roaring forties* but not in the Caribbean.

Later Maria was able to give a more coherent account of what had happened.

"*Antares* had just surfed off a big wave and was in the trough when I happened to look aft," she said. "There was a wall of water towering above us, traveling much faster and higher than the regular waves. At first I thought it would break over us and I braced myself for the impact. The stern began to lift higher and higher though, until the boat stood almost vertical on the bowsprt pointed into the dark trough.

"I started slipping off the seat and that's when I screamed. I was very scared and absolutely did not want to die.

"What happened then I do not know. There was a crash, roar and hiss. Foam and spray boiled all around us, the boat whirled about, pointing into the wind for a moment. Then, like a toy, *Antares* was pushed around once more, the sails filled and she was on course again.

"All was over in a matter of seconds," she finished, rather weakly, as if recounting a bad dream.

There must have been tremendous forces at work for *Antares* to be tossed around twice, 180 degrees. I had no reason to doubt Maria's account and realized that we had narrowly escaped being pitchpoled.

Conditions deteriorated further during the late afternoon hours. *Antares* screamed along from wave top to wave top. I thought it wise to reduce sail, taking down the storm main. Only the number two jib remained. It was to be our only sail for the next three days.

Both of us knew that it was imperative to maintain a regular routine of watches and rest especially under the prevailing conditions. Fatigue would overcome me if I remained at the helm for indefinite periods of time.

Sooner or later, Maria would have to face the elements again. She did not disappoint me, for when I relieved her from her first night watch, she seemed calm and in command of her emotions again.

"These have been the longest three hours of my life." she confessed, "but I am not afraid anymore."

I was immensely relieved by her attitude because now I was confident that, together, we could face anything on the seas.

We became fully attuned to a world gone wild and could almost anticipate a shift in wind or the approach of a wave. There was hardly an opportunity to talk to each other for we had to keep portholes and hatch cover closed. The wave tops had secondary breaking waves which doused us frequently above decks. There was no reason to get things below as wet as they were aloft. But we did not need many words—there was a bond between us, a will to stand up to the elements, to fight and come away as the winners.

It was hard and tiring work; all our senses had to be alert, for the boat, more than ever before, demanded our undivided attention. This state of heightened tension and acute awareness had a serious drawback. Both of us found it very difficult to sleep. Fitful catnaps was all we could manage and we became envious of Igor who slept the days away, supremely confident of the next bowlfull of cooked flying fish. We had seen hundreds of them sailing and skimming above the water's surface, seemingly the only living things to enjoy the turmoil of the storm. Every morning I collected several of them on my regular rounds of the deck. I always found Igor eagerly awaiting me at the foot of the companionway.

On the afternoon of March 22nd, there was a slight but noticeable let-up in the wind. We decided that the little jib was still enough sail, for we did not know if the gale would abate finally or was gathering strength just beyond the horizon.

For the first time in three days, I was able to sleep for a whole hour and felt so refreshed that I unwrapped my camera and took a few pictures of the following waves. Maria then went below and she, too, fell asleep the moment her head was on the pillow.

No sooner had I taken over the watch than I was drenched by two consecutive following waves. Perhaps we had slowed down a bit; it was time to hoist more sail.

During the night and the next morning, wind and waves had subsided considerably. We could see the horizon again. The big question arose—where were we exactly?

For the past twenty-four hours we had held a westerly course and by our DR it was time to turn south. Heavy rain clouds piled up high in that direction, a sure indication of land. By noon the sea was relatively calm, the wind down eight to ten knots.

Maria winched me up the main mast and I retrieved the halyard. With all sails set we skimmed along, enjoying the silence after the hideous racket of the gale. I let Maria sleep and remained at the helm almost all afternoon. There had been no flying fish on deck that morning, and I made an attempt to catch one of the small tunas I had seen jumping for as far as the eye could reach.

I had no luck. Instead I witnessed a smart round-up that the sharks executed with deadly accuracy. The jumping tuna concentrated in an ever narrowing circle, while the triangular fins of the sharks remained at its outer edge. As if on command, they moved into the tuna circle and the waters boiled with the frantic efforts at escape by the smaller fish. Then it was all over, the surface calm and innocent of the drama of survival which had taken place only a few yards away from *Antares*.

The winds continued light. We thought it safe enough to leave all sails up during the night. I rested uneasily and at one point could hear the wind increasing. Maria called, but I was already on my way to help with the sails.

A squall had hit us squarely broadside, but Maria already had brought the boat into the wind.

After I had finished with the sails, Maria pointed toward the south, where the bright lights from Cristobal were reflected from the low cloud cover. And soon we had plenty of company as freighters and tankers moved in and out of the breakwater of Limon Bay.

By dawn, we ourselves slipped into the bay and hoisted all sails to make it to the yacht club. We tacked to the west of the bay and turned about to have a good run, by-passing the warehouses and piers of the port.

But we had not come high enough to make it this time and had to tack to make another try. We sailed this time more to the northwest, crossing the fairway to the locks. At that moment, one of the largest ships we had ever seen and which we thought was on the way to the locks, veered and bore down on us.

Son of a gun, it was on its way to the fuel dock!

We did some quick maneuvering to be out of the way of the black monster. Only then could we make a second attempt to reach the club.

Antares swept across the bay and had gathered enough momentum to get past the port facilities and in the lee of the wind.

The Cristobal Yacht Club is tucked away in a side channel and not easily reached without engine power. Once away from the shelter of the port building, we caught another sailful of wind and rushed up toward the club.

While I took the main down, we just scraped by the bowsprit of another boat. I went forward to prepare the anchor while Maria guided us into the tiny anchorage off the club's fuel dock. The chain rattled, Maria lowered the mizzen and let go of the jib sheet.

Well done. That was good teamwork. Later, we were told that the entire crew of the racing yacht *Ondine* had cheered and clapped at our maneuver. We had been too busy to hear anything of the sort.

The anchor alone was not enough to hold us safely in such a narrow space. We tied a line to a buoy and another to the fuel dock, to keep us from bumping into our neighbors While I was at it, a young fellow came along and helped me get the lines across. To our surprise, the first person we met in Cristobal was a Seattle native. The world seemed to be getting smaller by the minute.

Maria was happy to come away from what she called "the Caribbean's bag of tricks."

I felt a twinge of regret. The sailing had been grand and I knew it would be a long time before we found such good winds again. But we did indulge in a bit of conceit, for we had managed this last crossing without any damage to the boat.

"We must be learning something, after all," was Maria's comment.

The yacht *Victoria* put into Cristobal three days later. She had made the passage from Aruba in five days and the crew had not experienced the same conditions as we had encountered. Its owner, a gregarious skipper, invited us for "happy hour" and we renewed our acquaintances since our first meeting in Curaçao. The salon was filled with several other sailors, and under the influence of the excellent drinks, the stories flowed easily from loosened tongues.

We listened spellbound to two Scandinavian young men, telling how they had fought for twenty-three days to reach Cristobal. Just one day out of Aruba, the rudder from their thirty-seven foot boat had broken. After the engine failed, they used a sea anchor and the sails for steerage. Theirs had been a special kind of endurance!

A new rudder already had arrived from Sweden and had been installed, but the engine still had not been returned from the repair shop in Colon. It was apparent that in Panama things did not get done any faster than in the Dominican Republic. In any case, we took our hats off to them, and secretly, the chip off our shoulders!

As much as I loathed the prospect, I had to turn my attention to Frieda again.

Since I suspected the transmission to be at fault this time, I laboriously took it apart and found not a thing wrong with it. I probed a bit further and out came the clutch with broken bits and pieces. I had found the culprit. Maria and I set out to find a new one in Colon or a place which could repair the old one. By day's end we had met with several very nice and interesting people but still had no clutch.

At the club we met a guy called Yogi and Yogi the Bear he was. Stout, heavy, and sporting a dark beard, but as it turned out, with a heart of gold. He was one crew member of the *Whimsey*, bound for Los Angeles via Hawaii. Presently, their boat was anchored on the mud flats across from the club. He was in search of one more lineman, as they were three crew members besides the captain. As I had it in mind to go to Panama City anyway to hunt for a new clutch, I agreed to help them through the canal.

The next morning we had quite a bit of wind and rowing in the darkness over to the *Whimsey* was quite a challenge. Maria had to row the dinghy back and she had the wind directly ahead of her. But I knew she would make it safely back. She could row excllently as she had been a member of a rowing club during her ten-year stay in Germany.

The passage through the canal went very smoothly and was absolutely enjoyable. The captain, Paul, was a very nice soft-spoken man, and one of the other crew members, it turned out, was Yogi's wife, Greta. She was tiny and slim, and just the opposite of her at least 200-pound husband. We had a very simple dinner that evening, because they were almost out of food. They had a slow passage from Jamaica to Cristobal and their cash was short, too. It was late when we finally went into our bunks.

Next morning, the first thing to do was to go to the bank. By coincidence, Paul expected his money at the same bank that I did. My check was there but his was not. Somewhere, something had gone wrong. As I had more than I needed at that moment, I gave him enough cash so that he could buy all the groceries he needed.

Afterwards, I took a bus to Panama City where I hired a taxi and though I do not speak Spanish, the driver quickly caught on when I showed him the clutch I carried in my parcel. He knew just the right place.

Five hours later, the driver had grown progressively frustrated, much more than I could say for myself. He had criss-crossed the city from end to end. At each stop I had met with only negative head shakes, but at each shop I had been given another address until we came full circle and there was no place left to go.

My last recourse was to phone my daughter in Seattle and have her send a new clutch to Balboa. When it would arrive was something only the gods knew. Until it did, the question remained open as how to get *Antares* from Cristobal to Balboa. A tow by one of the Panama Company's tugs, which occasionally go through the locks, was, financially, out of reach for us.

During my absence, Maria had met and talked to one of the Cristobal club's carpenters. One of his friends was the owner of a machine shop and apparently was able to make our repairs. I grew very doubtful about the whole thing when the machine-shop owner drove us the next day to his place. He parked his big, American-made car among a collection of ramshackle buildings and walked ahead of us in the direction of a shack which looked as if it would not survive the next puff of wind.

To my amazement, the shack contained a row of very modern machines and the place hummed with activity. Our man placed the clutch on a workbench and explained to one of the workmen what had to be done with it. He then turned to me and said rather proudly, "We can fix anything here."

Behind his back, Maria crossed her fingers and sent a glance heavenward.

Two days later we had the clutch back; the job had been very well done. It was amazing what could be done with a piece of derelict engine part if one found the right place. However, I was baffled at the bill—it was double the price of a new one.

But such are the tribulations a skipper may encounter along

the way. In some ports one can get things done for free, and in others he can be grossly overcharged. One grows philosophical about such things. We found that our expenses evened themselves out nicely in the course of the voyage. I set to work to put the clutch back in and when I finished, the propeller turned again.

On April 4th the crew of the *Whimsey* boarded *Antares*. They had come by train from Balboa to return my favor and now crew for me as linemen.

To our delight, the same pilot, Bill, who had taken the *Whimsey* through the canal, had been assigned to *Antares*. I was especially grateful to have a pilot aboard who was an avid sailor and magnanimously overlooked Frieda's poor performance. With Bill's happy disposition and a compatible bunch of linemen along, the whole crossing turned into a lark. Maria kept us all well supplied with outstanding food and drink, a fact very much appreciated by everybody on board. On Gatun Lake we had such good wind that Bill allowed me to hoist the sails. We made better headway under the sail than with the engine power.

We had a terrific afternoon sailing across the lake. The wind favored us all the way to the Gaillard Cut. Here we had to lower the sails and *Antares* crept under power at three knots toward the first lock on the Pacific side of the canal. By 2300 we tied up at our buoy at the Balboa Yacht Club. The transit had taken eleven hours. Bill did not seem to mind a bit, and if he did, he never let on. On leaving he especially thanked Maria for the good food and we parted as good friends.

Word came from my daughter in Seattle that a new clutch had been shipped and should be at the airport of Panama City on a certain flight. As our efforts to contact the airline agency failed repeatedly, we decided to make a trip to the airport.

We boarded the bus in town at the worst possible time. School was out and the buses were crammed with high-school kids on their way home. The airport is miles from the city and it took the better part of two hours to reach our destination. We had to stand most of the way, but all Panamanian buses are radio-equipped and music pours out at the highest possible level. All teen-agers aboard the bus were acquainted with the lyrics and they sang, whistled and tapped their feet to the rhythm of the music. The noise was ear-splitting. When we finally got off the bus at the airport, Maria shook her head and twirled her fingers in her ears.

"My word," she sighed, "I thought I was going deaf in there."

We waited patiently at the desk of the shipping agency until the clerk gave up his search and told us that our parcel had not yet arrived from the States.

"You should have called us," he said.

We told him we had.

"Oh, I am sorry," he replied. "Here is our schedule. We open only at certain hours of the day."

The bus which took us back to town apparently had some clutch problems, too. It ground its way from bus stop to bus stop, stalling frequently, and the riders started to make derisive comments to the driver. Ultimately the bus broke down altogether, and we had to change transportation halfway to the city. One thing nice though!—we did get our money back. I felt sorry for the driver, he looked so frustrated and forlorn, as one let down by his best friend.

The Easter holidays were upon us. Stores and public offices would be closed for four days, from Good Friday to the next Tuesday. We celebrated the occasion in our own fashion, taking *Antares* across from the club to beach her for a much-needed bottom cleaning.

When the tide had run out sufficiently, we went overboard and stared in disbelief at the bottom of the boat. From bow to stern, it was evenly covered with a one-inch layer of grayish-whitish coral. There were few barnacles; just that gritty concrete-like growth.

We hacked and scraped away at it for eight solid hours. It was both arduous and tiring work. Moreover, this time there was no Manuel to help or distract us. Ignoring the protest of our sore muscles, the next day we attacked the rest of the growth on the bow section. From the tidepools nearby, we hauled buckets of clear seawater to wash the hull and by 1400 we had progressed so far that I could start painting.

Maria deserted me at this point for a walk on the beach. When she returned, she emptied the seashells from the pockets of her shorts and joined me in putting the finishing touches of antifouling around the aft section of the boat.

With the incoming tide lapping at my feet, I still found time to go over the hull with white paint. It might be of interest to tell that most of the barnacles we had scraped off *Antares*' keels the year before, are still distributed all over the beach, some alive and well.

We returned the next day to the club and filled up with water and fuel. The club secretary gave me a message that the clutch had arrived and was now at the Customs House. To clear it, I had to go to the Trade Center and fetch the clearance papers for it. This office is situated at the other end of Panama City. By the time I had gone there to fetch them and returned to the Customs office in Balboa, it had closed for the day. We had planned to leave early the next morning; therefore, I was at the Customs House when it opened at 0700.

For one more time I went through the mill of bureaucracy and fretted not a little, as the parcel seemed to have been lost among thousands of others. Finally I held the precious thing in my hands. By now it had cost me as much as one made of gold.

I remounted my bike, pedaled back to the club and was aboard by 0830. Maria helped to get parcel and bike on deck and said, "Good, you got it. Let's celebrate. Breakfast is ready."

We checked our charts once more for the course to Punta Mala for by now we had to forego our intended visit to the Pearl Islands. Time and financial considerations forced us to desist from the planned sidetrip to the archipelago.

The Panamanian government demands that visitors have visas, and yachts need a special permit to make stopovers at any of the islands. The permits are issued for a fee of $50, a sum we could not spend at this time. We had a bit over $100 with us, which would, hopefully, cover our stay in Golfito, Costa Rica.

Running with a nice northerly wind, we steered for Taboga Island. How fast we were sailing was anybody's guess for the knotmeter had gone on strike. But nothing else mattered as much as being on the way again.

CHAPTER 11

COSTA RICA

We had left Taboga and Tabogita Islands behind, as well as a row of other minor islets and assorted rocks. Just below Punta Chame we pulled our first tuna out of the water.

From this point, if one steers straight south, Punta Mala will be to starboard at a safe distance.

But we did not reckon with the currents in the Gulf of Panama, for at 0200 Maria awoke me with the news that the light from Punta Mala was visible already, but several miles to port.

This meant a long night for me again. We had to steer southeast, thus coming into the shipping lane. Around Punta Mala all ships coming and going to the canal tell each other "Hello" and "Good-Bye," which is nice but unnerving for my first mate.

We had a lot of company that night, which I spent in the cockpit for the greatest part of it. By 0600 the point was about a mile away and I thought that with the light wind, Maria very well could handle the boat alone for a couple of hours.

I had just undressed and savored the moment of being in my bunk at last, when I had to wave good-bye to it. The point was not through with us yet.

From one minute to the next the wind shifted to the northeast and gained a velocity of thirty knots. With all sails up, this was no joke. We were lucky that I had not put up the genoa, also. The sudden gusty wind would have laid us flat on our ear.

I took the mainsail down quickly and had a look around. How fast the calm morning had changed, and how fast the wind had whipped up the seas to a heavy chop. Maria was sure that we could now ride it out comfortably with jib, staysail and mizzen. Finally, I could keep that date I had with my bunk.

From Punta Mala we followed the coast to Morro Puercos where the northeasterly petered out and a southwesterly greeted us. It blew with intermittent force and by late afternoon we had not gained much ground. After a spectacualr sunset the wind died down completely. We had come to that part of the Panamanian coast where winds are rare and very light.

Off and on we lost sight of land, difficult to distinguish because of a heavy layer of haze over the mountains. The next two days were overcast and we had little chance to take sunsights.

Our course was roughly northwest toward Isla Coiba and we assumed that we had come to its southern shore when we sighted land one morning. We steered toward it, changing course to the north to verify our position. We were sure to have cleared Punta Mariato but had been adrift for most of the night and the sight of the coast was therefore even more surprising.

"Things do not look right," Maria said. "Besides, there is land to the east, also."

Half an hour later, after checking charts and the *Sailing Directions*, there was no more doubt in our minds. This was Isla Cebaco.

"Since we are here, why not sail around it?" asked Maria. "There is no reason to let the scenery go to waste."

I felt agreeable to the idea, for a light offshore breeze had come up. The island is fifteen miles long, hilly, and densely covered with lush vegetation. We spent most of the day circumnavigating it, finding it very attractive and well worth the time.

To the northwest of the island is another smaller one, Isla Gobernadora, which we left to port as the passage between the two islands did not look too promising. To the north there was the rocky and indented coast of the mainland. Ahead to the west and thirty miles away, the northern tip of Isla Coiba. Off this point lies Isla Rancheria and northwest of it, Isla Canal de Afuera, leaving a five-mile-wide channel open to the west northwest toward Punta Burica.

I felt uncomfortable and confined, as always when in waters where local knowledge is a must. Maria felt confident, though, and I was amused by the fact that our roles were reversed that night. It should be a memorable one, for above the mountains of Coiba Island a thunderstorm was brewing and we soon could hear it rumble in the distance.

The night turned velvety black and oppressive. The lightning flashes which had kept themselves over the mountains, started to intensify as they moved over us toward the mainland. Indeed, they became so intense and bright that we had to close our eyes at each hissing flash. For a brief moment the low hanging clouds, illuminated by the lightning, had the appearance of land nearby, which made us strain our ears for the sound of waves breaking on shore. But there was nothing else; only a gusty wind which changed direction, blowing from opposite quarters every few minutes. This kept us busy tacking to and fro until, quite suddenly, we could distinguish the halo of a light among the hills of Isla Coiba. Whatever we did, that light had to remain to port or aft of us no matter where the wind came from.

Toward 0300 the elements calmed down considerably, the wind steadied and the expected downpour never did materialize.

At 0600 I went on deck in time to see Isla Rancheria, still wrapped in morning mist, ahead of us. Everything was all right. We had contemplated sailing between Coiba and Rancheria Islands, but a close check through the binoculars convinced us that it was impossible. The islet is connected to Coiba Island by a rocky reef with vicious-looking black teeth sticking out of the white surf. I must mention here that our chart is not very accurate on this point, as it shows a twelve-fathom passage which, to us at least, was not visible.

We sailed all day with light but constant winds. The storm from the night before had swept the sky clean. The air was so clear that the many small islands to the north of us were sharply outlined against the horizon. For the better part of the morning, I took bearings with the headbearing compass and had a close check on our position.

Our course was northwest until reaching eight degrees of latitude, where we would then change to west toward Punta Burica. In contrast to her confidence of the previous night, Maria fretted all afternoon, searching the horizon for a sign of the Islas Ladrones. Her worries were laid to rest when she found their rocky pinnacles at sunset ranging to the south southwest.

"This will make for a restful night," was her comment.

We rounded Punta Burica early in the afternoon of the next day. It looked very different from the last time we had been there. Today, an angry surf broke heavily on the shore of the small island and on the reef which connects it to the peninsula. This forced us to give it a wide berth to the south and keep to the deep water two miles offshore.

Golfito, our next port of call, was roughly fifty-five miles away. With the vanishing winds went our hopes to make port that same day. We ghosted all night in the general direction of Punta Banco, the eastern point of the entrance to the Golfo Dulce.

The morning came, hot and windless, the point two miles ahead.

We resigned ourselves to having to motor the rest of the twenty-five miles into port. But luck was with us. A southerly wind came up and the sails unfolded to it in no time. I even hoisted the genoa, which I had been repairing during my off watches and which I had not quite finished yet.

This turned out to be a most enjoyable sail. *Antares* pulled ahead over the smooth waters, gliding past golden sandy beaches, palm-fringed and watched over by densely wooded hills and mountains. It was so beautiful that we almost regretted the moment as the entrance to the landlocked harbor came in view. We pulled the sheets in and on a broad reach skimmed into the bay.

By 1500, and far ahead of our ETA, the anchor was down and boat and crew at rest. For a while we just sat in the cockpit and drank in the surroundings. Both of us already knew that it would be very difficult to leave this bay. Somebody who had been here before us had told us "Golfito is muggy."

This is correct. At times it is, when the south wind blows. For as long as we stayed there, we had mostly breezes from the north and the occasional downpours did not bother us in the least. Whenever they happened to come, we were always ready with soap and a towel.

One night we had to rescue our dinghy, for it had filled two thirds with rain water and was almost awash. Usually, we left it standing right side up on the cabin roof so Maria could use the rain water which collected in it for rinsing out our clothing.

There were no authorities interested in coming aboard and though we tried several times to see the harbormaster, we never set eyes on him. He was always somewhere else. The only official to ask permission to board us was a man from the Health Department, who checked our boat for possible breeding places of mosquitoes. Since malaria is endemic in many of these parts, the Costa Rican government has made an all-out effort to control the disease by a careful check on all possible sources of infection.

Our boat received a clean bill of health and it did not cost a penny. The official had anticipated our reaction to this wonderful news.

"What? You mean we do not have to pay for the inspection?" I asked.

"No," he answered, smiling. "In this port you do not have to pay for any service."

We told him of our experience in Puerto Armuelles and he knew of many yachtmen who had gone through the same mill we had.

"Panama is a country governed by the military who always need lots of money," he said. "Costa Rica has done away with the armed forces and uses the money, once destined to maintain them, for educational purposes and such actions as controlling tropical diseases."

We thought this to be about the wisest decision such a small country could make. There were many more nice things to be learned about Costa Rica, and as the days passed we became so beguiled by its people and its beauty that the wish to remain here became almost overpowering. Had it not been for pressing business matters I had to attend to personally, we would have taken up residence then and there in Costa Rica.

From our anchorage in the immediate vicinity of the commercial pier, we could once more observe the loading of the banana boats. Since the train which brought the fruit to the pier often had passenger cars attached to it, we inquired about the possibility of a ride through the country.

On a Sunday afternoon we embarked in the somewhat rickety passenger train for a round-trip which would take us along the "banana belt" of the region. Soon the 'train inspector,' as he called himself, discovered the two strangers aboard and sat down beside us. He derived obvious pleasure from our interest and spared no effort answering our many questions. It was thus that we came to know a bit more about the harvest, packaging and shipping of bananas. The fruit is harvested only a day ahead of the scheduled arrival of a banana boat. The single bunches, as we find them in our supermarkets, are wrapped in plastic bags and packaged in cardboard boxes. These are loaded onto the waiting trains and are transported immediately to the pier, where they are placed by conveyor belt into the refrigerated holds of the ship.

The sooner the green bananas are stored into the hold of the ship the better. No fruit is shipped that has been two days or longer in the boxes. If a ship should be late to take on its perishable cargo, a new crop is harvested. We asked what happened to the fruit which could not be shipped out; was it wasted? Apparently not, for it was sold locally or processed for marmalade.

As the train wound its way through miles of banana plantations, we observed that all the green banana trunks had been wrapped in plastic bags. First we thought that this might be a means to hasten its ripening, but our new-won friend told us that the plastic protected the fruits from insects, especially a certain kind of wasp.

Conversation was difficult but not impossible in the noisy compartment, which was filled with people trying to make themselves heard above the clatter of the train.

There was a half-hour wait at the end of the line in a small town close to the Panamanian border. The area around the station had all the aspects of a frontier town.

The train inspector joined us for a refreshment at one of the barnlike establishments where he insisted on paying for our drinks. By now we had become his guests on the train as well and he would not let us pay for the fare back to Golfito.

A rain shower had overtaken us, leaving the countryside sparkling in the late afternoon sun. The land is so green and so obviously fertile that except for the dirt roads there was hardly a patch of bare soil to be seen.

Alternating with the light green of the banana trees are row upon row of very dark green stands of palm trees. Their bright red, cherry-like fruit hang in large clusters and are used to process a locally-used cooking oil. The remnant of the pressed fruit is used then as feed for swine.

By the time we ran out of intelligent questions, the conversation had turned to more personal matters. The train inspector told us all about his kids and wife and was not a little proud that at the moment a member of the American Peace Corps, a young nurse, had set up quarters in the family's home and was actively participating in its daily life. He was especially happy about this opportunity to have a guest from the States at his home, for one of his teen-aged sons could practice and learn English while teaching Spanish to the American.

When we told him how we had fallen in love with his country, he warmed to the subject and informed us that the Costa Rican government highly favors and facilitates the influx of retired Americans and Europeans. It stood to reason that such a clever move could only be of benefit to the country. Retired people do not seek jobs nor intend to add children to the growing population. More likely they will provide jobs for unskilled and skilled labor in the form of household and garden help.

Economically, retired families are a good asset to any community. We had a lot to think about when we returned late to *Antares* and to Igor, impatiently awaiting us from his perch on the main boom.

The next two days we had to devote to *Antares*. Frieda had been making highly disagreeable noises, and I thought it wise to install the new clutch. By now I was so familiar with every nut, bolt and part that I did not waste too much time on this job. It had been high time, though. The old repaired clutch was on its last leg.

A much more knotty problem was the knotmeter (pardon the pun). We were sorely in need of a dependable speed indicator, for it is difficult to judge how fast a boat is sailing, especially when there is no land in sight.

Our sail from Balboa to Golfito had taken exactly one week, which gave us an average daily run of fifty miles. Not very encouraging. Therefore, I planned for us to sail as far west and away from the coast as possible until we found more favorable winds. This in turn meant many weeks at sea where we had to keep an accurate DR based on our daily mileage.

Antares was easily beached a few yards east of the pier. There was no growth on the slick, newly-painted bottom and the propeller from the knotmeter was intact and clean. I then found that the cable which runs from the tiny propeller to the dial housing and counter was broken in half.

This posed another problem, for I was left with a length of only six feet of cable. After many measurements and practical considerations, I found a place for the dial inside the cabin. I installed it in the housing below the tell-tale compass.

The provisioning was no problem, for Golfito has a produce market as well as a regular supermarket. The problem was to buy sensibly and use the rest of our money wisely. We always found that there was a gap between the things we needed and those we wanted.

Our fare aboard had in no way been monotonous for, so far, we had never been longer than three consecutive weeks at sea without entering port. This had enabled us to replenish and complement our meals from canned goods. Our diet had been varied and, in my opinion, healthy.

In Balboa we had bought a sack of grapefruits one of oranges and a whole flat of semi-ripe tomatoes. It had been no special hardship for us to keep ahead of spoilage, only two grapefruit and four oranges had gone overboard. Citrus fruits are the best thirst-quenchers in these hot latitudes. And they kept well in the airy compartment I had built especially for this purpose in the bow.

On the whole trip we seldom regretted the lack of refrigeration aboard. Maria found ingenious ways to conserve foodstuffs and to cool our drinks. She wrapped a wet towel around a container of fruit juice or tea and left it overnight on deck or in a shady nook in the daytime.

We had adapted easily to the more primitive lifestyle aboard, and found countless ways to make life comfortable. The independence from electrical or electronic gadgets not only gave us a sense of freedom but their absence sharpened our wits and ingenuity when major or little every-day problems threatened to disturb our peace of mind.

It was here in Golfito, more than anywhere else, that I realized the time had come in which I did not have to continuously fight head on or work myself every day into exhaustion.

Maria, who has a much more introspective view of life, had long tried to influence my thinking and had always wished for me to slow down the hectic pace I was so accustomed to. But, it is not easy for a man like me to learn to relax. By that, I do not mean to grow lazy or practice procrastination and let things slide. I rather think that I learned to appreciate a good rest between the "sooner" and the "later," without feeling guilty about it.

Perhaps I had been a bit scared, too, of the image of the old retired man who slowly slips into apathy and wastes away the rest of his life in a rocking chair. The trick was to find the middle road between the two extremes.

I think I have.

As much as we regretted it, we had to set sails and leave 'paradise' behind. On April the 26th, much too soon for our taste, Golfito fell astern as we moved into the Golfo Dulce and set course for Cabo Matapalo, its western entrance.

CHAPTER 12

BOOBIES ON THE BOWSPRIT

Outside the Golfo Dulce flukey winds greeted us warmly. The sailing was slow at an average of two knots, and a black cloud had nosed about the horizon to the south all day.

Before sunset, the squall started to move toward shore and us. Its approach was rapid and inexorable. From the ragged cloud edge of the fast-moving front, a dark funnel snaked and twisted to the water's surface. The sight was awesomely beautiful and somewhat paralyzing.

I always had admired the dramatic photographs of such twisters published in books or magazines. Therefore, my first instinctive reaction was to lift the camera to my eyes and take pictures.

Meanwhile, Maria grew anxious at the helm, begging me to start lowering the sails.

"That thing is moving toward us," she said. "Just look at the turbulence at its base. It will tear us apart the moment it hits."

My picture-taking had not lasted longer than two minutes. The funnel was now less than a mile and a half away.

I handed Maria the camera, saying, "Here. Take it below and stow it well. Get Frieda going, and secure things lying about in the cabin."

While Maria did as told, I started to pull the sails down and lashed everything lying about loose to the decks. I not only had admired the pictures of twisters, I also had read the reports which had accompanied them and was fully aware that we could suffer severe damage should we remain in its path.

Fortunately, less than a half mile away, the funnel began swaying like a child's toy. Its watery walls became transparent and it disappeared seconds before the front reached us.

Day turned to night as the black clouds raced over us. A phenomenal downpour enveloped us in cascades of warm rain. The wind was not as strong as we had expected. I raised the staysail and mizzen to gain steerage and searoom.

An hour later the rain stopped, the storm moved on over the mainland, growling and pawing at the mountain tops. There came a sudden calm in which *Antares* rocked in the swell, while the setting sun turned the myriad raindrops on stays and lifeline to sparkling golden stars.

The skies cleared and a light northwesterly breeze moved us at two to three knot speed, due west. But for a few exceptions, this was to be our main average speed during the next weeks. The winds never were steady enough to get us way out to sea as we had planned.

Along the Central American coast, we found winds and currents favorable for a coastwise run. Squalls with heavy downpours, followed by complete calms, prevailed along the Costa Rican shores. Above it, along El Salvador and Guatemala, northerlies and northeasterlies gave us good daily runs of up to eighty miles. For a region in which variables and calms are a plague for the sailor, this last run was a matter of great rejoicing for us.

We tried only once to collect rainwater for drinking purposes, in the dinghy. It proved to be a failure. In the calm which follows a squall, *Antares* rocked so much that the water sloshing left and right in the dinghy, splashed in wide arcs over its sides onto the deck. Until the rocking subsided somewhat, we could not even think of bailing the water into jerry cans without endangering our limbs from a certain fall on the slippery decks.

"I wish I was an octopus," said Maria sadly, watching the fresh water run along the toerail into the sea. We did manage to save about twelve gallons of somewhat brackish water, useful enough for rinsing clothing or washing the salt from our bodies after our daily swims.

By May 4th our position was eighty miles southwest of Champerico, in Guatemala. We had reached the Gulf of Tehuantepec again. Nothing dreadful happened, unless one wants to call the absence of wind dreadful! Flukey, varying breezes and occasional squalls ruffled the surface of the mirror-like sea.

One morning we discovered a booby perched on the pulpit. Maria was delighted and Igor was furious. He marched forward with trembling whiskers and eyed the intruder with obvious disgust. The booby continued to groom and preen himself, totally ignoring the cat's presence.

The next day there were three boobies on the bowsprit.

"Things are getting crowded up front," I told Maria.

"Yeah, and Igor thinks the riff-raff there is spoiling the neighborhood," she laughed. "He looks positively insulted."

One more day passed and we counted seven birds on the bow, a fact which started us worrying about the sanitary conditions of the crowded tenement. The boobies, however, were unconcerned; for hours on end they groomed themselves feather by feather. Nothing could disturb them, not even when one of us busied himself with sails or sail changes. Their only reaction was to stop grooming and watch us with wary and alert eyes.

"They are cute," said Maria. "They are so trusting and tame."

When yet another bird tried to perch on the stern railing, we had to draw the line. Maria shooed it away and told it to fight it out with the tenants up front. It found a loud and rowdy resistance from its cousins on the pulpit.

After many attempts to alight there had failed, it clamped its webbed feet resolutely around the life line. Its stubborn determination must have cost it a terrific muscle cramp, for its feet are really not suited to hold on to such a thin wire perch. Indeed, during the night it must have lost its grip, for it fell with a mighty splash in the water. When I came on watch, Maria was still giggling uncontrollably.

"You should have heard him squawk at me as I sailed past him," she said. "He sounded so exasperated."

It was hard to believe, but by morning it had returned, grimly determined to hold its place. With the movement of the boat, it whipped up and down in a highly precarious fashion.

We had been wondering all these days what kept the birds alive, for we had never seen them feed or dive for fish. On and off they flew ahead of the boat, sat in the water in a group resembling a family council, but soon caught up with us, flying ahead of the boat when we had sailed past them.

The mystery was solved one day, unexpectedly, as we sailed along at a good clip with one of the rare livelier breezes in the area. On those occasions we always trailed our fishing line.

Maria woke me with the cry of "Booby, booby," instead of the usual "fish, fish, fish" which is always followed by a strike and heralds the cancellation of the planned corned-beef dinner.

About twenty feet astern a booby was being dragged along, its wing entangled in the line.

"Quick," said Maria, "help him. We don't want to hurt the poor fellow."

I pulled the line in carefully and heaved the bird on deck. As I worked to free it from the line, it tried to peck my hands. I then disregarded all ceremony and turned the bird upside down, holding it by its feet. At that, it squawked weakly, gurgled and coughed. . . .At my feet lay five flying fish, as perfect and fresh as from a refrigerator. Our surprise turned to hilarity as Maria promptly scooped up the fish and cooked them for Igor.

"Your worries are over, cat," she said. "Your dinner is as far away as an upside-down booby!"

The bird, which had so unexpectedly yielded a dinner for our cat, deserved special consideration and we let it sit on the rim of the dinghy. It remained there, apparently none the worse for its experience, and groomed itself contentedly for the rest of the day and following night.

Among the group of birds on the pulpit was one with a bright-orange swatch of paint across one wing. It must have come in conflict with an irate crewman of a merchant ship.

Boobies can wreck havoc on a freshly painted deck. Fortunately, there was not much of a mess on our bow, for most of their droppings fell into the water. A few buckets of sea water took care of the rest of it. We never did mind the company of the boobies. They were not particularly beautiful or bright, but very tame and to a certain point, even endearing. They provided us with enough entertainment to take our minds off the miserable sailing conditions.

One bright morning, as the sun burned off the haze obscuring the horizon, we gaped in amazement at a gigantic sand dune.

"Oh, no," cried Maria. "Do you know where we are?"

I had to admit ignorance.

"There is only one part on the chart marked 'conspicuous sand dunes,'" she said. "And that is five miles west of Salina Cruz." Something was terribly wrong again.

Two days ago we had checked our position with a passing freighter and our DR had been less than five miles away from our actual position. With this information we accordingly had shaped our course for Puerto Angel. For the past forty-eight hours there had not been much wind and sailing.

Occasionally, we used the engine when the swell became unbearable for us and too strenuous on the rigging. Because of the hazy condition, most of the sunsights I had taken were of no use. It was highly unpleasant to find ourselves eighty miles off course. This could not all be due to the currents, or could it?

To soothe my feelings, Maria read a paragraph from the *Sailing Direction* which refers to the gulf: "The navigation of sailing vessels is often very difficult and tedious, owing to the embarrassment of calms and varying drifts."

It was not much of a consolation. For now we faced the task of having to retrace those eighty miles to be out of the Gulf of Tehuantepec. Only during the evening hours of the second day did the light southwest wind increase and it ended by kicking up quite a fuss. We tacked across it all night and whipped around the capes between Puerto Angel and Sacrificios Harbor.

The next morning we rocked in perfectly calm waters four miles northwest of Puerto Escondido.

"Hey, we made good headway last night," exclaimed Maria. We had, indeed, and we hoped and wished in vain for another good blow. For two consecutive nights we still could make out the flashing light from Puerto Escondido lighthouse.

More and more I wished we could have sailed far out to the west in quest of better winds. From here on the winds prevailed from the west northwest, blowing exactly from the quarters to which we wished to sail.

Often we wondered about the fate of the *Whimsey*, which had set sail from Balboa directly to Hawaii. I was sure that they would have had better winds and pictured them pulling ahead with a boiling wake astern. Only many months later, did we receive a letter from her skipper in which he narrated their passage.

They had fared as badly as we did along the coast, for at times they had been becalmed for days on end, having had to use power for almost twelve days consecutively. But the *Whimsey* had the advantage of being able to carry a large amount of fuel in its spacious tanks.

As for us, the wish for wind, WIND! was all that filled my mind. It was not easy to keep those promises we had made to ourselves to take conditions as they came and just relax. How could I keep my cool when I awoke each morning looking upon the very same mountains I had seen at sunset?

We became intimately acquainted with the Mexican coast. Undeniably, it was worth it, for we never tired of its beauty and endless variety. At times, though, the sight became unnerving.

The distance from Puerto Escondido to Acapulco is a bit over 200 miles. We sailed, motored and drifted at the rate of thirty miles a day. On May 17th we anchored offshore eighteen miles east of Acapulco. Frieda had given up and we needed a rest. We had sailed roughly 1,300 miles in twenty-five days, an average of about sixty miles a day. It was not as bad as we imagined, at times. Of course, we would not be home in time for my youngest daughter's graduation.

"Maybe we will make it for the Fourth of July," said Maria. Such was our conversation as we sat in the cockpit and watched the sea turn to molten copper with the rays of the sinking sun.

After dinner we agreed upon keeping watches—the anchor was sixty feet down with almost 200 feet of chain and line. It was holding well, but we could not help feeling uneasy. A mile west of us, at the mouth of a lagoon, Mexican fishermen kept us company all night. They used very bright lights to attract the fish and we liked to watch the pattern of light and shadow on the smooth surface of the water. To keep myself occupied, I decided to do a bit of night fishing myself and by morning I had five bottom fish, including two eels, in a bucket of water—enough for lunch for all three of us.

The slow and painful progress west by northwest continued. We had problems with the engine and problems with the knotmeter. The taffrail log lied flagrantly, giving us only two-thirds of the actual mileage we had made.

So what?

We had come to accept the unavoidable and to cope with adversity.

There were compensations, such as a rousing symphony concert we listened to from our tape recorder on a sunny day, stretched out in the cockpit without a care in the world. Our small tape-set often had provided us with this pleasure, but there were special moments in which nature and modern technology met and fused in perfect harmony.

Should one of us become discouraged, impatient or downright grouchy, the other found ways in which to ease and dispel his negative mood. When I felt that Maria was in need of an uplift, usually I filled two glasses with some of our super-duper goodies acquired in St. Thomas. We then would sit close to each other in the cockpit, and I always managed to steer the conversation to the past or into the future and our plans for it. It never failed to take Maria's mind off the present. I felt gratified when her mood changed and she became her own self again.

Whenever I was in the doldrums, Maria practiced a special brand of "Galgenhumor" (a German term, designating a grim joke made in the face of death at the gallows). One evening, waiting for me to get the feel of the two-knot wind playing hide and seek with the sails, she turned to me and asked, "Wanna hear a couple of bad jokes?"

"Alright, shoot."

"Just imagine that besides us Krauts there are three other sailboats around us somewhere. One has an English crew, the other is French and the third is an American.

"Now, what do we do in these circumstances? We say, 'What? Winds against us? Currents, too?'

"We fight. We pull the sheets in tighter. We say 'Fight, push, work, Work, WORK!!' Right?"

"Right!"

"No! Stupid!"

"The English skipper will survey the situation and say, 'Oh deah, oh deah. We seem to have run into a bit of trouble. We shall have to hang on a bit longer. The wind must change sooner or latah.' And for him, it DOES! It's not for nothing they say that God is an Englishman!

"The French sailor has, meanwhile, turned around, sailing with the winds and the currents he will face his first mate and declare, 'Ma cherie, fill us a glass of wine. I know a snug little cove not far from here. We will be very 'appy there.'

"It's not that the French are quitters. They just know how to live!

"Now, the American does not waste time or words. He will shift the chewing gum from one side to another, calmly take down the sails, and turn the ignition key. He is driving home, the heck with the wind. I like the guy—he's always prepared."

Fifty miles from Manzanillo, Maria had news for me. "We are out of cooking oil. And out of butter. The margarine is running low." (Oh deah!)

"We will have to put into Manzanillo."

"It's taking a risk, we have no clearance."

"I don't like dry bread."

"By the way, the flour is getting low, too." (Oh deah, oh deah!)

"How much money have we got left?"

"About ten dollars." (OH DEAH!!)

We did put into Manzanillo, but we had to put up a fight to get into port. It was downright nasty how the headwinds started to blow at a twenty-five to thirty-knot speed. The barometer had fallen considerably, all the more reason to be in a safe anchorage.

By 2100 *Antares* swayed at anchor behind the breakwater of Manzanillo harbor. We slept for a solid twelve hours and awoke to a brilliant sun shining into our faces.

A pert and neat thirty-nine-foot sloop was anchored not far away. Its crew rowed over to *Antares* for a visit. We learned that the *Fair Lady* was on her way to the Marquesas and would continue on to the Philippines from there.

The husband-and-wife team had their adorable three-year-old son along. It was delightful to watch his sure movements around the boat and dinghy. Growing up on a boat and having spent most of his little life at sea, he was as familiar with his environment as any other child on the swing of his backyard.

The *Fair Lady's* crew had tracked the storm which had caused us so much trouble the day before. It was centered 350 miles to the west of Manzanillo in the vicinity of the Revillagigedo Islands. We had been just on its outer fringes and therefore had not experienced its full force.

We spent a quiet Sunday devoted to the restful occupation of doing absolutely nothing. Early on Monday morning, we rowed ashore and into town, where we felt highly conspicuous and extremely guilty, expecting at any moment an official-looking person to step up to us and ask for our papers. Our fears were unfounded, of course, because yachts are not boarded by port authorities in Manzanillo, unless one stays at anchor for an inordinately long time.

With our remaining $10 we really could not exactly raid the local market. We did stow away an extraordinary amount of staples, though, for we unpacked ten pounds of flour, four pounds of lard, four pounds of margarine, two quarts of cooking oil, four pounds of rice, one large jar of mayonnaise, one dozen eggs, eight matchboxes and a small fish for Igor!

The *Fair Lady* crew had put off their departure on account of the storm, and we profited from their surplus produce supply in the form of a head of cabbage, tomatoes, onions and limes.

That afternoon we sailed to the resort of Las Hadas and anchored off the breakwater of the marina across from the swimming cove of the hotel. We noticed immediately that the breakwater had been improved and enlarged. It now eliminated almost completely the strong surge and undertow we had experienced the year before in the marina.

Since we had parted with our last $10 in Manzanillo, we could not tie up at the marina to fill up with potable water.

But there were ways in which a fill-up could be accomplished. Before nightfall, the beaches and the marina are virtually deserted, as all the guests are preparing for dinner. We simply loaded all our jerry cans into the dinghy and rowed to the marina, where nobody bothered us while we filled them with the most precious wet to be found in the whole of Mexico.

In a perfect calm, on May 31st, we lifted anchor and motored out of Santiago Bay. San Diego was still 1,200 miles away and the winds, at this time of the year, would be blowing from the most unfavorable quarters, between west and northwest.

From this point of the coast, I fully intended to sail out for at least 200 miles and then tack back north, the winds permitting. My plan met with resistance from Maria, however, who had thought we would keep close to the coast until we reached Cabo Corrientes.

Our lines got crossed, and the atmosphere aboard was charged with mutiny. Maria resented having to give up a single mile of the hard-won northing we had so far achieved. I did give it an honest try and tacked back to shore observing our progress against the most conspicuous landmark for Santiago Bay, Piedra Blanca.

This is a huge rock, at least 250 feet high, almost circular in shape and tinged white from bird droppings. It rather looks like a misplaced iceberg in this latitude.

Close to shore, in shallower waters, the chop was miserable, the currents much stronger, and I could not see the point in sticking to our present course. It would be best to turn once more west by southwest and be away from the coast.

Two days later, with greatly diminishing winds, we turned to a more northerly course. Our progress remained painfully slow with runs of thirty, forty, or fifty miles a day. Almost every day we lost about ten miles to the currents flowing strongly southeast.

At the height of Cabo Corrientes, the last booby who had kept us company circled *Antares* a few times in a farewell gesture and flew away toward land. We felt a certain sadness at his departure, for we had grown accustomed to the bird's presence around the boat.

"Good-bye, little fellow, it was nice to have had you aboard."

Under cloudless skies, with light variable winds, we moved slowly into the cooler regions northwest of the mainland of Mexico. This brought us closer to the shipping lanes, where we met with merchant ships and fishing craft.

Unfortunately, the VHF radio had stopped functioning shortly after we left Las Hadas. We discovered this only because we had arranged to contact the *Fair Lady* after our departure at a certain hour. From there on we would have no means of checking our position with other craft. This was the more disturbing, for Maria had found among our books on the shelf the long-missing instruction booklet which accompanied our sextant.

After a careful check, I had to admit to what Maria had long since suspected—the index mirror of the sextant was out of alignment. It could only be corrected on land, wherever I could find the straight line of a building or bridge.

It was no wonder then, that even with a closely watched DR we came upon land not at Cabo San Lucas, but thirty miles to the northeast of it at the port of San José del Cabo.

We did not know this at the time—only the next morning, having come close to shore. Maria consulted our travel 'bible,' the ever-accurate *Sailing Directions.* By the landmarks, she ascertained our position, which was a load off my mind, for I had feared that tidal currents might have brought us far deeper into the Gulf of California.

In the lee of the cape we motored in windless and calm seas toward Cabo San Lucas. The light-green waters indicated shallows, where we observed great numbers of sharks, the most we had seen on a single spot so far. Small fishing craft and a sailboat ghosting east, probably in the direction of Mazatlan, were our early-morning companions.

By 1030 we sighted the two pinnacle rocks which mark the southernmost tip of the Baja Peninsula. These rocks rear straight from the sea to heights of over 200 feet, ghostly white from bird droppings, and with very steep sides. Punctually at 1100, the wind started to blow, hauling around the Cape with an ever-increasing intensity. Just for a moment we considered putting into the small bay off the town of San Lucas, a mile east of the cape.

Instead, we hoisted staysail and mizzen and stood off the shore. By noon we took the mizzen down and let the boat drift, for I needed a few hours of rest. I had been on the helm most of the night as I always am when approaching an unknown stretch of coast.

I was awakened two hours later by the sound of a sail flapping wildly in the wind. Maria had attempted to hoist the mizzen again, the wind had let up a bit and she did not cherish the idea of losing too much ground with the southerly drift we were making.

I dressed and went on deck, where I found her almost in tears.

"I am not even able to hoist this sail by myself," she exclaimed in frustration. I told her to calm down, that we would set the sail together, for the mizzen is troublesome to hoist in a strong wind because it always entangles itself with the line of the boomlift.

For the rest of the afternoon the wind held and we sailed our old course of west by southwest and tacked back in the morning toward north by northeast. The seas were very rough and it was wet sailing.

What bothered us most, though, was the fact that the wind seemed to come directly from the Arctic regions. This sudden change in temperature had Maria frantically searching for our warmer turtlenecks, woolen socks and gloves.

Our bodies reacted violently to the cold. The kidneys worked overtime during the next two days, ridding our bodies of all the surplus moisture accumulated for the last year in warmer zones.

Then an event occurred which overshadowed all these little inconveniences and would drastically change our lives aboard.

For the seven years I had owned *Antares* I had always tried to set the sails so that she would self-steer. I often had succeeded in my efforts, but only for short periods of time. Emphatically I had declared that *Antares* would never self-steer. The moment had come where I had to bow for forgiveness for this rash statement.

Antares had never been at fault, it had always been me who had not found the secret and I felt like a dunderhead for having taken so long to discover it.

In my former attempts, I had always set the sails and then the rudder. When the boat went off course, I corrected the rudder setting. My mistake had been here, because the rudder may be corrected, of course, but the main correction has to be made on the mizzen sail, which now becomes less of a driving sail and more a steering device. With a reefed main, jib and or staysail and mizzen, the boat steered itself beautifully. Never again were we forced to stand our three-hour watches, except when we had to tack or motor or when the winds became too light.

The slavery at the helm had ceased so abruptly that it took time to adjust to the fundamental changes it brought about. Quite suddenly we had time on our hands, time to read, to talk, to write. Time to have meals together, to play with the cat, which sensed the change and spent hours glued to our laps.

Time to talk about the future, make plans and discuss our actions. Best of all, there was time for love even, often neglected and regretfully put off for a more relaxed time. Here was our chance to fall in love with each other all over again. What an enjoyable experience!

From Cabo San Lazaro to Bahia Ballenas, the Baja coastline recedes to the east for a good sixty miles, forming a wide-open bay. The currents here have a strong trend toward the east and south, consequently we had to watch our course closer than ever. The shoreline is low with many sandy beaches, the higher land behind being mostly hidden by fog and haze. Great numbers of whales are to be found in these waters. We spent hours on deck watching, fascinated, as they majestically moved out of our way.

North of Bahia Ballenas the land is visible again, for the mountains are close to shore with all landmarks easier to make out.

After a short period, we almost despaired with the slow progress we could accomplish. We once more accepted the circumstances and the challenge they represented. The winds started to blow furiously with speeds of twenty to thirty-five m.p.h. from noon to sunset, tapering off during the night, decreasing to very light in the morning hours.

On June 29th, almost a month out of Manzanillo, I sighted Turloe Head, the eastern entrance cape of Turtle Bay. We had sailed at least double the distance of 850 miles between these two ports, in our constant tacks off and toward shore.

The more amenable things had been used up from our stores, such as butter, cheese, cookies and crackers, fresh produce and the last bar of chocolate. Fuel was extremely low as well as engine oil and water.

Below Cape San Lazaro we had caught our last fish which had given us a respite from canned ham and corned beef. For the last week the menu aboard had been acceptable, but quite monotonous.

What we would do for currency, we did not quite know at this moment. The excitement of being at anchor and at rest for a while was uppermost in our minds.

Turtle Bay is surrounded by an arid landscape of rolling hills and is well protected from the prevailing winds. We anchored across from the village of St. Bartolomeo, 200 yards from a group of black rocks, which were now, at low tide, densely populated with cormorants.

Snow-white seagulls played tag with the small waves breaking on the sandy shore. A pier, extending 150 feet from the fish-cannery building, was deserted. Small houses, gaily painted in all the colors of the rainbow, huddled in sleepy quietness among the promontories beyond it.

The only sound disturbing the utter stillness came from a fishing vessel anchored close by, upon which a Mexican youth dozed in the sun with a blaring portable radio at his side.

Only one other sailboat was anchored here, the *Flying Cloud*, from San Diego. We rowed over to it and knocked discreetly on the hull.

"Ahoy, anybody aboard?"

On silent pads, a black cat slinked over the decks and inspected us out of green, inquisitive eyes.

"It seems we have come to our kind of people," said Maria. Then, a lean and bearded face appeared out of the hatch. We introduced ourselves and asked for information about the possibilities of communications to the U.S. in the village.

David, the owner of the *Flying Cloud*, had been for almost a month in Turtle Bay and could tell us all about it. There was no telephone, no post office or bank, only a telegraph office to which one could have money sent from the U.S.

This was good news. We returned to *Antares* and initiated a thorough search for any stray coins and dollar bills hidden in nooks and corners of pockets and handbags.

The results were rather discouraging, until Maria, in a sudden flash of memory, started to dig among her things in the compartment under her bunk. Out came a neat black box containing several memorial coins she had taken along as souvenir tokens for friends and relatives in Brazil.

For once I was glad about one of those odds and ends women are wont to carry along "just in case." Armed with four dollars and five cents, we hurried to the telegraph office. Oddly enough, the cost of the fifteen-word telegram was exactly four dollars. Maria's coins did not go into the cash register, but were seized upon enthusiastically by the operators to be used as pendants on neck and wrist chains for their assorted girl friends.

We fervently hoped that the telegram would reach my daughter in Seattle, in charge of all my finances, before the Fourth of July celebrations. Maria had long since run out of cigarettes. She now smoked some very odd-looking things she fashioned from typewriting paper and filled with pipe tobacco, which Charlie had left behind. But, as Maria philosophically said, it was better than no cigarettes.

Our minds at ease, with the prospect of money soon again coming into our hands, we returned aboard and did a few necessary cleaning chores, for we had invited David to join us later on in the afternoon for a cup of coffee.

He had spent the last week alone in the company of his cat, for his wife had flown to San Diego. At 1700 he came alongside, but not alone. Barbara had just come back from the States.

This was a pleasant surprise. We liked the young couple very much and spent many hours talking about experiences. Maria prepared a quick dinner for all of us, which was not so easy in view of our depleted supplies. We had seen an imposing-looking American fishing boat anchored close by and learned from David and Barbara that it had been there for the last three months.

The skipper of the *Comanche* spent a lonely life watching over the boat and anxiously awaiting word from its owner for a return trip to San Diego. He seldom left the yacht, except for quick trips to the telegraph office. When he was in need of a few supplies, David and Barbara did most of the shopping for him.

Before leaving, they asked us to make a visit to the *Comanche*, for Jerry welcomed any distraction from his lonely vigil.

While waiting for the reply from home, we set about doing all the small and tedious jobs which accumulate while under way. Maria settled down to sail stitching, and I went overboard to check on the intake of the head. As I had suspected, a large cluster of gooseneck barnacles had thoroughly clogged it. I had to dive several times and felt completely chilled when I returned on deck. Not only was the water unexpectedly cold, I felt out of sorts in a general way and had to desist from my intention to clean the whole bottom on that occasion.

The next two days I felt listless, had little appetite and getting out of my bunk in the mornings seemed to be an unnecessary effort. Worst of all, what we call "the runs" had me racing to the head at odd hours of the day and night.

Where I could have picked up a flu bug during our month-long travel at sea, was a mystery to us. And "Montezuma's Vengeance" could not be responsible, for we had not had anything to eat or drink on shore.

On the afternoon of July 1st, Dave came by our boat to tell

us that a telegram awaited us at the office.

Rowing to shore, we already made plans for our buys and how soon we could be on the way again. At the telegraph office we found a message from my daughter in which she asked to which bank she should send the money we had asked for. Somehow my telegram to her had not expressed my instructions clearly enough.

Our initial disappointment turned to anxiety. All we had left was five cents! The only other recourse would be to ask David for a loan of four dollars for another telegram. When we reached the pier, his dinghy was bobbing alongside ours. He and Barbara could be anywhere in the village.

We rowed then to the *Comanche* and while I worked at the oars, I searched desperately through my mind for the proper approach to a total stranger of whom I would have to ask the loan of a few dollars.

I need not have worried, for Jerry quickly sized up our situation and, handing me a ten-dollar bill, told me to hurry back to the office for it would be closed after 1600.

Ten minutes later, we reached the office panting and sent another telegram to Seattle, with very detailed instructions.

Now that the tension was gone, we strolled slowly along the dusty road of the village. Left and right the houses had a thick coating of the fine powdery dust through which one could still see the pink, green and yellow paint. The glass panes of the windows, though, were all shiny clean and in front of many houses, people had moistened the road, washed the fronts of the houses and watered the tiny gardens full of blooms. These patches of green and bright colors stood in stark contrast to the austere landscape surrounding it.

Everybody answered our greetings readily as we walked past. The village had by no means the disquieting appearance of decay or poverty we had seen in other places. There was a mood of holiday, of satisfaction, reflected in the faces of the people. We found signs of prosperity everywhere, as men worked on new houses or additions to old ones—not mere huts, but solid constructions made of concrete blocks.

When we reached the pier, the beach around it was swarming with kids playing in the surf. School was out and they enjoyed the romp in the water the way only children are able to. Enjoying the afternoon sun while keeping an eye on the children, many adults strolled along the shore or sat on the rocks above the waterline. It was a picture of utter contentment, security and confidence.

With the six dollars left from the ten Jerry had lent to us, we had been able to purchase a few items we deemed necessary for our comfort. After checking our canned goods, Maria suggested we invite Jerry for a good dinner aboard *Antares*. She took off alone in the dinghy, for I was still nursing that confounded flu.

When she returned several hours later, she was bubbling over with excitement.

"Do you recognize that yacht which just came in?"

"No," I said. "Who is it?"

"It's the *Victoria*, and we are invited for happy hour around 1700."

While we had been talking, Maria had handed over the side a chart, a bag containing six large cans of sardines and—lo and behold—three packages of cigarettes and a small VHF radio unit.

Climbing back aboard, she told me that Jerry would not be coming for dinner and that we were to try the radio unit to see if it worked on our hook up—it was a spare one that Jerry had aboard the *Comanche*.

I had checked our antenna and repaired a cracked ceramic fastening, otherwise there was nothing amiss with it.

I hooked up the unit Maria had brought along, but this must have been in disrepair also. We wrapped it up and both of us rowed to the *Comanche* to give it back to Jerry and spend some time in his company. When we got to the boat, we found that, finally, his boss had arrived and Jerry was radiant at the prospect of leaving, finally, for San Diego. He introduced us to the owner of the yacht whom he had told of our predicament.

This man, whom I had just met, felt sorry that he had not taken along enough cash, for all he could spare at the moment was sixty dollars. He asked if I would please accept it, for he could fully understand our situation.

Indeed, wonders never ceased on that memorable evening. Sitting in the cockpit of *Victoria* lavishly supplied with drinks, we found that seemingly everybody knew what had happened to us. Before we left, Pablo gave me an envelope containing one-hundred dollars in traveler's checks.

"You can repay me when we meet in San Diego," he said.

This spontaneous, unselfish help pouring in from all sides almost overwhelmed us. Unexpected and heartwarming experiences like this had not been unusual ones, for we felt that solidarity among sailors was present everywhere we met.

From the *Victoria's* and *Comanche's* generous loans to the cans of cat food for Igor donated by the *Flying Cloud*, we had been the recipients of much help and sympathy from fellow boaters.

"Who says the seas are lonely?"

I wished I could have been of help to David, for the engine aboard his boat was in disrepair, and he was unable to purchase the spare parts in Turtle Bay. He had decided to take off by sail only and take his chances.

The *Flying Cloud* left one morning at 1100, only to return by 1730. She had encountered strong headwinds and David and Barbara, not troubled by time, reflected that it would be best to wait until the winds changed later in the season to a more south or southwesterly direction.

For us, the departure date was coming closer.

We had filled up at the pier and purchased most of our provisions. It was surprising how many things we found in the small stores of the village.

The money from Seattle had not arrived yet. As I walked on the morning of the 7th to the telegraph office, I vowed it would be for the last time. When I stepped into the tiny building, the operator beamed at me. "Your money just came in," he said.

I did not receive the cash in dollars, but in local currency, which amounted to the grand total of 4,000 pesos. I had trouble in putting this large amount of money away in my wallet and distributed it into several other pockets.

All this loose cash put me in a spending mood. I rowed back to *Antares* to fetch Maria and have her join me in a last minute shopping spree.

In one of the stores, we found a thermos bottle which we sorely needed, for all our others had broken under way. Maria had spent her birthday at sea, without much fuss, and I could make it up to her now by buying her a colorful Mexican poncho.

On a side road we found a grocery store that we had not raided yet, and Maria gleefully pounced on a large package of dates lying on the counter. She asked the storekeeper where on earth they came from.

Apparently date palms are not uncommon on the east side of the Baja Peninsula, where the land is more protected from the fierce winds blowing along its western shore.

And so, we returned to *Antares* laden with 'treasures.'

The hour was 1130 I did want to be off and Maria agreed that we could have lunch on the way. We hoisted the dinghy aboard, lifted anchor and soon had the sails set.

Turtle Bay fell behind, well guarded by the circle of bold and arid hills, sharply outlined against the clear blue sky.

Outside and away from the shelter of the land, the wind blew steadily, as always, from the northwest. I set a westerly course, balanced the sails and went below. *Antares* was on her way, the helm locked and unattended.

In the afternoon we motor sailed for two hours to charge the batteries. Maria came on deck, too, sitting close to me in the cockpit. Both of us enjoyed the warm sunshine, took turns at the helm and chatted the time away.

The winds were good, our daily runs an estimated sixty to sixty-five miles; no record but much better than those runs along the coast, where at times we had sailed hard for forty-eight hours and gained seven miles of headway.

The nights were mostly overcast, the darkness almost a tangible, overpowering presence. The moon, on its last quarter, did little to illuminate the surrounding sea. When it had set, *Antares* sailed through a black velvety void, in which speed, direction, even reality lost their meaning. Only the white masthead light occasionally shone on the foaming crest of a wave forward of the bow.

Maria had suggested that we keep at least one light on for, as she explained, there just might be another sailboat running without lights, its crew confident that they were the only ones on the whole ocean.

On our second day out, the wind shifted more to the west. We tacked and set course to the north. By our calculations, we would sail well to the west of Cedros and San Benito Islands.

Only twice did we sight freighters passing us on starboard, their hulls well below the horizon. Otherwise, the sea was empty; there seemed to be no life in it.

One morning, I found a squid on deck and I thought to myself, "Where there are squid there must be fish." I put the squid on our hook as bait. We trailed it for hours. There was not even a nibble.

"Squid is not on the menu today," said Maria.

Two seconds later, the stopper for the fishing wheel flew off and the line started to run off. Both of us moved into action. Maria pulled in the line from the taffrail log to prevent it from tangling with the fishing line I was now hauling in. Maria readied the catcher and stood by expectantly.

The line felt taut, then slack and taut again. Something flashed in the water. There must be a fish on the line keeping up with my pull. When I had the 200 to 300 feet of line coiled in a heap on deck, the head of a young seal popped out of the water. He glanced at me and disappeared quickly below the surface. He had been playing with the squid and tugging at the line, fooling me all the time into thinking I had a big catch on the hook.

For the next hour I had my hands full rewinding the line on the reel. The little rascal, meanwhile, cavorted around and beneath the boat, fully appreciating the audience of a man, a woman and a cat watching his antics.

More seals appeared toward evening. A shark fin showed its triangular shape above the water. Their interest seemed to concentrate now on the spinner of the taffrail log, but unlike the boobies, there was no way in which one could shoo away a seal or a shark.

My worst suspicions were confirmed the next day when I found the log line slack, the spinner cleanly bitten off. I fastened the spare spinner to the log line and hoped, against all odds, that this one would not be taken for an appetizer also.

The morning of July 11th was calm, the sea oily. Wide kelp beds and large numbers of pelicans indicated the proximity of land. When the fog lifted, by midmorning, above an impressive headland, neither of us could pinpoint it with accuracy. We must have made a considerable amount of leeway while beating against the coastal winds, for my DR had placed us thirty miles off the coast.

It was important that we find our position and determine if we had come upon the coast north or south of the Sacramento Reef. This treacherous, three-mile-long obstruction which lies exactly in the path of a north-bound vessel can be sighted easily during a calm. Dense kelp masses and a heavily breaking surf define its contours and position.

With a light breeze, we motored along the coast, as always, awed by the rugged beauty of mountains and mesas stretching inland.

Before we could agree on any of the landmarks, the breeze

intensified and developed into a good-sized blow. There was no possibility now of making out any obstruction ahead of our path in the short white-capped chop. It would have been foolhardy to remain close to shore. We tacked and turned west, the land soon obscured by mist and flying spray.

Our life had been easy and comfortable while staying off the coast. Close to it, one difficulty piled on top of another. It was not enough that the headwinds had us tacking across a miserable short chop. The appearance of an increasing number of Mexican fishing vessels forced us into a state of constant and nervous alertnesss by day and night.

To compound our discomforts, Frieda developed new quirks and temper tantrums. The head flooded the already disintegrating carpets and all burners of the stove simultaneously belched masses of black smoke into the cabin. It coated the cabin ceiling with a sooty, oily layer and sent us coughing onto the deck.

While we waited for the fumes to disperse below, we found that the second, spare spinner had suffered the same fate of the first. Some creature out there must be suffering by now from a colossal bellyache, for the spinners I had used were large, foot-long, heavy bronze affairs.

From Cape Colnett, which is easy to identify, the winds fell light and variable. With numb fingers and bleeding knuckles, I worked on Frieda, doing the best I could under the circumstances. My back and limbs ached from the exertion of folding my body into the engine compartment in strange positions, which would have done honor to a contortionist.

I had the engine purring again as we motor sailed toward Punta Cabras, a rocky promontory to the south of Punta San Thomas. A half-dozen small fishing boats clustered around the point. This reminded me of the many Mexican pesos still bulging my wallet. Besides, it had been a long time since I had tasted a good fish dinner. I guided the boat to the edge of the kelp bed and slowly pulled Frieda out of gear.

Maria had gone to the bow and talked to the men in the boats. Unfortunately, they had not been fishing but harvesting kelp, which is vacuum-packed at a fish cannery and exported to Japan. The moment I had taken the engine out of gear, it had stopped and I grew desperate while I tried to get her going again.

It was no use. She was hot and would not start for the next hour or so. In the lee of the point, there was barely a breath of wind. The swell pushed us farther into the kelp bed and much too close to the outlying rocks. By now we were two scant wave-lengths from shore.

While I hoisted the mizzen, hoping to get a bit of steerage, Maria, in a state of panic, ran forward and hailed the closest fishing boat.

I told her that we would not need help, for *Antares* had turned now and pointed her bow seaward. We might possibly make our way out of this dangerous spot. She did not believe me, though, and continued to cleat a line to the bow. As the fishing boat roared alongside, she threw it into the waiting hands of the men. These open pirogas are equipped with powerful 75-H.P. outboard motors. In a matter of seconds we had been pulled away from the point and out of the kelp bed.

The sails filled with the light offshore breeze. The danger was past. We paid the man with one of the larger Mexican bills, to which we added a bottle of gin for their quick help. This must have made their day, for they did not return to work but roared off toward their nearby village.

In Maria's opinion, we also deserved a drink to calm our jitters. She brought a bottle and two glasses into the cockpit and we had a toast.

An hour later Frieda could be persuaded to start once more. This at least gave us the illusion that our speed was a bit better, she adding her feeble support to the vanishing wind, which was barely enough to fill the sails.

With the sun close to the western horizon, we reached Punta San Thomas. A high cliff reared perpendicular out of the sea, its narrow ledges throwing fantastic shadows on its steep, smooth face. Excitedly, Maria handed me the binoculars. The ridges were densely populated by thousands of pelicans. We pondered if the birds had selected this inaccessible spot to nest, or if it just afforded a roosting place.

Our interest had diverted our attention from the course which we had been steering. By the time we turned our eyes seaward again, the propeller was churning hard in the masses of kelp which stretch for half a mile from shore.

It was more of a ridiculous situation than a dangerous one, for we were far enough offshore. Maria went forward and from the bow gave hand signals to guide us out of the kelp beds.

By far more dangerous to us was the dense fog which hides the coast from sunset to sunrise. In the light and flukey winds, the miles between Ensenada and San Diego stretched as endlessly as a worn-out elastic band.

On July 18th, we sighted Point Loma, at 1000. It was a perfectly calm morning during which we nearly despaired, for the closer we came to San Diego, the slower Frieda would run. For the last two miles we hoisted the main sail to a regular afternoon westerly wind and, coming about at the south end of Shelter Island made for the dock of the San Diego harbor police for clearance. Port as well as Customs and Immigration officials were not only efficient, but the most courteous and friendly we had met with for a long time.

At last we were home. Well, almost. Seattle was another 1,200 miles away.

CHAPTER 13

HOMEWARD BOUND

At the height of the vacation season, most marinas in San Diego were filled to capacity. To forego a long search, I thought it best to moor at the police dock. We were granted a ten-day stay. The cost was about the same, though we had to dispense with the amenities of a shower and had a slightly longer walk into town.

We did not get much rest, for our list of things to do, to buy and to repair had grown considerably. Supermarkets, laundromats and well-stocked marine-supply stores were close at hand. It was easy to adapt again to the availability of all the modern conveniences. Food prices hold a certain balance the world over. We found that we could calculate our food budget much as we did at home.

The prices for marine hardware, fittings and labor costs for repairs were a shock; something to get used to all over again.

Because of a sore back, I was not able to dive for a hull inspection. Instead I contracted the services of a professional diver, who cleaned the hull and bottom of the boat. He thoroughly checked and freed all intakes and outlets from accumulated silt, growth and paint. When he surfaced, he reported to me that the intake from the salt-water cooling system had been heavily clogged, perhaps the reason for Frieda's overheating.

In reality, as I was to find many months later, the valve of the seacock was frozen and allowed only the merest trickle to reach the cooling system.

This fault could only be detected by taking the seacock completely apart, something that had never occurred to me, for the valve turned easily. I never suspected that the stem was corroded and had broken off inside!

The long walks to the different stores did not do much to improve my ever-aching back. It was much easier and less painful for me to make use of our folding bikes for our daily shopping trips. One morning, as I was busy pumping up one of the tires of the bike, it tipped over, teetered at the edge of the dock and disappeared, supplies and all, between boat and dock into fifteen feet of water. Foolishly, we watched the waters eddy as bubbles and bits and pieces of garbage began to surface.

But this was no laughing matter, for the San Diego port authorities pride themselves on having the cleanest harbor on earth. Maria stretched out on the dock and fished out eggshells, orange peels, milk cartons and assorted odd items floating up from the depths.

Meanwhile, I looked for a quick way in which to recover the bike. I fastened the largest, three-pronged fishing hook in my collection to a line, added a weight to it and began to dredge alongside the dock. It caught on something and both of us heaved on the line.

"I must have hooked something else, the bike is not that heavy," I said to Maria.

"It feels more like an anchor," she replied.

One more mighty pull and the bike was in sight with the hook not on the handlebars or the spokes as I had hoped, but clean through the tire and innertube of the rear wheel. Where else could it have lodged so securely?

Maria hosed down the bike while I took hers for the ride into town. At this point she did not mind my going by myself. She disliked intensely having to pedal in the traffic. She mostly ended up by pushing the bike for miles along the curb. This was a highly impractical way to go shopping.

We made one big mistake in San Diego. That was in going for a visit to its famous zoo on a Sunday. This meant sharing the day with three-fourths of the city's population, plus the influx of thousands of tourists.

The zoo has a great variety of exhibits concentrated in a

relatively small area. It is especially well organized to handle large numbers of visitors. At that time the zoo personnel was especially excited about the arrival of several specimens of koala bears from Australia. Of all the exhibits, these cuddly marsupials were the stars of the day and the most endearing show-stealers.

We did not have much time left to visit any of the other attractions of the city. We celebrated a happy reunion with the owners of the yacht *Victoria* and learned that they had, for the time being, decided to give up their trip around the world. They would sail the *Victoria* to San Francisco, refit her and put it up for sale.

As always, we had a standing invitation to visit them at their future mooring in San Francisco, but we had to decline. I had no intention of putting into any other port between San Diego and Seattle, our home port.

Antares was ready to sail on July 26th.

Every afternoon, brisk westerly breezes usually set in, blowing until sundown.

We joined the fleet of smart sailing craft going out for an afternoon sail, a bone in their teeth, a foaming wake at the stern. We rounded Point Loma, set our course for the south tip of San Clemente Island—and thirty minutes later the wind fooled us and went to blow somewhere else.

The swell was very confused and uncomfortable.

Digruntled with this state of affairs, we motored on due west. We intended to sail along the south coast of San Clemente in a northwesterly direction to St. Nicholas Island. With the rest of the islands and the main coast to starboard, we hoped to be away from the shipping lanes. This was no idle consideration in view of the heavy fog in the area.

The fog extended much more south and west than we had anticipated. By sunset the dark cloud waiting on the western horizon quickly moved inland, wrapping us in a moist, silent and cottony world. The next four days were a hair-raising experience. The late morning, warm, sunny and windless, gave way to cooler afternoons with light and variable winds.

During the nights, a row of nightmarish sounds, muffled by the dense fog, made us tense with the expectation of impending disaster. The beat of the surf, the thump of a distant engine or the mournful warning of a foghorn set our nerves on edge.

Brief glimpses of a rugged, rocky shore, or a ship's bow

rushing by, only served to heighten the sense of unreality and danger, when they instantly and silently disappeared into the milky void. I felt a strongly growing kinship with the *Flying Dutchman* as we groped about the area, ghosts ourselves and very unhappy with our lot.

On July 30th we sighted and identified Anacapa Island. We had come a bit too high and resigned ourselves to the fact that we would have to sail the next thirty miles west through the Santa Barbara Channel to regain open water.

Only by the next evening were we to reach San Miguel Isand, the westernmost of the channel islands.

We did not dare to turn west at this point, for out there lurked Richardson Rock. With the sun setting and darkness approaching, who wants to get acquainted with a pile of rocks in the middle of the night?

I handed the genoa, hoisted the jib and tacked toward Point Conception. By 0200, Maria sighted the light of the cape. We had made good speed, the way west was clear. With a long-held sigh of relief, we turned to the open sea.

The wind was from the northwest and *Antares* churned along at six to eight knots, steering herself marvelously.

I let Maria sleep for the rest of the night. She had been nursing a monumental toothache for the past two days, which had not left her much chance for a good rest.

We breakfasted together and I then spent most of the day sleeping away the accumulated fatigue of the past five days. Maria went quietly about her chores, glancing now and then at the tell-tale compass in the cabin. From time to time, she went on deck to check the horizon, which remained empty of any sign of land or ship.

The sky was so heavily overcast that I did not have a single opportunity to take a sunsight. Without the taffrail log to register the mileage, it was no easy task to keep an accurate DR, for we tacked frequently, changing course according to the winds.

On a beautiful morning, we greeted the sun for the first time, shining in a deep blue sky. Most of the day the wind was just enough to fill the sails. Our progress was slow, but the sailing was very pleasant. It was the right time to get a haircut, a shave and take a washbowl bath. I felt newborn. Back to the sextant. Let's see where we are. Just south of San Franciso—five to six miles off the coast.

During the afternoon we fell on our cat, Igor, to cut his long and curved claws before he became permanently attached to the carpet or the upholstery. We had expected a struggle, but Igor let the procedure go on without flinching or batting a whisker. Good cat. For dinner we would open a can of his most favored food! With the passing of time, he had become more gentle and apparently more dependent on our attention and affection for him.

That evening, judging ourselves to be north of the Farallons, we turned west with a good northwesterly. The helm had to be attended on this night run, a must when in a shippng lane.

As we could not be 100% sure of our position, it would be an uneasy night until we had put at least fifty miles out to sea.

Throughout the voyage, a well established pattern of rules had developed, which stayed with us. Important landfalls always happened at night, on Maria's watch and mostly when I had just fallen asleep. Emergencies arose when either of us was otherwise occupied in the head.

Not to break with this honorable tradition, Maria awakened me at the right moment out of a wishful dream.

"There is a flashing light ahead. I think it is Noon Rock," she said, and went back to the cockpit. When I came on deck, there was not only a flashing light, but a circle of several other steady lights to the south of us. It was all very puzzling and made no sense whatsoever.

The wind had risen to force four and five. We had to beat hard into it, causing us almost to jibe. The flashing light remained elusive. Observing it through the binoculars did not disclose any contours or any signs of on what or to what it was attached.

Since there was no reason for both of us to feel cold and miserable, I sent Maria below for a rest. Too nervous to sleep, she pored over the chart for a while, but was unable to make heads or tails of the mysterious lights.

The puzzle was solved after almost two hours of anxious sailing and peering into the night. A whole fleet of fishing vessels had hovered on the horizon, virtually motionless. The slight changes in position, if any, had been imperceptible.

The flashing light revealed itself as the puzzling strobe signal atop the mast of one of the vessels. When the last of the lights had fallen astern, I could let *Antares* go by herself again. I went below, and, sipping a cup of hot chocolate, wrote in the log book: "Winds 10-15 miles, from the NW. Seas rough, sky overcast, cold."

San Francisco today had a high of 75 degrees and a low of 56. For heaven's sake, this is AUGUST!!

These conditions prevailed for the next three days. We spent them mostly below, making our lives as comfortable as possible. Even so, Maria suffered from a brief spell of claustrophobia. She fled on deck, where she remained for the better part of an hour ventilating her mind. When she returned, we sat down to a game of chess to keep her thoughts occupied and concentrated on something other than the narrow confines of the cabin.

We started to slam hard into the waves, and, with the increasing winds, our angle of heel grew proportionally to the pressure on the sails. Something had to be done. Down with the main, up with the storm main; much easier than reefing. Our trysail has a considerable pull comparable with the reefed main. I found the jib torn at the leech and I had to take it below for stitching.

Maria discovered a five-inch tear along a seam of the mizzen. We slogged along for a time, Maria was busy stitching the tear and other weak points she found while working on the mizzen. She worked all afternoon on it and when we had the mizzen up again, our heading and speed improved.

The repair on the jib took two days of hard work, during which both of us stitched the heavy dacron folded in triple and 'fourple' layers.

Clad in our foul-weather gear, which after a year and a half of use did not afford much protection from the water anymore, we went forward and hanked the jib. Now the boat was balanced at its best. Flying spray and heavy seas came over the bow. We returned below to the warm and cozy confines of the cabin, back to our neglected books and chess board.

Antares rose and fell with the waves, sometimes shuddering from stem to stern with the impact of mighty cross swells. The booming noise, amplified in the cabin, gave me reason to wonder how long the boat could hold out against the onslaught of the seas.

I asked Maria how she felt about packing and readying an assortment of emergency supplies and stowing it in the dinghy. She looked at me across the table, considering for a moment what I just had said. For a second she seemed to listen to the wild song of the wind, to feel the motion of the boat; then she said, "No, it won't be necessary, we will see it through."

Then she added with a quick smile, "Besides, it would be a miserable spot to have to bail out, wouldn't it?"

Her confidence in the boat's strength had always been unshakeable. I felt good that she still should think so.

Only by August 13th did the gale abate somewhat. Our spirits still were high in spite of the discovery of several annoying and persistent leaks. The pump on the forward head let a steady trickle of salt water flow along the cabin sole.

Water had accumulated in one of the storage compartments under my bunk. Bedclothing and mattress had been soaked, a sign that the leaks came from above the waterline. I had always feared that the many times *Antares* had been lifted out of the water might have made hair-line cracks in the fiberglassed hull.

I traced the leak to the light socket above my bunk. Each time the boat heeled or a wave rolled over the decks, water seeped from under it, dribbling on the bunk or running along the hull and disappearing into the compartment.

While Maria held a bucket under it, I removed the socket, insulated the wire ends and dried the immediate area. Then I stuffed a large amount of rags into the hole, hoping that my bunk would become usable again.

We had to empty the compartment of the cans stored there and find another dry place for them. Most of them could be stored in the now empty ice box in the forward section of the bow. We removed over a gallon of water from the compartment and declared it off limits for the rest of the voyage, for every few days it had to be mopped dry.

All this had taken hours of hard work in the heeling, lurching and bouncing boat. Most simple chores turn out to be major affairs, when conditions outside are at their worst.

After the gale had blown itself out, the winds fell light and variable. Our course had been west by northwest, the coast was hundreds of miles away. This was the way we had planned it, for now, no matter where the wind came from, we could run between northwest to north and northeast, without having to fear bumping into the coast and being forced to tack away from it.

We had plenty of searoom but no position. On the few occasions on which the sun had peeked from under the overcast, the swell had been so high that I had not been able to get her down to the horizon long enough for a good altitude measurement. I had corrected the error in the index mirror in San Diego, but had the correction been good enough?

For the next few days I would not be able to find out, for now a heavy overcast stretched from horizon to horizon in a dreary, grey uniformity. Light breezes coming from the southwest, south or southeast, stirred the sails now from here, now from there.

The helm had to be manned, for in the light winds the boat did not self-steer as well. The seas were still heavy, the rocking hard to cope with. It was here that, while attempting to shave, I did one of those remarkable balancing acts one has to do when on a rocking boat, as I was intent on keeping from poking myself in the eye with the shaving brush. My back protested against the twist I had just executed. Soap in the eye would have been preferable to the pain I experienced at that moment.

When I had finished shaving, I could no longer stand upright. Alarmed, Maria helped me to my bunk, rubbed my back with alcohol, wrapped me in a blanket and made me swallow a painkiller.

It soon took effect and, mercifully, I fell asleep. When I awoke, Maria had changed sails, attended to the boat's needs, corrected our course and baked a bread. I was not hungry but accepted a bowl of cool orange slices and sipped a cup of coffee. With it came another pill, and I slipped off into dreamland once more. Probably due to the calming effect of the medication, I experienced the most lovely and colorful dreams.

For two days I was to remain in my horizontal position, feeling useless and guilty that Maria had to take the full load of the work. She was cheerful, though, and assured me that it was good training for her. I had never been out of commission before for two days while sailing and we could be thankful that we were blessed with improving weather conditions.

On the second night, though, we were completely becalmed and spent it rocking horribly with the swell. By daybreak I could stand it no longer. I crawled out of my bunk and started to work on Frieda. At 0630 I had her running. Against Maria's loud protest, I heaved myself up the companionway and steered for an hour due northwest into the swell.

For the rest of the morning, we took one-hour turns. My back improved a bit after each watch. It was not quite as painful to move about anymore. As a southerly breeze started to blow in the afternoon, I was able to hoist the genoa and booming it out, we were now running before the wind beautifully.

On August the 19th, I slept in until 0900. I awakened with a sensation of well-being. The night watch had been uneventful; the boat had needed little attention. At daybreak I had gone out briefly and checked wind, sails and heading. Then I had gone back to my bunk and slept like a baby. Still a bit drowsy, I lit the stove and put the kettle on. Looking out through the porthole, my eyes wandered from the deck to the horizon and snapped to complete wakefulness.

A ship!

By golly, there was a ship heading toward us! I dressed quickly and went outside to watch its approach, until I could read the name on the bow.

A deep and pleasant voice answered my call over the VHF. As we had experienced so often before, the officer on watch did not mind having an early-morning chat with me and giving us our position. We wished each other a bon voyage and signed off.

When I compared the position with my DR from the evening before, it put us forty miles farther to the west. As we had been going all night north by northeast, I had been quite far off, but it was good to know for sure that we still had a lot of leeway from the Oregon and Washington coasts.

This had been a good start for a day which was to be perfect. The sun shone bright, the wind kept the sails filled and taut, drawing without a flap. *Antares* rushed on, over a deep-blue and sparkling sea, steadily north by northeast, toward home. This was the kind of sailing we had often dreamed of. As we have no brake on the shaft the propeller hummed happily all day, as it always does when we sail six knots and over. We felt an intense joy mingled, sadly, with the first realization that our voyage was drawing to an end.

From August 20th to 23rd, the weather turned squally, ugly and disagreeable. High winds reaching force six to seven and heavy rainfall, followed by miserable calms, made our lives difficult once more. Heavy seas, lumpy and confused, fell on deck while we fought the wind during the frequent sail changes.

On the night of the 24th the granddaddy of all squalls overtook us with all sails up. Winds from the south, gusting to eight, whipped the swells to mountains. Rain poured in cataracts, soaking me to the bones.

Well, this was more than fair. On the day before, Maria had

been soaked on each watch, while I had been on the helm during the dry spells.

Only by 0630, was I able to heave to and lower the main. I still could not understand how the sails and rigging had withstood the tremendous pressures. I had fought at the helm for two hours as the heavy seas, born with the south wind, clashed with the northwesterly swell, throwing *Antares* off course by as much as thirty degrees. These had been the scariest hours I could remember having spent on the helm.

When the squall subsided, it left us rocking in ten-foot swells and with unstable winds blowing now from one quarter, now from the other. Through a thin cloud layer, the disk of the sun was visible for brief moments. This prompted me to take a few sun sights. According to those, our position was still eighty miles west off Cape Flattery.

To alleviate the terrific beating the swell subjected us to, we motored for most of the following thirty-six hours. When we sighted a light with a ten-second interval, we excitedly studied our old chart of Vancouver Island. There was no such light. It made us feel inept and foolish.

This feeling changed to bewilderment when another light appeared over the horizon by dawn and we could not find any corresponding reference on our chart.

"The best we can do now is to go there and find out," said Maria. "Perhaps all the lights have been changed. After all, it is an old chart."

I thought this to be very unlikely, but we had not much choice, for the seas were oily from the absence of wind, the swell heavy and hard to bear.

Fog over the mountains obscured any landmarks we could have recognized. We must have been twelve to fifteen miles away from the light, for it took us until noon until we came close to it. By then, the sun had broken through the clouds and had burned off the fog over the lovely mountains of the island.

Ahead lay the entrance to Tofino, its lighthouse still blinking into the sun. Maria was a bit disappointed, for she had hoped to make Barkley Sound on that morning.

Ucluelet, the westernmost harbor at the entrance of Barkley Sound, was a good thirty miles away. "It would be nice to put in there for the night," she said.

We motor sailed all afternoon, feasting our eyes on the many shades of green, the rugged coast and lofty mountains. We listened to radio programs originating from Seattle and Victoria. Fiddling with the radio dial, I came upon a Canadian station which broadcast notices to mariners. It had almost finished and it was not very clear, but I caught the tail end and heard mentioned that the timing of several lights along the west coast of Vancouver Island had been changed. I made a note of it, to put the new timing on the corresponding lights on my chart.

It was good to be familiar with the rocky and narrow entrance to the harbor of Ucluelet, for we did not arrive there before nightfall. It was packed full with fishing vessels. We had no other choice but to raft up to a yacht moored at the public dock.

After having spent the past thirty days at sea, it was heavenly to be able to sleep the whole night through undisturbed in the protection and utter calm of the harbor.

In the morning, a quick walk to the local market to get us fresh milk, butter, a few fruits and vegetables. Back at the boat, we cut the lines right away.

The day would have been perfect had the wind cooperated. It blew exactly from where we had to go. By the end of the day we had gained a bit over twenty miles. Toward evening the weather turned nasty again. The wind direction had not changed but it blew now much stronger and rain was coming down in buckets. The reception committee was absent.

We tacked across the wind all day and continued to do the same all night. But it was really no fun. We could not see any mountains, nor islands, nor any lights. It was pitch dark; we could not see a hand before our eyes. It was a fitting welcome from the Pacific Northwest. We wondered what had ever happened to the westerlies which had been forecast for the past two days.

At dawn a heavy fogbank lay ahead. Not a speck of wind was left, and what the swell did to us is unmentionable.

"Come on, Frieda, be a good girl we still have a lot of miles to go," I said.

Frieda did cooperate before I went below, all fagged out from the night's labors. Maria remarked glumly, "With our luck, we might have to claw our way home to the very last mile."

An hour later, through the thinning fog, we made out Pachena light. We had made ten miles during a full night of fearful sailing. By the time Carmanah light peeked out of the fog, we had already agreed on spending the night at anchor in the protection of San Juan Harbor.

Our plans were rapidly overthrown when the long-announced westerly arrived in the early afternoon. It blew away the last shreds of haze. To starboard was the dark outline of the Washington coast. Sails up, engine off.

Antares almost flew across the Strait of Juan de Fuca. Forgotten was the miserable night, the rain and cold. We were on our way home.

By 1730, *Antares* swayed at anchor in Neah Bay. We had come full circle from where we had taken off seventeen months ago. We had set out with many assumptions, dreams and ambitions. The sea had humbled us, taught us a lesson and dispersed the last vestiges of any mistaken notions about it. But it had not broken us. It had left room for dreams and plans. What we had long known became a certainty. This would not, could not be our last and only voyage. We talked until late and made notes. The list grew and grew.

"We need new sails, and a new sextant."

"Frieda needs an overhaul, and I want a spice rack."

"We had too many woolens. Next time we take more shorts along."

"What for? We do not wear much anyway."

"Silly! For when we are in town!"

"No new shorts. I need shackles and blocks and lines and an anchor."

"Who's going to pay for all this?"

"We might have to work for a while."

"Why don't we write a book?"

"Don't be facetious, let's go to sleep."

The next morning we overslept. I had wanted to leave at 0700 and here it was already 0900. Before I could go too far, first mate said, "Hold it, Skipper. Let's have breakfast first. What's the hurry, anyhow?"

"It's still August, we will make it in a day or two."

Our holiday mood persisted in spite of drizzle and cold, calms and flukey winds.

We stopped over in Port Angeles and Port Townsend.

On August 31st we set sails from there to Seattle.

Antares ghosted south on Puget Sound, on the last forty-odd miles of our trip.

She logged 15,000 miles, faced and survived destruction, gales and calms; had been and still would be our home.

Her sails were grey and bellied out, patched and stained. The varnish was peeling from her brightwork. She had seen strange seas, stranger lands and people and unknown stars.

When Mount Rainier came in sight, Maria poured us a glass of wine and we toasted to each other. On lifting her glass, she said, "Here is to us old folks. We are living proof that everything is possible when you are young at heart."

"Cheers, my first mate, you have become a great sailor."

Erased were all the fears and all the worries. The joys would remain forever, a never-ending source of pleasure.

At this moment there was no yesterday, no tomorrow, only the immediacy of the present, of this day in which a hand took our lines and a voice said, "Welcome home, sailors."